Tropic]

E. J. Banfield

Alpha Editions

This edition published in 2024

ISBN : 9789362097170

Design and Setting By
Alpha Editions
www.alphaedis.com
Email - info@alphaedis.com

AUTHOR'S NOTE

In my previous books the endeavour was to give exact if prosaic details of life on an island off the coast of North Queensland on which a few of the original inhabitants preserved their uncontaminated ways. Here is presented another instalment of sketches of a quiet scene. Again an attempt is made to describe—not as ethnological specimens, but as men and women—types of a crude race in ordinary habit as they live, though not without a tint of imagination to embolden the better truths.

I thankfully acknowledge indebtedness to my friends Mr. Charles Hedley, of the Australian Museum (Sydney); Dr. R. Hamlyn-Harris, Director of the Queensland Museum; and Mr. Dodd S. Clarke, of Townsville, N.Q., for valuable aid in the preparation of my notes for publication.

DUNK ISLAND.

PART I
SUN DAYS

IN IDLE MOMENT

"'Are you not frequently idle?' 'Never, brother. When we are not engaged in our traffic we are engaged in our relaxations.'"—BORROW.

On the smooth beaches and in the silent bush, where time is not regulated by formalities or shackled by conventions, there delicious lapses—fag-ends of the day to be utilised in a dreamy mood which observes and accepts the happenings of Nature without disturbing the shyest of her manifestations or permitting 'the-mind to dwell on any but the vaguest speculations.

Such idle moments are mine. Let these pages tell of their occupation.

As the years pass it is proved that the administration of the affairs of an island, the settled population of which is limited to three, involves pleasant though exacting duties. It is a gainful government—not gainful in the accepted sense, but in all that vitally matters—personal freedom, absence of irksome regulations remindful of the street, liberty to enjoy the mood of the moment and to commune with Nature in her most fascinating aspects. Those who are out of touch with great and dusty events may, by way of compensation, be the more sensitive to the processes of the universe, which, though incessantly repeated, are blessed with recurrent freshness.

The sun rises, travels across a cloudless sky, gleams on a sailless sea, disappears behind purple mountains gilding their outline, and the day is done. Not a single dust-speck has soiled sky or earth; not the faintest echo of noisy labours disturbed the silences; not an alien sight has intruded. What can there be in such a scene to exhilarate? Must not the inhabitants vegetate dully after the style of their own bananas? Actually the day has been all too brief for the accomplishment of inevitable duties and to the complete enjoyment of all too alluring relaxations.

Here is opportunity to patronise the sun, to revel in the companionship of the sea, to confirm the usage of beaches, to admonish winds to seemliness and secrecy, to approve good-tempered trees, to exchange confidences with flowering plants, to claim the perfumed air, to rejoice in the silence—

"Not learning more than the fond eye doth teach,

Which pries not to th' interior."

How oft is the confession that the fullest moments of life are achieved when I roam the beaches with little more in the way of raiment than sunburn and naught in hand save the leaves of some strange, sand-loving plant? Then is it that the individual is magnified. The sun salutes. The wind fans. The sea sighs a love melody. The caressing sand takes print of my foot alone. All the world might be mine, for none is present to dispute possession. The sailless sea smiles in ripples, and strews its verge with treasures for my acceptance. The sky's purity enriches my soul. Shall I not joy therein?

Though he may be unable to attain those moments of irresistible intuition which came to Amiel, when a man feels himself great like the universe and calm like a god, one may thrill with love and admiration for Nature without resigning sense of superiority over all other of her works or abating one jot of justifiable pride.

Even in tropical Queensland there is a sense of revivification during the last half of August and first of September, and the soul of man responds thereto, as do plants and birds, in lawful manner. Perhaps it is that the alien dweller in lands of the sun, when he frisks mentally and physically at this sprightly season, is merely obeying an imperative characteristic bred into him during untold generations when the winter was cruelly real and spring a joyful release from cold and distress. The cause may be slight, but there is none to doubt the actual awakening, for it is persuasive and irresistible.

The lemon-trees are discarding the burden of superfluous fruit with almost immoderate haste, for the gentle flowers must have their day. Pomeloes have put forth new growth a yard long in less than a fortnight, and are preparing a bridal array of blooms such as will make birds and butterflies frantic with admiration and perfume the scene for the compass of a mile. The buff-and-yellow sprays of the mango attract millions of humming insects, great and small. Most of the orchids are in full flower, the coral-trees glow, the castanospermum is full of bud, loose bunches of white fruit decorate the creeping palms, and the sunflower-tree is blotched with gold in masses. The birds make declaration of attachment for the season.

Great trees, amorous birds, frail insects, perceive the subtle influence of the season, and shall not coarse-fibred man rejoice, though there be little or nothing to which he may point as special evidence of inspiration? He may feel the indefinable without comprehending any material reason why. He may confess, although there is but a trifle more sunshine than a month ago—and what influence a trifle where there is so much—and scarcely any difference of temperature, that Nature is insisting on obedience to one of her mighty laws—the law of heredity. Why, therefore, refrain from justifying the allusion? Why persist in declining the invitations of the hour? Far be it from me to do so. Is sufferance the cognizance of this Free Isle?

All my days are Days of the Sun. All my days are holy. Duty may suggest the propriety of contentment within four walls. Inclination and the thrill of the season lure me to gloat over the more manifest of its magic. Be sure that, unabashed and impenitent, shall I riot over sordid industry during the most gracious time of year to hearken to the eloquence and accept the teachings of unpeopled spaces.

Such is the silence of the bush that the silken rustle of the butterflies becomes audible and the distinctive flight of birds is recognised—not alone such exaggerated differences as the whirr of quail, the bustle of scrub fowl, and the whistle and clacking of nutmeg pigeons, but the delicate and tender characteristics of the wing notes of the meeker kinds of doves and the honey-eaters, and also the calculated flutterings of the fly-catchers. In the whistling swoop of the grey goshawk there is a note of ominous blood-thirstiness, silent though the destroyer has sat awaiting the moment for swift and decisive action.

Seldom, even on the stillest evening, may the presence of the night-jar be detected, except by its coarse call, while the sprightly little sun-bird flits hither and thither, prodigal of its vivid colours and joying with machine-like whirring. The sun-bird exemplifies the brightness of the day. All its activities are bold and conspicuous. Aptly named, it has nothing to hide, no deeds which will not withstand the scrutiny of the vividest rays.

To work out its destiny the night-jar depends on secret doings and on flight soft as a falling leaf. It is a bird of the twilight and night. Startled from brooding over its eggs or yet dependent chicks, it is ghost-like in its flittings and disappearances. In broad daylight it moves from its resting-place as a leaf blown by an erratic and sudden puff, and vanishes as it touches the sheltering bosom of Mother Earth. Mark the spot of its vanishment and approach never so cautiously, and you see naught. Peer about and from your very feet that which had been deemed to be a shred of bark rises and is wafted away again by a phantom zephyr.

The chick which the parent bird has hidden remains a puzzle. It moves not, it may not blink. Its crafty parent has so nibbled and frayed the edges of the decaying brown leaves among which it nestles that it has become absorbed in the scene. There is nothing to distinguish between the leaf-like feathers and the feather-like leaves. The instinct of the bird has blotted itself out. It is there, but invisible, and to be discovered only by the critical inspection of every inch of its environment. You have found it; but not for minutes after its instinct has warned it to possess its soul calmly and not to be afraid. So firm is its purpose that if inadvertently you put your foot on its tender body it would not move or utter cry. All its faculties are concentrated on impassiveness, and thus does Nature guard its weakest and most helpless offspring.

While you ponder on the wonderful faith of the tiny creature which suffers handling without resistance, the shred of bark, driven by the imperceptible zephyr, falls a few yards away, and in an agony of anxiety utters an imploring purr, or was it an imprecation? That half purr, half hiss has been the only sound of the episode. It is a warning to be gone and leave Nature to her secrets and silences.

A month's abstinence may not be a very severe penance for an island on which the rainfall averages 124 inches per year; but when vegetation suffers from the cruelty of four almost rainless months, promises and slights amount to something more than mere discourtesy. How genuine the thanksgiving to the soft skies after an incense-stimulating shower. Insects whirl in the sunshine. Among the pomelo-trees is a cyclone of scarcely visible things. Motes and specks of light dance in disorderly figures, to be detected as animated objects only by gauzy wings catching the light and reflecting it. Each insect, wakened but an hour ago by the warmth of the moist soil, in an abandonment of the moment, is a helioscope transmitting signals of pure pleasure. Drops still linger on myriads of leaves, and glitter on the glorious gold of the Chinese laburnum; the air is saturated with rich scents, and the frolicking crowd, invisible but for the oblique light, does not dream of disaster. Their crowded hour has attracted other eyes, appreciative in another sense. Masked wood-swallows, swiftlets, spangled drongos, leaden fly-eaters, barred-shouldered fly-eaters, hurry to the circus to desolate it with hungry swoops. The assemblage is noisy, for two or three drongos cannot meet without making a clatter on the subject of the moment. They cannot sing, but clink and jangle with as much intensity and individual satisfaction as if gifted with peerless note. It is the height of the season, and a newly matched pair, satisfied with an ample meal, sit side by side on a branch to tell of their love, and in language which, though it may lack tunefulness, has the outstanding quality of enthusiasm. But why waste clamorous love-notes on a world busy with breakfast? The sportful, tail-flicking dandy flits and alights so that he may address himself solely to his delighted and accepting spouse, peering into her reddish eyes the while, and in ecstasy proclaiming, in tones as loud and unmusical as her own, that life overflows with joy when mutual admiration surcharges the breast.

The noise stays a company of metallic starlings in headlong flight from the nest-laden tree in the forest to the many-fruited jungle. Though they most conscientiously search the fronds of coco-nut palms for insignificant grubs and caterpillars, starlings do not hawk for insects. Held up by the excitement—for by this time other birds have darted to the feast—the starlings alight among the plumes of the laburnum, interrogating in acidulous tones, their black, burnished, iridescent feathers and flame-hued eyes making a picture of rare vividness and beauty.

How thin becomes the throng! Last night's shower, the morning warmth of the soil, have brought forth a gush of life that wheels and sparkles in the sun and becomes bait for birds. Are droughts designed by Nature to test endurance on the part of animal and vegetable life? Leaves fall from evergreen trees almost as completely as from the deciduous, and even the jungle is thickly strewn, while every slight hollow is filled with brittle debris where usually leaves are limp with dampness and mould. The jungle has lost, too, its rich, moist odours. Whiffs of the pleasant earthy smell, telling of the decay of clean vegetable refuse, do issue in the early morning and after sundown; but while the sun is searching out all the privacies of the once dim area, the wholesome fragrance does not exist.

Drought proves that certain species of exotic plants are hardier than natives. Wattles suffer more than mangoes, and citrus fruits have powers of endurance equal to eucalyptus. Whence does the banana obtain the liquid which flows from severed stem and drips from the cut bunch? Dig into the soil and no trace of even dampness is there; but rather parched soil and unnatural warmth, almost heat. Heat and moisture are the elements which enable one of the most succulent of plants to bear a bunch of fruit luscious and refreshing, and when heat alone prevails, the wonder is that the whole patch of luxuriant greenness does not collapse and wither. But the broad leaves woo the cool night airs, and while the thin, harsh, tough foliage of the wattles becomes languid and droops and falls, the banana grove retains its verdancy, each plant a reservoir of sap.

A noteworthy feature of the botany of the coast of tropical Queensland is its alliance with the Malayan Archipelago and India. Most of the related plants do not occur in those parts closest to other equatorial regions in the geographical sense, but in localities in which climate and physical conditions are similar. Probably there are more affinities in the coastal strip of which this isle is typical than in all the rest of the continent of Australia. One prominent example may be mentioned-viz., "the marking-nut tree." When the distinctiveness of the botany of the southern portions of Australia from that of the old country began to impress itself on the earliest settlers, the miscalled native cherry was the very first on the list of reversals. The good folks at home were told that the seeds of the Australian cherry "grow on the outside." The fruit of the cashew or marking-nut tree betrays a similar feature in more pronounced fashion. The fruit is really the thickened, succulent stalk of the kidney-shaped nut. The tint of the fruit being attractive, unsophisticated children eat of it and earn scalded lips and swollen tongues, while their clothing is stained indelibly by the juice. Botanists know the handsome tree as SEMECARPUS AUSTRALIENSIS, but by the indignant parent of the child with tearful and distorted features and ruined raiment it is offensively called the "tar-tree," and is subject to shrill denunciations. The fleshy stalk beneath the fruit is, however, quite wholesome either raw or cooked, but the oily pericarp contains a caustic principle actually poisonous, so that unwary children would of a certainty eat the worst part. The tree, which belongs to the same order as the mango, has a limited range, and there are those who would like to see it exterminated, forgetful that in other parts of the world the edible parts are enjoyed, and also that a valuable means to the identification of linen is manufactured from it. A tree that is ornamental, that provides dense shade, that bears pretty and strange fruit, an edible part, and provides an economic principle, is not to be condemned off-hand because of one blot on its character.

An Indian representative of the genera produces a nut which when roasted is highly relished, though dubiously known as the coffin-nail or promotion nut, but there is no reason to believe that it is specially indigestible unless eaten in immoderate quantity.

One of the many bewilderments of botany is that plants of one family exhibit characteristics and habits so divergent that the casual observer fails to recognise the least signs of relationship. Similar confusion arises in the case of plants of the same species producing foliage of varied form. One of the figs (FICUS OPPOSITA) displays such remarkable inconsistency that until reassured by many examples it is difficult to credit an undoubted fact. The typical leaf is oblong elliptical, while individual plants produce lanceolate leaves with two short lateral lobes, with many intermediate forms. As the plant develops, the abnormal forms tend to disappear, though mature plants occasionally retain them. There seems to exist correlation between foliage and fruit, for branches exhibiting leaves with never so slight a variation from the type are, according to local observation, invariably barren. The leaves, which, when young, are densely hairy on the underside, on maturity become so rough and coarse that they are used by the blacks as a substitute for sandpaper in the smoothing of weapons. The fruit is small, dark purple when ripe, sweet, but rough to the palate.

During the fulness of the wet season, a diminutive orchid, the roots, tuber, leaf, and flower of which may be easily covered by the glass of a lady's watch, springs upon exposed shoulders of the hills. So far it has not been recorded for any other part of Australia, or, indeed, the world. Science has bestowed upon it the title of CORYSANTHES FIMBRIATA, for it is all too retiring of disposition to demand of man a familiar name. Probably it may be quite common in similar localities, but its size, its brief periodicity, and inconspicuousness, contribute to make it, at present, one of the rarities of botany. Beneath a kidney-shaped leaf a tiny, solitary, hooded, purple flower shelters with becoming modesty, the art of concealment being so delicately employed that it seems to preserve its virginal purity. There is proof, however, that the flower does possess some "secret virtue," for if the plant be immersed in glycerine the preservative takes the hue of the flower. Nature having ordained that the plants should be elusive, they appear in remote spots and unlikely situations with foothold among loose and gritty fragments of rock, and with cessation of the sustaining rains disappear, each having borne but a single leaf and produced but a solitary flower. The leaf does not seem to be attractive to insects, nor is the flower despoiled or the tuber interfered with. The first dry day sears the plants, and succeeding days shrivel them to dust and they vanish. What part in the great scheme of Nature does the humble flower fulfil? Or is it merely a lowly decoration, not designed to court the ardent gaze of the sun, but to brighten an otherwise bare space of Mother Earth with a spot of fugitive purple?

Widely different are the ant-house plants, of which North Queensland has two genera. One is purely an epiphyte, growing attached to a tree like many of the orchids. In both genera the gouty stems are hollow, a feature of which ants take advantage; they are merely occupiers, not the makers of their homes. Few, if any, of the plants are uninhabited by a resentful swarm, ready to attack whomsoever may presume to interfere with it. It is discomposing to the uninitiated to find the curious "orchid," laboriously wrenched from a tree, overflowing with stinging and pungent ants, nor is he likely to reflect that the association between the plant and the insect may be more than accidental.

Some of the commonest wattles exhibit singularity of foliage well worth notice. Upon the germination of the seeds the primary leaves are pinnate. After a brief period this pretty foliage is succeeded by a boomerang-shaped growth, which prevails during life. Botanists do not speak of such trees as possessing leaves, but "leaf-stalks dilated into the form of a blade and usually with vertical edges, as in Australian acacias." If one of these wattles is burnt to the ground, but yet retains sufficient life to enable it to shoot from the charred stem, the new growth will be of pinnate leaves, shortly to be abandoned for the substitutes, which are of a form which checks transpiration and fits the plant to survive in specially dry localities. Several of the species thus equipped to withstand drought are extremely robust in districts where the rainfall is prolific. There are no data available to support the theory that such species in a wet district are more vigorous and attain larger dimensions than representatives in drier and hotter localities. In her distribution of the Australian national flower, Nature seems to be "careless of the type," or rather regardless in respect of conditions of climate.

Human beings, and occasionally animals lower in the scale, deviate distressingly in their conduct from the general. Plants, too, though lacking the organ of brain, are subject to aberrations of foliage almost as fantastical as the mental bent which in man is displayed by the sticking of straws in the hair. "Phyllomania" is the recognised term for this waywardness. One of the trees of this locality, the raroo (CAREYA AUSTRALIS), seems singularly prone to the infirmity, for without apparent cause it abandons habitual ways and clothes its trunk and branches with huge rosettes of small, slight, and ineffective leaves, evidence, probably, of vital degeneration.

Among the beautiful trees of this Island there is one, PITHECOLOBIUM PRUINOSUM, possessing features of attraction during successive phases of growth. The young branches, foliage, and inflorescence, are coated with minute silky hair, as if dusted with bronze of golden tint. The dense, light, semi-drooping foliage produces a cloud-like effect, to which the great masses of buff flowers add a delightful fleeciness, while the ripe pods, much twisted and involved (to carry similitude as far as it may), might be likened to dull lightning in thunderous vapour. The tree flourishes in almost pure sand within a few yards of salt water, and, being hardy and of clean habit, might well be used decoratively.

Standing with its feet awash at high tide, the huge fig-tree began life as a parasite, the seed planted by a beak-cleaning bird in a crevice of the bark of its forerunner. In time the host disappeared, embraced and absorbed. Now the tree is a sturdy host. Another fig envelops some of its branches, two umbrella-trees cling stubbornly to its sides, a pandanus palm grows comfortably at the base of a limb, tons of staghorn, bird's-nest, polypodium, and other epiphytal ferns, have licence to flourish, orchids hang decoratively, and several shrubs spring aspiringly among its roots. But the big tree still asserts its individuality. It is the host, the others merely dependents or tenants. Most of the functions of the tree are associated with the sea. Twice a year it studs its branches with pink fruit, food for many weeks for a carnival of birds, the relics of the feast dully carpeting the sand. Before the first fruiting the old leaves fall, and for a brief interval the shadows of branches and twigs, intricate, involved, erratic, might be likened to unschooled scribblings, with here a flourish and there a blot and many a boisterous smudge. Soon—it is merely a question of days—the swelling buds displace millions of leaf-sheaves, pale green and fragile, which fall and, curling in on themselves, redden, and again the yellow sand is littered, while overhead fresh foliage, changing rapidly from golden, glistening brown to rich dark green, makes one compact blotch. And when the wind torments sea and forest, and branches bend and sway, and creepers drift before it, the white blooms of the orchids, so light and delicate that a sigh agitates them, might be "foam flakes torn from the fringe of spray" and tossed aloft.

The technical description of a fairly common tree—IXORA TIMORENSIS—is silent on a quality that appeals to the unversed admirer almost as strongly as the handsome flowers, which occur in large, loose panicles at the terminals of the branches. Boldly exposed, the white flowers as they lose primal freshness change to cream, but last for several weeks. The omitted compliment from formal records is the singular fragrance of the flowers—strong, sweet, and enticing, though with a drug-like savour, as if rather an artificial addition than a provision of Nature. During December the perfume hangs heavily about the trees, being specially virile in the cool of evening and morning. Being confined to the tropical coast, away from the centres of population, and flowering at a season when visitors avoid the north, the scented Ixora has so far remained uncommended. Those who are familiar with it in its native scene dwell on its unique excellence, and are proud to reflect that when a comprehensive catalogue of the flowering and perfumed plants of Australia comes to be compiled it will stand high in order of merit, being unique and characteristic of the richness of that part of the continent in which it exists naturally.

Twice during lengthy intervals have I been perturbed by the conduct of the sea-swallows (terns) which breed in this neighbourhood. They select for their nurseries coral banks, depositing large numbers of eggs beyond the limit of high tides. In obedience to some law, the joyful white birds began to lay in September, five or six weeks earlier than usual. It seemed to be a half-hearted effort to maintain the strength of the colony, the unanimous and general purpose being postponed for three months, when numerous clutches and marvellously variegated eggs embellished the coral. But that which was a perfectly safe and wise undertaking in September was a foolish and dangerous experiment in December. The tides then approach their maximum, flooding areas denied three months previously. Wholesale tragedy was inevitable. The full moon brought bereavement to many parents, for the sea overwhelmed the nurseries, or the best part of them. Many wise birds had laid their eggs above the limit of the highest tide. Others screamed in protest against the cruelty of the sea, for eggs and fluffy chicks do not surely represent legitimate tribute to Neptune. Several fledglings were found half buried in sand and coral chips, some with merely the head with bright and apprehensive eyes obtruding. Why were not the whole of the parents of the colony prudent when in default the penalty was inevitable? Five score were wise, five hundred were foolish, and the natural increase from the second brood must have been seriously diminished. Several of the parent birds had brooded over their eggs until overwhelmed by the surges and drowned. Some on the tide limit squatted buried to the eyes in sand and seaweed. Of one the tip of a wing only protruded. It was alive, fostering unbroken eggs.

The metallic starlings have again built on a favourite tree—not massive and tough, but a slim though tall Moreton Bay ash, the branchlets of which are not notoriously brittle. They withstand a certain weight, beyond which they snap. Why do these otherwise highly intelligent birds so overstrain branches with groups of nests that "regrettable incidents" cannot be averted? First there came to the ground a group of four, and then twenty nests, all containing eggs or helpless young. By these and similar mishaps during the season the colony suffered loss to the extent of at least a hundred.

"But, like the martlet,

Builds in the weather on the outward wall

Even in the force and road of casualty."

How often, too, do we find nests in places absurdly wrong? Wonderfully and skilfully constructed nests are attached to supports obviously weak, and eggs are laid on the ground right in the track of man and less considerate animals. Some birds seem to lay eggs and rear young solely that snakes may not lack and suffer hunger, while how large a proportion of beautiful and innocent creatures are destined to become prey to hawks?

Years ago scientific visitors to a coral islet found almost innumerable sea birds and eggs. The multitude of birds and their prodigious fecundity inspired the thought that the "rookery" for the whole breadth of the Indian Ocean had been discovered. Investigations showed that the islet was also the abiding-place of a certain species of lizard which subsisted entirely on eggs. It was calculated that not one egg in several hundred was hatched out; yet in spite of such an extraordinary natural check the islet was enormously overpopulated. Thousands of birds every year laid eggs for the maintenance of fat and pompous reptiles, without reflecting that there were other and lizardless isles on which the vital function of incubation might be performed without loss. Years after other men of science sought the isle. Birds seemed to be as numerous as ever, but the lizards had disappeared. Had the birds been wise enough to perceive that the plague of lizards had been sent as reproof for overcrowding, or did the lizards become victims to physical deterioration incident upon gluttony and sloth?

"Into every instinctive act there is an intrusion of reasoned act." No doubt; but in the case of the terns—sea-frequenting and sea-loving—which had not the wit to lay their eggs beyond the reach of spring tides, the reasoning is the merest intrusion. Yet an instance of what seems to be the reasoned act of a wasp may be cited. The insect had selected a dead log of soft wood as a site for its egg-shaft. It was at a spot to which the occupations of the season took me daily, so that the boring operations were watched from beginning to end. The work was done rapidly and neatly, and when all was ready for the deposit of the eggs the insect constructed from papier-mache-like material a disc-shaped lid exactly fitting the mouth of the excavation, to which it was attached on its upper edge by a hinge. Then round and about the disc similar stuff was plastered, so as to form an irregular splash, imitative of a bird's droppings to the-degree of perfect deception. In the centre was the lid with the hinge, and whensoever the insect visited its nursery the lid swung up, closing behind it. On departure it fell into position. Unless the insect by its presence betrayed its secret, the shrewdest observer at close quarters would have been misled.

There are reasons for the belief that green tree-ants understand and respect the laws of neutrality. There are several communities in the mango-trees, and since some of the trees overhang the fence, the top wire is used as a highway. When a gate is opened traffic is suspended. In a minute or two of a busy day there will be considerable gatherings on the latch-style, and if the intervening space is narrowed by the swing of the gate the impatient insects begin to make a living bridge across the perilous gap. At one particular gate, which is opened and shut many times a day, it has been noticed that the ants never seem to resent interruptions or to be vexed by them. If they happen to get on the hands or fingers, they submit to be restored to the gate; but go to the formicary on the mango-tree half a dozen yards away and offer a friendly finger, and you will find dozens of pugnacious individuals ready to defend their home. Do they recognise that they are but pilgrims of the fence, enjoying certain rights on sufferance, that it is a path of peace on which belligerents must not intrude, a neutral tract under the custody of the law of nations, which ants, as well as men, must respect? Whatsoever the reason, the deportment of the truculent ant on the highway is that of an upholder of peace at any price. It is to be doubted if the animal world holds more illustrious examples of heroism than a green tree-ants' nest. Two or three individuals may be despised as long as their assaults are confined to the less sensitive parts of the body; but let a huge colony up among the branches of an orange-tree be disturbed, and the first army corps instantly mobilised, and it will not be cowardly hastily to retreat. So eager for the fray are the warriors, so well organised, so completely devoted to the self-sacrificing duty of protecting the community, that two distinct methods of advance and attack are exercised forthwith in the midst of what appears to be calamitous confusion. Swarming on the extremity of the branches among which the formicary is constructed, the defenders, projecting their terminal segments as far into space as possible, eject formic acid in the direction of the enemy. Like shrapnel from machine guns, the liquid missile sweeps a considerable area. Against the sunlight it appears as a continuous spray, and should one infinitesimal drop descend into the eye the stoutest mortal will blink. Attacks are made singly and in detachments. Heroes actually hurl themselves from the branches, and, failing to reach the enemy, run along the ground and, scaling his legs, inflict punishment on the first convenient patch of unprotected skin. Detachments muster in blobs, fall in a mass to the ground, and charge. If one of these forlorn hopes happens to be successful, the observant man will retire with little of his dignity remaining.

It is interesting to note how readily birds acquire tastes for the sweet fruits which man cultivates. One of the honey-eaters, the diet of which ranges from nectar to the juice of one of the native cucumbers, as bitter as colocynth, has become an ardent advocate for the thorough ripening of bananas. While on the plant the fruit is not appreciated, but after the bunch has been hung for a week or so and the first fruits are changing colour the bird is enthusiastic. Formerly bunches were ripened in a thatched building for the the most part open, and the bird got the very best of the bunch. Now the process takes place where the bird has to venture through wire-netting. It has no fear, entering without ceremony, loudly complaining when inadvertently disturbed, and flying to other parts of the house to express remonstrance when the supply is exhausted.

Scarcity of surface-water sharpens the powers of observation of some birds and increases the trustfulness of certain species towards human beings in a region wherein they are held to have rights on equality with those of their superiors in the animal world. For years, during the few weeks which generally intervene between the disappearance of accustomed water reserves and the beginning of the wet season, with its super-abundance, the metallic starlings have been wont to obtain refreshment from a hollow far up a huge tea-tree, the supply in which seemed to be inexhaustible. The tyrant's plea, necessity, ordained the destruction of the never-failing tree, and now the starlings descend by the hundred into the deep and shady ravine whence water is pumped, and drink also from the cattle-trough and bathe therein with noise and excitement of happy children on the beach. It is quite within the mark to compute the starlings by the hundred. The trough is edged nearly all day long by thirsty or dirty birds, while scores sit round among the shrubs waiting turn and commenting on the frolics and splashings of others in excitable tones. When, perhaps, there are but a poor dozen or so round the trough, you may chance to see the birds in attitudes more varied than those of Pliny's doves, and catch the shadows of burnished necks darkening the water, as in that famous mosaic, and even the glistening reflection of the red, jewel-like eyes. Other birds, with far less assurance and shrill clamour than the lovely starlings, visit the trough regularly and by the score. Two species of honey-eaters are seldom unrepresented. The barred-shouldered dove, the spangled drongo, the noisy pitta, the red-crowned fruit pigeon, the pheasant-tailed pigeon, are less frequent visitors; and though the purple-breasted fruit pigeon—the most magnificent of all—talks to his mate in coarse gutturals from the trees above, he has not been seen actually drinking. So shy and furtive a bird would choose his time for refreshment when there is little likelihood of interruption. In the ravine there are often metallic starlings by the dozen, and little green pigeons—for those domiciled come and go at all hours of the day. Occasionally a sulphur-crested cockatoo comes sailing down to the diminishing pool through interwoven leafage noiselessly as a butterfly; but scrub fowls, scared by the apparition in white, scamper off with a clatter, scattering the dead leaves. In such narrow quarters, birds are under restraint, and show anxiety and apprehension. There is no sport or play. They drink quickly and with faculties strained, and flutter off excitedly on the least alarm. Well may they be suspicious, for is not the cool spot attractive to the sly enemy, the green snake, which conceals its presence by faithful resemblance to the creepers among which it glides? Here, too, come millions of industrious bees, and in the dusk the big pencil-tailed water-rat, which the masterful dog kills with as little ceremony as he does the bird-scaring snakes.

It was late for cockatoos to start on their daily flight to the mainland from the big tree close to the twin palms half-way up the hill, and as they flew hastily and in close company they scolded each other in unmannerly terms. The language must have been vexing, for as they sped along far above the passionless sea one jostled the other. It was just the sort of action to provoke hungry, peevish birds to vindictiveness. That which had been jostled turned on the offender with angry shrieking, and instantly a clamorous fight was in progress. Claws became interlocked, and they fell each with distended crest, like a gilt-edged cloudlet following the setting sun. Shadow and substance met with a splash. The sea momentarily swallowed the combatants. Then a yellow note of exclamation appeared, and with laboured flutterings, using his enemy as a base, one rose and struggled to the beach oaks. Frantic wing-beating showed that the other bird was in serious difficulties. It was a hundred yards out, but the enjoyment of a sunbath after a sea frolic enabled one to proceed to the rescue without preliminaries. Half drowned and completely cowed, the bird was now confronted by a more awful peril than that of the sea. A bedraggled crest indicated horror at the steady approach of the enemy man, whose presence stimulated the sodden bird to such extraordinary efforts that it succeeded in rising and in making slow, low flight to the beach.

At dawn a bat flew into a spider's web spun during the night, the extremities of the wings being so entangled that struggling was almost impossible. A big spider pounced on it. Not a minute elapsed from the entanglement until the bat was released, but the venom of the spider had done its work. There was not a sign of life. The spider is dark grey in colour, bloated of body, slothful, and of most retiring disposition. Huddled up into almost spherical form, it lurks in dark places, which it soon makes insanitary. In the open it crouches among dead leaves which have gathered in the fork of a tree, and will construct a web which spans the coconut avenue with its stays. From one aspect its rotund body invites a good-humoured smile, for the marking exactly simulates the features of a tabby cat, well fed, sleepy, and in placid mood. Venom of virulence to kill a bat almost instantly would be severe enough to a human being. This dirty, obese spider deserves little consideration at the hand of man.

A moonless, cloudless night. The little praam takes the ground in the bay a few yards from the beach, and in the midst of a constellation of "jelly-fishes" spherical in form and varying in size. The larger are so many pale blue orbs floating lazily in a luminous mist, the only visible manifestation of life being a delicate but rhythmical deepening of the central hue. The wash of my wading seems not to affect them. I become conscious of the sudden appearance and swift disappearance of lesser spheres of startling brilliance. They emerge from nothingness, pause for a moment, and shoot towards me with extraordinary impulse. Each is a mere globule, resplendently blue. The tint intensifies as with accelerated velocity the atom flies until of its own excessive energy it explodes with a shell-like flash, leaving a sinuous trail of golden light. To burst into sight, gather force, to flash and slowly vanish— such is the sum of life of a speck of sea-jelly. To be the centre towards which scores of the watery meteors gravitate, to witness their apparently spontaneous beginning, their swift, brief, but ineffectual career and lingering end, delights this night of darkness. How many of the race of man are there whose post-mortem glory outshines life tenfold?

Beneath a slab of dead coral on the reef there was revealed one of those primitive and curious marine animals which has no common name, but which science recognises as SYNAPTA BESELLI. It is a relation of the béche-de-mer, of snake-like form, with a group of gills differentiating the head. Playing about it were three or four little fish which immediately took advantage of the only remaining cover, the body of the Synapta, snoodling beside it so artfully that they were quite concealed. The protector did not appear to resent the close company of the fish, which remained perfectly motionless. In a few seconds the Synapta began to extrude its feathery gills, which had been partly retracted on disturbance. I counted the gills, and while my forefinger indicated the sixth, a little fish, not previously noticed, appeared at the focus and edged off to the margin of the pool, now and again making decided efforts to regain its sanctuary. It was about an inch long and a third deep, ruby red, with pink undersides and pink, transparent fins. Three narrow bands of silver edged with lavender extended across the shoulder. Life gave it jewel-like lustre. The companionship between the slow and feeble Synapta, one of the most primitive of sea things, and the brilliant, agile fish may be another instance of commensalism.

No one who parades a coral reef can fail to be impressed by the various means adopted by its weaker denizens to evade the consequences of conspicuousness. Among the vast multitude of creatures, mostly hostile to each other, few are more remarkable than the crabs, not only on account of form and habit, but for care of themselves during the periodic casting of their shells. They therefore represent an entertaining study and a never-ending source of pleasure to the observer, who, as he happens on some fantastic member of the family, wonders, remembering his Shakespeare, what impossible matter will Nature make easy next. Dreamy little ripples were laying on the strands sprays of seaweed, torn from the reef which was not quite out of the influence of the easterly swell. The conditions were ordinary, but one fragment made itself noticeable by slight, almost undiscernible, but still distinctive efforts to regain the water, whence it was separated by a few inches. Seaweed alone was visible as it rested on the palm of the hand. Presently it moved hesitatingly and with infinite slowness, and, being reversed, revealed itself as a "watery" crab under living disguise. The specimen was sent to the Australian Museum, Sydney, where it came under the hands of my friend Mr. Allan R. McCulloch, who devotes himself to the phenomena of the sea; and since his references to it are explicit and authoritative, they will be more acceptable than generalities from an uninformed pen: "The crab you sent is the second specimen known of ZEWA BANFIELDI, which I described from a dried specimen received from you some years ago. Not only the species, but the genus also, was unknown until you gave me the opportunity of describing this interesting beast. It is one of the spider crabs, or Oxyrhynchus, most of which have long horns projecting from the rostrum, and are more or less thickly covered with stiff curled setae, to which seaweeds, sponges, and other marine growths— selected according to the taste of the bearer—are attached. When these crabs shed their shells, which they must do periodically to allow of growth, they retire to a dark corner and draw themselves out of a slit between the back and the abdomen, legs and all, which must, I imagine, be a delicate and somewhat painful proceeding. After emerging, they are, of course, quite soft, and the setae on the carapace and legs are flexible. The crab then selects choice bits of weed from its old shell and fastens them to itself by the setae, which soon curl at the tips like the tendrils of a vine, and so hold them firmly. The weeds and sponges, requiring no roots, but merely a secure base, readily grow in their new position, and so cover their host with a sheltering disguise, enabling it to sally forth in quest of fresh loves and other adventures. I am sending the reprint with the original description and figure, also a sketch of the crab with its weedy garments. Much of the weed had become detached on its arrival here, which is, perhaps, fortunate, since the sketch would otherwise have shown merely a cluster of weeds." It could be well wished that the specimen had retained the whole of its floral cloak, for then the sketch would have shown its deceptive qualities in perfection. Masquerading as a spray of seaweed, the crab eludes its enemies, the mask being of such high order that even man, with his perceptions, does not penetrate it unless he exercises his reasoning faculties. Because he knows that a spray of seaweed is not endowed with independent movement, when it does walk about he, at first, is as incredulous as was Macbeth when told of that "moving grove" of Birman.

ETERNAL SUNSHINE

"North Queensland is my country. I love it. I live in it. I would die for it."—
DODD S. CLARKE.

To those who earnestly believe that a country exercises dominance over its
inhabitants, mental as well as physical, the present state of North Queensland
offers interesting problems. Save for a fast-disappearing remnant, gone are
the original occupiers of the land. The most listless, the least thrifty of the
old peoples, have given place to representatives of the most adventurous, the
most successful—men and women of British blood, of progressive ideas,
vaunting and independent spirit, but with slight respect for the traditions of
their race. Apt to regard their own land as all-sufficient, to resent the
incoming of strangers (especially those of dark complexion), determined to
exclude coloured labour from tropical fields, while demanding higher and yet
higher recompense for work which in other equatorial regions is deemed to
be servile, on what grounds do they base the hope of adapting themselves to
their environment, of becoming children of the soil?

The genius of the race forbids degeneracy. Marked and sudden improvement
may be expected if examples drawn from the lower animals and certain plants
are applicable. Huxley laid it down that "the animals and plants of the
Northern Hemisphere are not only as well adapted to live in the Southern
Hemisphere as its own autochones, but are in many cases absolutely better
adapted, and so overrun and extirpate the aborigines. Clearly, therefore, the
species which naturally inhabits a country is not necessarily the best adapted
to its climate and other conditions." Australian aboriginals having given way
before a race better fitted to flourish, what will the future of the new race be?
What ideal is at present pursued?

To one who firmly upholds the theory of the evolution of Australian types,
and who thinks he perceives convincing evidence in support of his belief, it
seems likely that on the tropical coast, where the influence of the sun is all-
powerful, rainfall abundant, and vegetation prolific, the type will not only be
more rapidly developed, but that it will be pronounced in bodily form, in
tongue, and in temperament. One of the reasons compelling towards such
conclusion is the decided desire—nay, the ambition—on the part of native-
born Australians to do glad and seemly homage to the sun.

If a traveller from distant and friendly lands were to accept as germs of a type
those who sport in the surf at fashionable watering-places, he might infer
from the display of brown backs and shoulders that Australia had not
escaped a smudge of aboriginal blood. But this ardently cultivated tint is
notoriously impermanent. Contradictory as it may be, the most earnest
advocates of the "White Australia" principle use more than the average

quantity of oil, which makes the skin to shine and embrown under the influence of the much-loved sun. Do not their shoulders bear testimony to the sun's wholesome salutations, and does not the too fair and thin-skinned individual smart under his peeling and display envy against the favoured ones who burn to the tint of old copper? Naturally, those who have the most intense longing for a coloured skin, who persistently seek to acquire it by exposure to the sun seconded by anointings, will prevail. In the course of a few generations—it would be idle to say how many—the type will be fixed and the unguent superfluous; in the meantime the use of coco-nut oil has become one of the confirmed customs of the country, as in Fiji and elsewhere in the Pacific.

If "beauty born of murmuring sound" may enhance the charms of maidenhood, is it too much to expect that sunburn, fervently desired, may not only permanently darken the complexion, but affect the mien of the race? And thus in years to come the white Australian may be of the past— transformed physically by the supremacy of soil and sun, and improved in disposition and character by economic observances as irrefutable as the laws of Nature. The horses of out dry, stony uplands have already developed hoofs in shape and texture well adapted to the country over which they roam, and have become surer-footed and more active and durable. Conditions and circumstances which in a few generations effect desirable changes in horses will assuredly be influential in respect of the physique and stamina and moralities of man. North Queensland will establish a type, just as Tierra del Fuego did many centuries since, and the type will be that which is best fitted to maintain itself. It will be brown of complexion, hardy and alert. North Queensland is expansive and varied. It comprises a marvellous range of geological phenomena, from which may be expected remarkable variants. The sheep-grower of the treeless downs will differ from the denizen of the steamy coast who supplies him with sugar and bananas. The man from among the limestone bluffs may be in temperament strange to the dweller on the black soil plains and to the individual who lives among barren hills seamed with copper. Readers of English books and magazines are familiar with the little prominence given to matters which stand for good and worthiness and the stress laid on the seeming disadvantages of life in tropical Australia. A favourite magazine may contain a series of articles, sumptuously illustrated, conveying information concerning country life in Canada. It is impossible not to visualise the miles of wheat-fields, the imposing elevators, the railways cutting across endless prairies or winding among wonderful mountains, snowcapped as a stage effect merely. The pictures of chubby children and buxom girls and sturdy boys tell of the healthfulness and invigorating qualities of the climate. Is it not always spring or summer in Canada? Would not the man who whispered of snow and ice be a renegade, a dastard, a rebel? North Queenslanders do not attempt to belittle the reputation of Canada as a field for the activities of the surplus population of the old country. We are of the same blood and breed, and merely ask for a proper understanding of our own good land. The comfort given to Canada is all in the family, and an Empire which extends from pole to pole must needs embrace differences of climate and productions.

Do not we all take upon our shoulders the burden of Empire? Here we bear our share stripped to the buff, while Canada bustles under an equally honourable but heavier load. Occasionally, no doubt, the most patriotic son of our Lady of Snows would joy in the heat of North Queensland noon; while the sweatful North Queenslander may often pant for the superfluous ice of his far-away cousin.

The denizens of the different parts of the Empire quite understand one another, and realise that to be great the Empire must disregard temperatures as it does prickly heat and chilblains. Only the casual visitor fails in this.

Sun Days are essential to the production of sugar and bananas and mangoes, to say nothing of pineapples and other fruits of the tropics. When we are called upon to endure extraordinary heat, we tell one another of the penance and find excuse for extra drinks. But neither the heat nor the comparison of personal experiences is of the injurious nature of some of the refreshments. The weather is not compounded of excesses, but of means. Is it not true that few countries in the wide world would be considered fit for habitation by human beings if the character of the climate was estimated by its extremes?

No North Queenslander will resent records of high temperatures. He will be quite content to be shown enjoying and flourishing in the heat in which sugar-cane thrives, for thereby is to be proved a fact theorists seem unable to grasp—viz., that such is the soundness and virtue of the British race that it adapts itself with equal success to the long, dark, cold winter of Canada and the perpetual summer of North Queensland. Who is to say that the Canadian in his thick woollens and furs is a healthier subject, a worthier type, than the North Queenslander, stripped to the waist in the full blaze of the sun, glorying in his own vigour, proud of his magnificent heritage, and scornful of the opinions of those who have never experienced that supreme zest of life unpurchasable outside the tropic zone?

With intent to picturesquely demonstrate that soil will tell, some are ready to assert that we owe Christianity to the horizontal limestone formation of Palestine. Accepting the theory with whole-hearted enthusiasm, and admitting that North Queensland comprehends tracts of country not dissimilar from the Holy Land, mark what the future may have in store for the race. Do you want old age?—Methuselah, Noah, Isaac. Strong men?—Gosselin, Samson, Saul. Beautiful women?—Ruth, Rebecca, Esther. Does not David, the man after God's own heart, appeal? Was not Solomon, the wise, the glorious, the prolific, a superior type? And, with all reverence be it said, was not the Founder of the Christian religion a solar product?

Hotter lands beyond the bounds of Palestine gave to the world men and women whose deeds and influence still astound and stimulate millions of mankind—the Queen of Sheba, Cleopatra, Pharaoh the Great, Moses the leader, whom the Lord knew face to face, Joseph the organiser, Mahomet, the benign Buddha, and all the sages, the poets, the historians, the architects of the gorgeous East. May not those who elect to live in lands of high temperature and who are strong in their faith cite apt and illustrious precedents, and make bold to say that none has exercised more influence on the minds and destinies of mankind than those born in the lands of the Sun?

FRAGRANCE AND FRUIT

"The woman saw that the tree was good for food, and that it was pleasant to the eyes, and a tree to be desired to make one wise."—Holy Writ.

While the remnant of the crop of citrus fruits still hangs on the trees, after providing refreshing food for six months and more, the blooms which promise next year's supplies decorate the branches. Is it not pleasing to have such graceful promises before the burden of the passing season has disposed of all its sweetness? Possibly these early flowers are destined to produce fruit for the admiration of living things upon which the gardener bestows anything but a welcome. It may come to maturity just after the wet season, when flies and moths feast and corrupt in riot which provokes to wrath. Inconsequent feeders, they probe the fruit and flit away after a sip which does not absorb a thousandth part of its keen juices, or they use a comely specimen in which to deposit eggs, which in the course of Nature become grubs. All such infected fruit the trees abandon until the ground is strewn with waste. Such disaster happens when the air is favourable to the breeding of quivering gauze wings; but there comes a time when the fruit suffers little or no ill, and then the heart of the orchardist rejoices as does that of the fisher when the wind comes up from the sea. Then does he accept fine promises in good faith, for it has come to be the fashion for certain varieties of citrus fruits to provide two crops, and the second, which ripens about the beginning of August, the superior in size, appearances generally, and distinctly in flavour. The fruit is just as juicy as that which ripens when the air is saturated with the moisture of the wet season, while its fragrance almost equals that of the snowy flowers whence it sprang. These facts hasten to this conclusion—that the orange-grower has something beyond mere money in compensation for his toil. Can it be called toil? Does he not for the most part, after the first and essential preliminaries are of the past, permit Nature to have her own wayward will with his dutiful trees? Does he always and invariably cut out the dead wood which tells of much too strenuous efforts on their part to justify their existence and his care? Does he attempt to exterminate the pretty flies which send to the ground a certain percentage, while yet the fruit is immature and bitter? Does he let the light of the caressing sun into the hearts of his pet trees by removing superfluous twigs? Well does he know that if he tended them as he should their bounty to him would be much magnified. Yet does he dream on, accepting that which comes, admiring leafage, bloom, and fragrant fruit, and always postponing the day when substantial aid and credit should be given. There is something to be said in favour of this happy attitude towards good-natured trees. Should it not suffice to have given them monopoly and choice? Many others, and some of far nobler proportions, have been exterminated for their special benefit and advantage. They have been grown from seed of most highly complimented fruit; their infancy and youth have been nurtured and protected; each has been assigned its proper place with due regard to the welfare of neighbours; less promising vegetation has been summarily checked; the first flowers have been sniffed with high delight, the first fruits sampled with extravagant praise. Having bestowed upon trees care and attention, while they were yet mere sprouts of tender green, and admired their sturdy development, and approved their best efforts, is it not yours to accept whatsoever they offer as reward and recompense for past labour and present appreciation?

From the artistic standpoint the most admirable of all the citrus-trees is the pomelo, which, however, lacks merit from the commercial side. The tree grows more sedately than the orange or the mandarin, but on a grander scale. The leaves are bigger, tougher, and the appendages on either side of the stalk (which botanists call the stipules) more developed. The blooms are greater, and endowed with a much richer perfume than the orange; the fruit is huge and fragrant, though somewhat disappointing to the individual who expects the sweetness of the mandarin; while, if the views of the learned in such attributes are trustworthy it possesses medicinal qualities which are foreign to its dainty, diminutive relative. It would be mere affectation to refrain from these compliments to the pomelo when the atmosphere is saturated with the perfume from lusty trees. Certainly one has to wait patiently for many a long year ere his trees greet him with white flowers which pour out perfume of rare density and enrich him with golden fruit almost as big as footballs. From nine to twelve years must elapse, but expectancy is not wholly measurable by the arbitrariness of time. The true standard is the desire, tempered by the patience of the custodian of the trees.

In August the pomeloes put on their most attractive appearances. The young leaves of lively tint contrast with the almost sombre green of the older foliage, and flowers in clusters give a most becoming adornment. Big and beautiful as they are, scent is their most conspicuous feature. Even in the open air it is rich almost to cloyness. It hangs about the tree while the wind is still, and the slightest movement of the air wafts it hither and thither. It stings sensitive folk with its intensity at close quarters, but when diffused is fragrance of ethereal delight. All day long birds frolic in the trees, some to cull the nectar, some to search for insects attracted for like purpose, some to nibble and discard white petals. All the moist soil beneath is strewn with snowy flakes, for at night flying foxes blunder among the branches, destroying more blooms than they eat. But why grumble? Birds which nip off petals and musty foxes which brush down whole posies in their clumsiness are but positive checks to overproduction. Do they not avert the unthankful task of carting away dozens of barrow loads of superfluous fruit? Last night at dusk there was a sensation of the coming of rain, though the air was still and the sky clear. I paused under the trees to expand my lungs with their scented breathings. A semi-intoxicated bird twittered drowsily among the branches,

"His happy good-night air,

Some blessed hope, whereof he knew,

And I was unaware."

Dozens of sphinx moths—big torpedo-shaped bodies carried by wings of soft brown and dull red—floated about, sipping where and when and as long as they liked. Sometimes the sphinx has almost an aggressive tone In his flight—hasty, important, brooking no interference. Last night's note was of supreme content. A rich and overflowing feast was spread and the insects hovered over the posies and sipped and fluted like merry roysterers, without a care or thought of the morrow. It was a love-feast, for the still night seemed to invite the trees to give of their richest and best; the psalm of the insects was audible, not to the distance whence the perfume was dissipated, but for many a scented yard. The trees seemed sanctified, and I stood bare-headed among them and gave my silent praise for a delightsome experience. Expectancy and patience had been overpaid.

THE SCENE-SHIFTER

"We are all going to the play or coming from it."—DICKENS.

In a few hours came "the season's difference." The scene-shifter worked with almost magical haste, with silence, and with supreme effect. The gloomy days and nights of misty hill-tops and damp hollows, where the grass was sodden and the air dull and irresponsive to sound, gave way to bright sunshine, cloudless skies, calm seas, echoing hills, and the tinge of that which for lack of the ideal word we call "spring." Spring does not visit the tropical coast, where vegetation does not tolerate any period of rest. When plants are not actually romping with excess of vital force, as during the height of the wet season, they grow with the haste of summer. And yet immediately on the dispersal of the mists of July the least observance could not fail to recognise that a certain and elaborate change had taken place. The mango-trees had been flowering for several weeks in a trivial, half-hearted way, but when the sun sent its thrills down into the moist soil the lemons and pomeloes began to sweeten the air; the sunflower-tree displayed its golden crowns among huge soft leaves, and the last blooms of belated wattles fell, showing that it is possible for tributes representative of May and September to be paid on one and the same date.

The scene-shifter came softly "as the small rain upon the tender herb," but with an orchestra of his own. Years of observation have shown that the weather does control the habits of some birds—birds of distinct and regular methods of life. Two such are common—the nutmeg pigeon and the metallic starling. Both species leave this part of the North during the third week of March, flying in flocks to regions nearer the equator. For several weeks the starlings train themselves for the long Northern flight and its perils, dashing with impetuous speed through the forest and wheeling up into the sky until they disappear, to become visible again as black dots hurtling through space when the sunlight plays on their glossy feathers as the course of the flock is changed. With the rush of a wind of small measure but immense velocity, the flock descends earthwards, among and over the trees, perfecting itself by trials of endurance and intricate alertness. The birds return during the first week in August, in small and silent companies, to reoccupy favourite resorts in common. The nutmeg pigeons are also of exact habit, the time for their return generally coinciding with that of the starlings. This year (1916) both birds were noticed just after the scene-shifter had swept the hills of mists, and now other birds seem to have awakened to the conditions which the starlings and the nutmegs brought with them from hotter lands. The swamp pheasants are whooping and gurgling, and that semi-migratory fellow, the spangled drongo—a flattering name, for he jangles but does not spangle—sits on the slim branch of the Moreton Bay ash which held last year's nest and chatters discordances in the very ears of his responsive mate. They will start building a loose nest on the brittlest branch forthwith, and while the lady sits on her three eggs he will screech defiances to the high heavens and perform aerial gymnastics with delirious delight.

The sun-birds are searching the lemon blooms. The breast of the gay, assertive little bird is far richer in tint than the brightest of the lemons. A minute ago one perched on a ripe fruit as if to shame it by contrast, and the fruit has since seemed a trifle dull of tint, and with light-hearted inconsequence the pair are now probing narrow throats of papaw flowers. The ground has been too much overgrown with grass and weeds for the comfort of the little green pigeons which come strutting down the paths for seeds and crumbs. Dry soil, which may be easily scanned and scratched, is more to their liking, so they keep to the forest, where in some places the undergrowth of wattles is so dense that the sun may not visit the ground, and the bare places glitter with seed.

When rain was seriously deficient, proof was given that some proportion of the wattle seeds eaten by pigeons are not digested. In the crevices of logs supporting the water-trough, which proved to be a popular refreshment spot of many species of birds, clamorous with thirst, seeds were deposited, and when the rains came the trough was fringed and decorated with pinnate leaves of sprouting wattles, some of which grew so strongly, notwithstanding the absence of soil, save that which occurs from the slow decay of seasoned bloodwood, that if summary measures had not been taken the trough might have been embowered. The season seems to have been too damp for the night-jars, though quite to the taste of all species of pigeons. In the course of a few minutes the voice of the timid, tremulous, barred-shouldered dove came from among the yellow-flowered hibiscus of the beach, while the pheasant-tailed pigeon sounded its rich, dual note, the red-crowned fruit pigeon tolled its mournful chime, and the guttural of the magnificent fruit pigeon—often heard, but seldom seen—came from the jungle close at hand. Not one of these birds was visible, nor was the fluty-voiced shrike thrush, which answers every strange call and mimics crude attempts to reproduce its varied notes. The blue kingfisher is investigating the tumour made by white ants in the bloodwood wherein the nest is annually excavated, and soon the chattering notes of the pair will be heard. A week ago few signs of the approach of the scene-shifter were discernible. He has come, and plants and birds respond to his genial and becoming presence—plants with richer growth and more abundant flowers, birds with the unreflecting gaiety of nuptial days.

BEACH PLANTS

"Remove the vegetable kingdom, or interrupt the flow of its unconscious benefactions, and the whole higher life of the world ends."—HENRY DRUMMOND.

Strolling on the curving footway of broken shells and coral chips marking the limit of the morning's tide, a vague attempt was made to catalogue the plants which crowd each other on the verge of salt water, and so to make comparison with that part of Australia the features of which provoked Adam Lindsay Gordon to frame an adhesive phrase concerning bright scentless blossoms and songless, bright birds. Excluding the acacias and eucalypts, said to have given sameness to the scenes among which the exotic poet ranged, a long list might be compiled; nor will the pleasant sounds of the afternoon be set down in formal order to the vexing of his memory, for possibly he never heard the whoop and gurgle of the swamp pheasant or the blended voices of hundreds of nutmeg pigeons mellowed by half a mile of still, warm air.

Nor may such unassuming vegetation as the grasses—at least a dozen varieties—find place in an enumeration which appeals primarily on the grounds of prominence, though it would not do to despise the soft and pleasant carpet beneath the orderly row of Casuarinas which the tide planted during the last big cyclone with gardener's art. The common name for the trees—"she" (or "shea" oaks, as the late F. Manson Bailey preferred)—mimics the sound of the wind among the branches, which the slightest zephyr stirs and, the storm lashes into sea-like roar. The bright green of the grasses sets off the dull green and bronze of the steadfast harps of the beach. At certain seasons and in some lights, when the sun is in the west, the minute scales at the joints of the slender, pendulous branchlets shine like old gold, producing a theatrical effect which, if not experienced before, startles and almost persuades to the belief that the complaining trees have been decorated by one who "has sought out many inventions." But the slant of the sun alters, the light fades, leaving them sombre in hue and whispering more and more discreetly as the night calm settles over the scene. Such communicable trees should stand together, commenting on passing events, booming in unison with the cyclone, and mimicking the tenderest tones of the idlest wind. During a storm, when the big waves crash on the beach and the Casuarinas are tormented, the tumult is bewildering; but however loud their plaint, very few suffer, though growing in loose sand; for the roots are widespread and, like the trunk and main branches, tough, while the branchlets stream before the wind.

Close behind the screen of Casuarinas is a magnificent specimen of a wide-spreading shrub, in form a squat dome, which commemorates the name of a

French naturalist—TOURNEFORTIA ARGENTA. The leaves, crowded at the ends of thick branchlets, are covered with soft, silky hairs of a silvery cast, which reflect the sun's rays. It would be gross exaggeration to say that the finely shaped shrub shines like silver, for the general hue of the foliage is sage green, but that it has a silvery cast, which in certain lights contrasts with the dull gold of its neighbours, is an alluring fact which must not be strained. Moreover, the shrub covers an almost perfect circle, about thirty feet in diameter, and since it is not more than ten feet high, its form is as if Nature had designed the creation of a circus of shadow, dense and cool, for the comfort of mankind.

At high-water mark stands one of the Terminalias with big terminal light green leaves, musty flowers, and purple fruit—gold, silver, and purple in close array—while over the sand the goat-footed convolvulus sends long, succulent shoots bearing huge pink flowers complementary to the purple of the beach-pea (CANVALIA OBTUSIFOLIA).

Under the she-oaks young coral trees have sprung up, but the red flowers are of the past, and so also have the gold and white of the Calophyllums disappeared. But in the evening the breeze brings whiffs of a singular savour, pleasant yet not sweet, which comes from the acre or two of native hops a few yards back. The bruised leaves thereof give off anything but an attractive odour, yet the faint natural exhalations from the plant are sniffed eagerly and to the revivification of pleasant recollections.

Among a crowd of massive shrubs sprawls a plant of loose habit known as CAESALPINA BONDUCELLA, the long clinging branches and the pods of which are armed with hooked prickles. It is a plant of wide range, for the bluish-grey seeds are said to be used in Arabia for necklets. In the idle days of the past the blacks were wont to enclose a single seed in a miniature basket woven of strips of cane for the amusement of infants—probably the first of rattles. It has seized for support some of the branches of a rare tree (CERBERA ODOLLAM) which bears long, glossy, lanceolate leaves, large, pink-centred, white flowers, delicately fragrant, and compressed oval fruit, brilliantly scarlet. The tempting appearance of the fruit is all that may be said in its favour, for it is hard and bitter, and said to be vicious in its effects on the human system; hence the generic title, after the three-headed dog, guardian of the portals of the infernal regions.

Grouped here and there are pale green, big-leaved shrubs (PREMNA OBTUSIFOLIA,) bearing flowers and fruit calling to mind the elder of the old country. The wood is deep yellow in colour, but apparently of no practical use.

Another small tree, suggesting in its regular and well-balanced shape the use of the pruning-knife, is GUETTARDIA SPECIOSA, the flowers of which are white with a tinge of pink in the centre and highly fragrant. The fruit is a hard, woody drupe, containing small seeds. TIMONIUS RUMPHII, belonging to the same Family, but of more frequent occurrence, bears small white flowers and globular fruit. The white, finely grained wood is said to resemble English sycamore. Though harsh and flaky, the surface of the bark seems to retain moisture, making it attractive to several species of fungi and epiphytal ferns, the most conspicuous of the latter being the stag's-horn. Few of the trees near the beach are free from such encumbrances.

To unaccustomed eyes the Pandanus palm is chief among the noticeable features of the flora of the coast of tropical Queensland. Two species are represented on these accommodating sands, each suffering no ill, from imbibing salt water, each exhibiting the peculiarity whence the genus derives its common name—the screw palm, the arrangement of the long, narrow, prickle-edged leaves displaying in the most regular and demonstrative style the perfect spiral. The single stem of youth frequently deteriorates and occasionally disappears altogether, adventitious roots, descending from various heights, forming an elaborate and sure and ever-developing support. The huge, bright orange-tinted fruit of the species known as Odoratissimus is highly attractive in appearance, and to the uninitiated offers pleasing hopes and delicious expectations. It is, however, delusive, being constituted of woody drupes in close clusters collected into a globular head, with meagre yellow pulp at the base of each group, the pulp having an aromatic and unsatisfactory flavour. Each drupe contains an oblong oval kernel, pleasant to the taste, but so trivial in size as to be hardly worth the trouble of extraction unless there is little else to occupy attention save the pangs of hunger. These defects do not detract from the parade of the tree— picturesque, singular, and replete with interest to the observer of the infinite variety of the vegetation of the tropics.

The cockatoo apple (CAREYA AUSTRALIS), which has several useful qualities, flourishes exceedingly. The ripe fruit, green and insipid, was wont to be eaten by the blacks, bark from the branches was twisted into fishing-lines, that of the roots used for poisoning fish, while the leaves, heated over the fire until the oil exuded, were applied to bruised and aching parts of the body. Extraordinary tenacity of life distinguished the tree, the axe, fire, and poison failing under some circumstances to vanquish it.

Another and closely related member of the same Family (Myrtaceae) is BARRINGTONIA SPECIOSA, which, so far as local experience is to be trusted, is restricted to the beaches, growing lustily in pure sand at the very verge of high-water mark. The glossy leaves of this many-branched tree often exceed a foot in length; the flowers, too, are large and singular in style, the petals being comparatively insignificant, while the numerous stamens attain a length of four inches and are of a lovely shade of red. Like its relative, the cockatoo apple, the flowers of the Barringtonia have a meaty smell, which seems to attract many species of insects. In keeping with other characteristics, the fruit is large, consisting of a thick, woody covering, as if Nature designed that the single seeds should be adequately protected during a protracted oceanic drift. It is often cast up on the sand, but the seed does not germinate as consistently as that of the cannon-ball-tree; but when it does it rarely fails to become established.

Two species of Ficus deserve to be mentioned, though this catalogue does not claim to be exhaustive. FICUS FASCICULATA, as the title implies, bears its inedible fruit in bundles, branches, trunk, and exposed roots, being alike fertile, and is almost as retentive of life as the cockatoo apple. Opposita is remarkable for varied form of foliage, referred to particularly elsewhere, and for the sweetness of its fruit.

One of the loveliest and most remarkable plants of the beach is the seacoast laburnum (SOPHORA TOMENTOSA), with its pinnate leaves of sage green, hoary with silvery fur as soft as seal-skin, and bearing terminal spikes of golden flowers with scent invoking slight comparison with mignonette. The thick, silky leaves, the yellow flowers, and the strange pods, are distinctive qualities, which atone for the absence of the special sweetness of the garden favourite. The pods begin as slender, silvery, dangling threads, which speedily lengthen and become constricted. When the breeze flusters the shrubs, revealing the undersides of the leaves at a reflective angle and shaking the tasselled pods, and the splashes of gold sway hither and thither, the character of the shrub as one of the most attractive ornaments of the beach is so truly displayed that it might be likened to the tree of the sun described by Marco Polo—green on one side, but white when perceived on the other.

This quality, however, is not special or peculiar. The brown kurrajong (COMMERSONIA ECHINATA) exhibits it even more conspicuously, and, when the dusty white flowers—displayed in almost horizontal planes—are buffeted by the winds and the white undersides of the leaves are revealed, the whole style of the tree is transformed as a demure damsel is by tempestuous petticoats.

With the grey-green of the Sophora is often intertwined the leafless creeper CASSYTHA FILIFORMIS, which in the days of the past the blacks were wont to use with other beach plants in the composition of a crude seine net. The long-reaching, white-flowered CLERODENDRON INERME and the tough, sprawling BLAINVILLEA LATIFOLIA, with its small, harsh flowers, yellow as buttercups but resembling a daisy in form, were also embodied in the net.

The Poonga oil-tree, the new and old leaves the colour of new copper, and the mature the darkest of green, bears spikes of pale lavender flowers, and makes a decided blotch among the light green succulent leaves of the native cabbage (SCAEVOLA KOENIGII), with its strange white flowers and milk-white fruit. All parts of the plant are said to be emetic.

Two varieties of VITEX TRIFOLIA, each bearing pretty lavender flowers, but in other respects sharply contrasted, are among the commonest of denizens of the beach. The one is a prostrate plant with sage-coloured and sage-scented leaves; the other a shrub or small tree with light green foliage, the underside of which is mealy-white, and flowers paler than those of its lowly kin. Each is pretty, and the creeping variety (known in Egypt as the "Hand of Mary") decidedly one of the most eager lovers of the sand, to which it keeps strictly.

Almost within reach from high water are representatives of a tall, shining-leaved shrub known as MORINDA CITRIFOLIA, the flower-heads of which merge into a berry which has a most disagreeable odour and a still more objectionable flavour. It is related that when La Perouse was cast away on one of the islands of the South Pacific, a native undertook to ward off the pangs of hunger by converting the fruit into an edible dish. But his manipulation seemed but to intensify original nauseousness, and the brave Frenchman and his companions found semi-starvation more endurable than the repugnant mess.

Magnificent representatives of the umbrella-tree (BRASSAIA ACTINOPHYLLA), unique among the many novelties of the tropical coast, are massed in groups or stand in solitary grace close to the sea. Queensland has a monopoly over this handsome and remarkable tree, the genus to which it belongs being limited to a single species occurring nowhere else in a native state. Discovered by Banks and Solander at Cooktown in 1770, the second record of its existence, it is believed, was made from specimens obtained on this island by Macgillivray and Huxley in 1848. Possibly the very trees which attracted their attention still crown their rayed and glossy leaflets with long, radiating rods thickly set with red, stud-like flowers. Such foliage and such flowers would appeal gloriously to an enthusiastic botanist, and to so devoted, indefatigable, and successful a searcher after the wonders and the higher truths of the world as Huxley.

Few of the ornaments of the beach are more noticeable than that known commonly as the sunflower-tree and by the natives as Gingee (DIPLANTHERA TETRAPHYLLA), with its big leaves, soft of surface when young, but harsh and coarse at maturity. The golden flowers, grouped in huge heads, are rich in nectar, attracting birds and butterflies by day and flying foxes at night. The fruit, enclosed in a crisp capsule, is tough and leathery, in shape a flattened oval, and is entirely covered with silken seeds lying close and dense as the feathers of the grebe. When numbers of the capsules open simultaneously, the seeds float earthwards like a silvery mantle or stream before the wind like a veil. Rarely the capsule falls to the ground complete, and then the parting of the valves reveals the fruit, in form not unlike a small fish covered with glistening scales. The soft white wood is generally condemned, but duly seasoned it becomes tough, and is durable when not exposed to the weather. Like other quick-growing trees, the Gingee takes no long time in arriving at maturity, and its life is comparatively brief. Often big trees die from no apparent cause, and the wood becoming dry and tindery, the limbs crash to the ground suddenly, and in a few months the whole substance disappears in dust and mould.

Though the flowering season of the Calophyllum is of the past, the tree which bestows on the beaches the deepest shade and is handsome in all its parts must not be disregarded, for does it not, ever and anon, strive after a higher purpose than the production of goodly leaves, white flowers, and nuts "harsh and crude"? On rare occasions the external covering of the nut turns yellow on the tree, and is then found to enclose a thin envelope of pulp of aromatic and rather gratifying flavour. Such a phenomenon seems to manifest inherent excellencies, a laudable effort towards self-improvement, a plea for assistance on the part of some approving and patient man, an indication of the lines on which he might co-operate. The tree does not need gloss for its perfect leaves or fragrance for its flowers, nor need the qualities of its pink wood of wavering figure be extolled. With the exception of the stamens, all parts of the inflorescence, inclusive of the long pedicles, are milk-white, and the perfume is as sweet and refreshing as an English spring posy. Chemists tell us that the oil from the kernels contains a green pigment which changes to yellow on saponification, and that the resin is emetic and purgative, and healing when applied as plaster. If botanical science can develop the meritorious tendencies the fruit occasionally exhibits, the Calophyllum would certainly rank as one of the most wonderful of all tropical fruits. And may it not be wise to indulge the highest hopes when it is borne in mind that at the head of the Family to which the Calophyllum belongs stands that queen of fruits—the mangosteen? Faith in the probable idealisation of the Calophyllum is justified by reference to the "Prefatory and Other Notes" to the late F. M. Bailey's great work, the "Comprehensive Catalogue of Queensland Plants," where is to be found these encouraging words: "When any particular plant is said to furnish a useful fruit, it must not be imagined that the fruit equals the apple, pear, or peach of the present day, but all so marked are superior to the fruits known to our far-back forefathers."

Two eucalypts—bloodwood and Moreton Bay ash (CORYMBOSA and TESSELLARIS respectively)—and two acacias are represented, the former developing into great trees of economic value, the latter being comparatively short-lived and ornamental. The young shoots of Acacia flavescens are covered as with golden fleece, and its globular flowers are pale yellow. The wood resembles in tint and texture its ally, the raspberry-jam wood of Western Australia, though lacking its significant and remarkable aroma. ACACIA AULACOCARPA displays in pendant masses golden tassels rich in fragrance.

The yellow-flowered hibiscus (cotton-tree) overhangs the tide, and the small-leaved shrub the blacks name Tee-bee (WIKSTRAEMIA INDICA), the pink, semi-transparent fruit of which is eaten in times of stress, springs from pure sand.

A tall, almost branchless shrub (MACARANGA TANARIUS), the Toogantoogan of the natives, grows in close clumps conducive to the production of light, straight, slim stems used as fish-spears. The bark peels readily in long strands, easily convertible into lines, and the sap from incised stems, which crystallises with a reddish tint, is a fast cement. Huge platter-shaped leaves are supported on long stalks from nearly the centre, whence radiate prominent nerves of pale green. Some plants exhibit leaf-stalks of ruby red, with central leaf-spot and nerves like in hue, producing the most beautiful effect. If the growth of the plant could be kept within bounds it would be gladly admitted as a garden shrub. The stems and the base of the leaf-stalk are coated with, glaucous bloom, like that of a ripe plum. The bloom, easily to be rubbed off, is said to derive its title from that Glaucus who took part in the Trojan War and had the simplicity, or the wisdom, to exchange his suit of golden armour for one of iron.

The length of the beach thus casually examined is not more than a quarter of a mile long, and no plant mentioned is more than a few yards from high-water mark, the soil being almost pure sand. Imagine some three square miles of country varied by hills and flats of rich soil, with creeks and ravines, precipices and bluffs, dense jungle and thick forest, hollows wherein water lodges in the wet season, and granite ridges, and then endeavour to comprehend the botany of one small island of the tropical coast!

To obtain demonstration of the vitalising and nourishing principles in maritime sands under the effects of heat, light, and moisture, it is necessary to retrace our steps and walk round the sandspit to the transfigured and degenerate mouth of that once mangrove-creek known to the blacks by a name signifying that a boy once tethered in it a sucking fish (Remora). Obstructed by a bank, the creek is dead and dry save when the floods of the wet season co-operate with high tides and effect a breach, to be repaired on the cessation of the rains. No more than four years have passed since the formation of the bank began. It is now a shrubbery made by the incessant and tireless sea from materials hostile, insipid, and loose-sand, shells, and coral debris, with pumice from some far-away volcano. On this newly made, restricted strip one may peep and botanise without restraint, discovering that though it does not offer conditions at all favourable to the retention of moisture, plants of varied character crowd each other for space and flourish as if drawing nutriment from rich loam.

Several botanical Families are represented, the genera and species being:

Casuarina equisetifolia (she-oak)

Avicennia officinalis (white mangrove).

Clerodendron inerme.

Premna obtusifolia.

Vitex trifolia.

Vitex trifolia, var. obovata.

Carapa moluccensis (cannon-ball-tree).

Erylhrina indica (coral-tree).

Sophora tomentosa (sea-coast laburnum).

Pongamia glabra (poonga oil-tree).

Vigna luteola (yellow-flowered pea).

Calophyllum inophyllum (Alexandrian laurel).

Terminalia melanocarpa.

Ximenia americana (yellow plum).

Scoevola koenigii (native cabbage).

Hibiscus tiliaceus (cotton-tree).

Wikstroemia indica. Macaranga tanarius.

Euphorbia eremophilla (caustic bush).

Dodonaea viscosa (hop-bush).

Passiflora foetida (stinking passion fruit).

Ipomea pes caprae (goat-footed convolvulus).

Ionidium suffruticosum, Form A.

Ionidium suffruticosum, Form B (spade-flower).

Blainvillea latifolia.

Gnaphalium luteo-album (flannel-leaf or cud-weed).

Vernonia cinerea (erect, fluffy-seeded weed).

Remirea maritima (spiky sand-binder).

Cyperus decompositus (giant sedge).

Erigeron linifolius (cobbler's pegs or rag-weed).

Tribulus terrestris (caltrops).

Triumfetta procumbens (burr).

Salsola kali (prickly salt-wort).

Mesembryanthemum aequilaterale (pig's face).

Anthistria ciliata (kangaroo-grass).

Paspalum distichum (water couch-grass).

Zoysia pungens (coast couch-grass).

Lepturus repens (creeping wire-grass).

Panicum leucophaeum (pasture-grass).

Andropogon refractus (barbed wire-grass).

Tragus racemosus (burr-grass).

Eragrostis brownii, var. pubescens (love-grass).

With the exception of some of the grasses and two noxious weeds, this assemblage is representative of plants which grow just beyond the sweep of the waves, and are prosperously at home nowhere else. One, the cannonball-tree, is so highly specialised that its presence is but temporary, for it endures but a single set of conditions—saline mud and the shade of mangroves. The thick, leathery capsule contains several irregularly shaped seeds, somewhat similar to Brazil nuts, but larger in size and not to be reassembled readily after separation. When stranded, germination is prompt, but the young plants, lacking essential conditions, invariably perish. One of the trailers—the caltrops—has trilobed, saw-edged leaves (harsh on both sides), yellow flowers of unpleasant odour, and fruit which, perhaps, formed the model of the war weapon of the time of the Crusaders. In whatever position it rests on the ground it presents an array of spikes to the bare foot. Though all its superficial qualities are graceless, it performs the admirable office of binding sand, and thus prepares the way for benign and faultless vegetation.

That his garden might not only be instructive but profitable to mankind, Neptune heaved on to its verge three coco-nuts, the goose-barnacles on two of which bore testimony to a long drift. That which retained the germ of life fell into the hands of a visiting black boy, who split it open to feast on the pithy and insipid "apple" within its shell at the base of the sprout. This mischance ruined for the time being the prospect of a fine effect; but the perseverance and prodigality of Neptune none may estimate. He will certainly bring from distant domain another nut which may escape the observation of the never-to-be-satisfied black boys until the young plant itself has assimilated its concentrated food, and begins to spread its glossy fronds in the face of the sun. In the meantime the garden displays four weeds, two of the nature of pests, two of discomfort merely; ornamental, scented, and flowering shrubs, and trees promising to be conspicuous and picturesque, so that credit is to be divided—the sea made the site, the adjacent land provided all the becoming plants.

What are the elements in this primitive spot which afford nutriment to vegetation of such varied character? Probably there are few of the beaches of islands within the Great Barrier Reef on which the majority of the plants do not exist. It is typical, therefore, not of isolated experiments on the part of Nature, but of conditions and processes repeated in similitude wheresoever in the region raw sand heals the wounds inflicted by the sea or the grumbling sea retreats before the sibilant, incessant sand.

SHADOWS

"The wish—that ages have not yet subdued—In man to have no master save his mood."

BYRON.

Before the coming of the obscuring grey of these wet-season days, when the tranquil sea absorbed the lustrous blue of the sky, I discovered myself day-dreaming for a blissful moment or two ere the crude anchor of the flattie slipped slowly to the mud twelve feet below. The rough iron and rusty chain cast curious crinkled shadows, and presently, as the iron sank into the slate-coloured mud and the chain tightened, the shadow was single but infirm. Light and the magic of the sea, which, though it takes its ease, is forbidden absolute rest, transformed it until imagination created similitude to a serpent in its natural element. Its half-concealed, formless head was verified by a flake of rust just where a watchful eye might have been, and the sun played upon it.

So here at last was the sea-serpent with alert eye and without end. It was all so realistic and endowed with such benignity and such gentleness of motion that I gazed at it with the gladness of a discoverer. In response to a slight motion of the hand, the sea-serpent wriggled as though in haste; but wriggle as it might the end never came.

The boat drifted back. The serpent became seriously elongated, but though the beginning was now a grey blotch in the mud, the end was not. I might beat up a little foam with the chain, and see below a giddy dance or at least lively flourishes and swaying. Yet there was something lacking—the end. But for that very commonplace default did there not here exist a very good beginning for another romance of the sea?

The phantom, born of light and limpid salt water and iron into which rust had deeply gnawed, gave zest to the pursuit of shadows. What is commoner under the tropic sun? The boat was now over the sand of the steeply shelving beach, where the water takes the tint of the chrysolite and creatures of fairy lightness come into view. Often on still days small sea-spiders sport under the lea of the boat, each of the eight legs supported by a bubble. With astonishing nimbleness, the spider slips and glides over the surface as a man in laborious snow-shoes over the snow. Having basked in the sun and frolicked with its kind, the spider abandons its pads, takes to its hairy bosom a bubble of air, and dives below. The shadows, not the spiders alone, gave pleasing entertainment. Each vague shadow and the eight bubble-shod feet formed a brooch-like ornament on the yellow sand—a grey jewel surrounded by diamonds, for every bubble acted as a lens concentrating the light. When the frail creatures darted hither and thither—the majestic sun does not disdain to lend his brilliance to the most prosaic of happenings—the shadows of the bubbles became jewels or daylight lightnings. The hour was so restful, the light so searching, that many of the spiders, long of leg and pearly-grey of body, gathered about the boat, the shade of which seemed to be grateful. A wave of the hand dispersed the gay assemblage, but in a few seconds the playful creatures—not too easily to be deprived of their place in the sun—reappeared from nowhere, and the beads and flashes on the floor of old Ocean once more began to glitter.

Small, slim fish took shelter from the intense light. Some hung motionless in the water; others nibbled daintily the green and lazy slime on the batten at the bilge, their gently waving shadows being barely perceptible, for their delicate, semi-transparent bodies absorbed but the merest particle of the brightness of noonday.

The unnoticeable swing of the tide took the responsive boat out from the beach, and again the serpent swayed sleepily. Down in the mud an organised conflict was taking place between a tiny soft-bodied crab and four molluscs which used whip-like tentacles with unceasing energy, while the crab defended itself with ever-ready claws. Borne down by numbers, it sank into the mud, the energy of the victors creating a tiny spiral of slush. A huge stingray passed on its way, the edges of extended wings rippling never so gently, its shadow half the size of the boat; and presently, with ghostly glide, a dull-skinned shark came into view with motion so steady and apparently effortless that it might have been a spectre. The pectoral fins swayed listlessly. The swirl of the tail was as tender as a caress. Passing the boat a few yards, it turned with a gracious sweep and nestled in its shade, and, though motionless, it was wide awake. The eyes on each end of the projecting extremities of the head blinked up at the boat. It was comfortable, but suspicious. Was its conscience quite clear? The hammer-head has not the reputation of being an active enemy of man. Why should it be distrustful? This hammer-head would not sleep in the shadow, so let it be made aware of the serpent. I took hold of the chain cautiously, the shark watching, and with a quick turn of the wrist the docile serpent lashed offensively. Then did the shark, frightened of a shadow, flee with mud-stirring haste, like the wicked when no man pursueth.

The hour of day-dreaming was past. I slip over the side of the boat to roll and splash in tepid water limpid almost to invisibility, and to test the wondrous buoyancy of the substantial part of man. Sit down, the lips just awash, so that the accurately ballasted portion cushions on the cleanly sand. Stretch out the legs so that the heels barely rest. Head thrown back and arms extended, fill the lungs to their utmost capacity with the placid, revivifying air, and you will find yourself so uplifted that the heels alone gently touch the sand. At each inspiration almost sufficient air is imbibed to float the whole bulk and machinery of the body. And when the radiant air is all one's own, why be niggardly? Let it be gulped greedily, strongly, wilfully, and let the smiling sea, responding to the embraces of your widespread arms, salute your lips with ripples.

"SMILING MORN"

"The light of the morning, When the sun riseth, even a morning without clouds; As the tender grass springing out of the earth By clear shining after rain."

Holy Writ.

A cloudless sky, the long grass wet with the night's gentle shower, a thin veil of mist on the hills, a glassy, steel-blue sea, the air saturated with the essences from myriads of leaves and scented with the last whiffs from the tea-trees and the primal blossoms of the wattles—such are the features of this smiling morn.

A spangled drongo—ardent lover of light and free air—talkatively announced the dawn long before its coming; the noisy pitta—bird of the moist soil and leafy gloom—triumphs in three notes. For an hour the scrub fowl have been violently noisy, but have retired to the recesses of the jungle, whence comes an occasional chuckle of satisfaction or a coarse, triumphant crow. The fasciated honey-eater has loudly called "with a voice that seemed the very sound of happiness"; the leaden flycatcher, often silent but seldom still, has twittered and whispered plaintively; the sun-birds are playing gymnastics among the lemon blossoms, and the centre of activity for butterflies is the red-flowered shrub bordering the wavering path.

Since—sometimes wantonly, often thoughtlessly—man interferes with plants, time out of mind the banqueting-table of the butterflies, is it not a duty to provide substitutes for devastated natural vegetation? When it is discovered that a plant, introduced to give satisfaction to the lust of the eye, provides from year's end to year's end nectar as unfailing as the widow's cruse of oil, is it not becoming to reproduce it plentifully so that excited and virtuous insects may be encouraged to return to former scenes? If not a duty, at least it is a source of happiness, for the particular insects which revel in the nectar of the perpetually flowering shrub are the two most gorgeous butterflies of the land—pleasantly known as Ulysses and Cassandra.

Science changes its titles so frequently that unless the intellect is to be increasingly burdened it is well to refuse to be divorced from the old and often explicit and fulfilling names. Cassandra is the lovely green and gold fly which dances in the air so delightfully when he woos his sober, fluttering mate. That of gorgeous royal blue with black edging to the wings and dandyish swallow-tails, which wanders far and wide and flies high and swiftly, is Ulysses.

This glorious morn the ruddy shrub is as lively as a merry-go-round with the feasting and antics of flitting gems, and there are others by the dozen attentive to less seductive fare. For half an hour the courtship of a perfect Ulysses has interfered with the staid ways of those not in holiday humour. Unlike Cassandra, there is little in appearance to distinguish the sexes, nor in the wooing does the dame exhibit staid demeanour. The object of Ulysses' love is almost, if not quite, as brilliantly decorated as himself. She is not, therefore, to be fascinated by the display of blue no more lustrous than that of her own proud wings. He may flit and toss about her, but she seems to take scanty notice of his affected aerial limpings. Her raiment is just as brave, and she has swallow-tails too. The wider black margin on her wings is no badge of subserviency, but rather an additional charm inciting tremulous fascination. She may soar over the mango-trees with ease as careless as his, and slide down straight to the red flowers with like certainty. She is not to be bewildered by his gyrations, nor thrilled by mock hostile swoops. However sprightly his activities, she has a mood to correspond and power to mimic. Indeed, is she not indifferent?—so much on an equality with him that she might say:

"If thou thinkest I am too easily won, I'll frown and be perverse, and say thee nay."

Might she not say more at the moment, since her airs are those of independence? Possibly she imagines hers to be the superior sex. Is she to be distinguished from her wooer as she flits from him disdainfully? Can she not imitate his most audacious feats? Ah! but for how long may she restrain primal emotions? The blue-mantled dandy understands his art. His wings beat with the passion of the dominant lover. He tosses himself before her, impeding her flight until she imitates his antics. Tossing is not the privilege of his sex. She exercises her right to toss, and the pair toss in delightful but bewildering confusion, like jewels sent skyward by a conjurer. And thus having established her rights if not her equality, she consents to play the part Nature decrees, and the pair tumble and toss over the mango-trees, while half a dozen others sip contentedly the red flowers.

Many other winged creatures flit and glisten in the garden and down along the grass-invaded path between the coco-nuts. Dragon-flies hover over the moist spots, transparent wings carrying coral-red bodies, and two sand-wasps pilot my steps, following the narrow ribbon of bare ground as a fish the course of a shallow stream, buzzing ominously as if in warning of some possible mischance. They are friends, and will in a moment swerve, and boom back to the shafts they have excavated in sand as depositaries for their eggs, and into which they will pack living caterpillars as fresh food for their young. They dig with such deftness and vigour that the sand is expelled in a continuous jet. When the mouth of the shaft, round to exactness, is lumbered with soil, the insect emerges backward and shovels away dog-like with its forelegs. Then it disappears again, until the sand-jet has made another encumbering heap.

These alert and furiously resentful insects are endowed with resourcefulness and "intelligence" in keeping with their physical activities. One had foraged a caterpillar in bulk and weight beyond its flight strength, and was, therefore, compelled to haul it along the toilful earth. On the wing the wasp finds its home unhesitatingly. On the unfamiliar ground it lost its bearings, and, moreover, the lumbering caterpillar had to be tugged through a bewildering forest of grass stems, among which it went astray. During a pause the wasp surveyed the scene, and, locating the shaft, after stupendous exertions deposited its prey conveniently thereto, to find itself confronted with a problem, since the diameter of the caterpillar exceeded that of the shaft. It seemed to reflect for a few moments, and then with feverish haste enlarged the shaft. Another difficulty had then to be overcome. Was it possible to force such a bulky and unwieldy body head first down—the habitual way? The insect came to a rapid decision in the negative. Backing into the shaft, it seized the caterpillar by the head and drew it down, presently emerging, and how it managed to squeeze past so tight a plug is another of the magics of the morn. Having butted with its highly competent head the caterpillar well home, the wasp selected a neatly fitting stone as a wad, and, filling the shaft with earth, strewed the surface with grass fragments, to the artistic concealment of the site.

On the beach is another industrious winged miner which has not learned the art of the rapid evacuation of the spoil, but follows the slower ways of the crab, carrying the sand in a pellet between the forelegs, and as it backs out jerking it rearward until a tidy heap is made. But it is a fussy worker, so charged with nervous energy that its glittering wings quiver even while down in the depths of its shaft, as you may assure yourself if you hearken attentively when neither the sea nor air makes competitive noises.

ANCESTRAL SHADE

"Time was when, settling on thy leaf, a fly Could shake thee to the root—and time has been When tempests could not."

COWPER.

If it were possible to recall the spirits of the departed of this Isle to solemn session and to exact from them expression of opinion as to the central point of it, the popular, most comfortable and convenient camping-place, there can be no question that the voice of the majority would favour the curve of the bay rendered conspicuous by a bin-gum or coral tree. Within a few yards of permanent fresh water, on sand blackened by the mould of centuries of vegetation, close to an almost inextricable forest merging into jungle, whence a great portion of the necessaries of life were obtained, and but ten paces from the sea, the tree stood as a landmark, not of soaring height, but of bulk and comeliness withal.

Generation after generation of careless coloured folk must have been born and bred under its branches. When the soil became rank because of continuous residence and insects of diabolical activity pestered its occupants, the camp would shift to another site; but there existed proofs that the bin-gum-tree localised the thoughts of those aimless, unstable wanderers to whom a few bushes stuck in the sand as a screen from prevailing winds represent the home of the hour and all that the word signifies and embodies. Many a one was laid to rest beneath its spreading branches, for it was the custom of the pre-white folk's days to swathe the dead in frail strips of bark, knees to chin, and place the stiffened corpse in a shallow pit in the humpy which had been in most recent occupation. If the dead during life had possessed exceptional qualities, burial rites would be ceremonious and prolonged. With tear and blood stained faces (for the mourners enforced grief by laceration of the flesh) incidents in the admirable career of the departed would be rehearsed in pantomime. The enactment of scenes from the life of the hunter and fighter might occupy hours. The art of the canoe or sword maker would be graphically mimicked. The life of the woman found rehearsal from infancy until she passed from the protection of her father into the arms of her lover. If she had died childless, a protesting infant or an effigy in bark would be placed on her shrunken bosom, so that she might not suffer the reproach of matrons who had preceded her to the mysterious better country.

The ancestral shade was a birth-place, an abiding-place, a cemetery, and the soil grew ever richer, and the thick-trunked tree displayed its ruddy flowers and gave of its best in nectar for birds and butterflies and gauze-winged, ever-flitting creatures.

It was not a comfortable tree to climb, for its grey-green branches were studded with wens each armed with a keen prickle, long and tough. It offered the hospitality of its shade to man, but little else, save flowers to gladden his eyes, though it stood as a perpetual calendar, or rather floral harbinger, of some of the most excellent things in life. At a certain season its big, trilobed, hollow-stalked leaves changed from bright green to pale yellow and lingeringly fell, and often before the last disappeared, flower-buds registered the date with almost almanac exactitude. Then, as the rich red began to glow here and there, and impatient small birds to assemble in anticipation of the annual feast, the old inhabitants of the Isle would comfort one another with reminiscences of the "Oo-goo-ju," the nutmeg pigeon, which was wont to congregate in such numbers that adjacent and easily accessible isles were whitened. There would be plenty of eggs then, and in a few weeks squabs quiveringly, helplessly fat.

It was a good tree, for it gave good tidings, and it centralised the shelter of the Isle. Its blooms were delightfully, dashingly red, and they lasted long— that is, if the camp—the soil rectified by sun and rain—happened to be in residence, for then the sulphur-crested cockatoos would be scared. Otherwise the profligate birds would sever the heavy racemes of flower in their eagerness for honey until the ground beneath glowed with a furnace-hued shadow. But there would be still plenty for the gay sun-birds and the honey eaters, while the grey goshawk would make the site of regular call, for the bibulous lesser birds could not always be on the alert, ready to dart into adjacent tea-trees. The hawk would abide its time, and have occasion, after its kind, to be grateful because of the tree and its seductive nectar which translated artless little songsters into shrill-tongued roysterers, careless of the ills of life, or at least less watchful for the presence of crafty enemies. Flying foxes would swoop into the tree at sundown to squeak and gibber among its repellent branches till dawn, when some, too full for flight, would hang among the lower limbs all day, sleeping with eyes veiled by leathery wings.

For many a long day the bin-gum tolerated no undergrowth. Despotic over its territory, the shade was clean but for a carpet of ferns, and its branches free from the embraces of orchids, save that which bears the ghostly white flowers which set off its own of bold red. But as it passed its maturity shrubs and saplings began to encroach, until it was the centre of a circus of upstart vegetation, though still stretching big, knotty limbs over the slim youths of yesterday. Anterior to this era a neglected fire had scorched a portion of its trunk. Decay set in. A huge cavity gradually appeared, betokening vital injuries. The soft though tough wood does not patiently endure the annihilating fret of time. Far up in a recess of this cavity a toy boomerang was found, placed there by some provident but forgetful piccaninny. At the date of the discovery of the missile the age of the resident blacks had passed away; but still the tree stood, stout of limb, while the encompassing saplings shot up until sun-seeking shoots caressed the branches and familiarised with the blooms, as if taking credit for the seasonal gaiety of the patriarch.

In the prime of life the wood of the bin-gum is of pale straw colour with a faint pinkish tinge, and tough though light. Sapless age makes it tindery, and the decaying fibre descends in dust—glissades of dust which form moraines within the hollow of the base. Then the end is not far off.

The old tree might have been credited with premonition of its fate. However fanciful to ascribe to it power of utterance, some phenomena, perhaps associated with the dusty flux draining its vitals, gave it distinct voice. On silent days it was often heard—a whispering, whimpering sing-song, pitifully weak for so great a tree, but not without appeal. Did it not suggest the sanctuary of some wood-nymph chanting never so faint a death psalm—a monotone which the idlest zephyr might still?

Disdaining to die while consenting to disappear, the great tree, proudly green of head, did not fall headlong, like a giant, in its pride, but subsided silently behind its leafy screen while all the winds were still, and as one who passes away full of years and with untarnished conscience.

Though the saplings and shrubs which fought for its place decently conceal its shattered relics, addressing glossy leaves to the face of the sun, is it quite vain to expect that its graceful proportions—a true and stately dome—will be transmitted to the most worthy of its descendants? Or that they will escape for so long a term the many mischances that befall soft-wooded trees? No; the bin-gum of the bay was unique. Afar off its flowers assumed a bricky shade, which contrasted with the sage-green background of huge and overtopping melaleucas, while but a strip of creamy sand intervened between its low and spreading branches and the shallow sea, with its varying tints of pale green and blue. So lovely and conspicuous a feature is not to be reconstituted under a century.

If it be permitted to assume that trees are sentient, that each—since it differs from all others in some material quality and condition—has its individuality, and that one may stand out from the rest as a figure and representative of its age, then was this old monarch which maintained its red robes to the last an examplar of the race whose births, nuptials, pastimes, deaths and burials it witnessed from the date when the good ship ENDEAVOUR slowly plodded along the alien coast. The dust of the witness is blending in common decay. A few months and not a trace will be discoverable, and what is left of those who rested in its shade? In the pages of history they will be unchronicled, for were not their lives less beautiful than the life of a tree, and their renown no more durable?

QUIET WATERS

"Like playhouse scenes the shore slid past."

KIPLING.

Lovable as is the open sea when the spray drenches the scanty clothing of the steersman and rains upon his lips salty salutation, yet is there rare delightsomeness in reverse of the wet frolic.

A few minutes past the deck glistened in the sun as each rollicking billow sent its herald over the bows, and here the surface of the river is almost rippleless. Shallows and uncertainties perplex its union with the ocean. Sombre green mangroves screen its muddy banks at full tide and trail leathery leaves and the tips of spindly fruit on its placid surface. Pendant roots and immersed branches create on each hand a continuous scroll of wavering ridges and eddies bordered with the living tints of the steadfast wall of leafage. The sun so burnishes the midstream ribbon that the boat seems to float on an invisible element. Though the topmost leaves of the mangroves fail to disclose any movement in the air, an unceasing and inharmonious hum tells of the sea idly shouldering the orange-hued sands outside.

The original inhabitants of the country knew the stream as Marang. None call it so; but half stranded on the bank at the mouth lies a raft typical of the past, and of the ease and resource with which those of the day are wont to avail themselves of Nature's suggestions in the art of crossing flooded waters. The name of the river has gone, but not that of the three buoyant logs lashed together with strips of cane which with sullen lurch, take the wash of the boat. The boys jerk their heads in the direction and murmur "wur-gun," and speculate on the last user. The day is young. For the time being the best the ancient river has to show—the quintessence of the season, superb October—shall be ours. The cloudless sky is richly blue, lighter in shade than the shapely mountain which seems to block the way miles ahead. The sun gives a taste of its quality, not to fret or discomfort, but merely to add a slightly richer tint to skin glowing with previous marks of his fervour and favour.

All the sounds of the little engine are maliciously exaggerated as the boat forges ahead. The silent green river has become vociferous with echoes, which snap and grunt, groan and hiss, in mockery of inevitable and earnest doings. Out at sea the merry moods of the boat and hasty and determined throbs of the engine are manifestations of something accomplished in the overcoming of distance. Here it is all mere idle fancy, while the echoes jeer. Surely the uncouth imps of the dimly-lit jungles need not proclaim their spite with such exaggerated fuss.

With but little effort of imagination the boat becomes stationary on a shining ribbon with strips of dark green on each side, and the banks glide past with never so gentle undulations. The tide screens most of the mud on which the many-rooted trees stand. Some are in full bloom, the hawthorn-like flowers breathing perfume as from an orangery soliciting the raids of millions of bees. Scents cling to the placid surface. It is as a stream of scent, bounded and confined by changeful tints as the sun toys with the shadows, and curve after curve, reach after reach, slip by. Sometimes the chattering boat heads due east. South she knows too, and then she bows her duty to the west, along reaches which run straight and clean as a canal; and round hairpin bends she sweeps with disdainful air, as if conscious of besoiling banks.

Gradually the monopolistic mangroves become more tolerant of the rights of other vegetation. Tea-trees with white papery bark and pale yellow flowers dripping with spirity nectar, the sunflower-tree with its masses of gold, an occasional wattle, and slim palms mirror themselves, and here and there compact jungle, with its entanglement of ponderous vines and smothering creepers, shoulders away the salt-loving plants. Scents may vary as the river's fringe; but only a delicate blend is recognised—the breathings of honey-secreting flowers and of sapful plants free from all uncleanliness. Many trees endure sadly the decoration of orchids in full flower, some lovely to look on and deliciously scented. The snowy plumes of one species sway gently, as if offering friendly greeting. A worthy similitude to the lily of the valley clings to a decaying limb, and a passing smudge of lustrous brown is but the reflection from a mass of the commonest of the Dendrobiums which encumbers a long-suffering host. Where forest trees and wattles guard the bank the water is of a different hue, as if the face of the river had absorbed less of the actualities of the sun. The screen of vegetation is not only higher, but it is varied and impresses its individuality. Only during the pelting rains of the wet season may this delightful stream be monotonous, for at intervals brief and narrow vistas open out on patches of yellowing grass, and beyond lie forest-clad hills.

All save the boat is wonderfully still. The birds are silent, for this is the first hot day of the season, and they have retired to the patches of jungle where shade and dimness afford relief from the sunlight spaces. For many a mile a cormorant, lacking valour to double on its tracks, has fled before the boat, settling out of sight ever and anon, only to be scared further from its nest. A mangrove bittern sitting humpbacked on a root and roused from its night thoughts has flown ahead, following the bends of the stream until it crossed a familiar loop and so evaded incessant harrying.

No murmur of the sea is audible, though the water is as briny as at the mouth. Mangroves still reinforce the muddy banks at intervals, and big barramundi swirl aside to give the boat precedence in the narrow way. If in no impetuous haste, one might drift with the tide up and down with but little exertion except during periods of flood, which quickly rise and quickly subside. Drifters become familiar with characteristics of the stream unknown to those who hurry up and down in an echo-rousing motor-boat. They see crocodiles basking on their sides, as many as seven on a sunny morning in the cool season, and many curse them in De Quincey's phrase as "miscreated gigantic vermin" because the rifle happens to be unavailable. Crocodiles have their moods. Sometimes they are lazy and indifferent and will not be disturbed though the boat may clink and chatter as it passes, and the then easygoing man disposes of them. More often the faculties of the crocodile are disappointingly acute. He is visible for such a fragment of time that the authoritative man who has promised sport looks foolish and tries to relieve the strain by the relation of anecdotes in which circumstances have not been all in favour of the illusive creature. He tells of the slumbering one which lay on a mud-bank with its jaws distended, weary of the monotony of the mangroves, and took but sleepy notice when upbraided for being a sluggard. And of that other monstrous beast which, with eyelids like saucers and a bulk which filled a narrow tributary of the river, floundered, splashed, and flurried into deep water, while the awestruck individual with the rifle was too astounded to fire a shot. He may tell, too, of another instance of good luck on the part of the crocodile. How, drifting down silently with the ebb, the black boy indicated the presence of game on a slide overhung by a deep verandah of mud; how a shot was fired and a big log splashed into the water and the little one remained bearing the bullet-wound, the real having been too big and impressive for sight.

The day is well spent among strange plants. Here is a tall hibiscus with coarse leaves, diversely lobed, and great pink, fragile flowers, each with a blotch of maroon at the base and each containing a fat and lumbering bee spangled with maroon-tinted pollen. A trailing eugenia bears dark red flowers shaped like a mop, and a tiny white lily with petals and strangely protuberant anthers scents the air as with honey and almonds.

The tide ebbs fast. All the country teems with entertainment, and the river, cool in the dusk, and black, reflects the dead mangroves, white and spectral, on its brink.

This breathless night the sea is as tetchy as petrol. Trailing fingers are terminals which ignite living flames, and the propeller of the little boat creates an avengeful commotion of light which trails far astern. Blobs of light are cast off from her bows as she rounds the familiar sandspit and glides to her moorings.

"THE LOWING HERD"

"Your cattle, too—Allah made them; serviceable, dumb creatures; they change the grass into milk; they come ranking home at evening time."— CARLYLE.

Remote from the manners and the sights of the street, here are we secure against most of the pains which come of the contemplation, casual or intimate, of other folk's sufferings. No hooded ambulance moves joltlessly, tended by enwrapt bearers, on pathless way; no formal procession paces from the house of death to the long last home. Immune from the associations which oft subdue the crowd, as well as from its too exciting pleasures, and participating only indirectly in its inevitable sorrows, yet we are occasionally forced to remember that troubles do come to all that is flesh, and that keen is the grief attendant upon enforced separations even among animals which cannot call reason to their solace. Man cannot claim to be the sole proprietor of the luxury of woe, and may he not draw edifying lessons from contemplating the transient sorrows of his pets and domestic animals? Is he to confine his schooling on the wholesome theme of the frailty of flesh solely to his own species? It is not to be denied that animals lower in the scale than mankind have acute sense of bereavement, though it is equally certain that in their case the healing influences of time are more prompt and potent.

An illustration may be cited. Two favourite Irish terriers, in violation of an all-precautionary training, molested a death adder, the emulation of each inciting the other to recklessness. When the fray was over and the wicked little serpent lay squirming in death, both dogs took joyful credit on account of the feat. An hour after one began to froth at the lips, and in another hour he lay dead. His son and companion, as well as rival in all rat and lizard hunts, softly approached the body, lifting each foot with almost solemn deliberation. He sniffed, and catching a whiff of the scent of death, sat on his haunches, threw back his head, and in loud and piercing tones lamented the tragedy until from very hoarseness he could howl no longer. He stood the solitary spectator of the burial, and as the soil was patted down tenderly, sniffed the spot, whimpered plaintively, and followed with downcast mien. Unable to fathom the mystery of death, yet fearful, if not resentful, he wandered about for days rebuking the moon, or its dire influence, and hailing passing steamers with weak whines. Time soon soothed the mental hurt.

Since I became a milker and tender of pet cows many instances have been revealed of the patience and amiability of these inestimable beasts. The man who owns the cattle on a thousand hills, who employs stockmen by the dozen, who sends off hundreds of fat, contented, happy, liberty-loving oxen in droves to end their days in an unknown locality amid the clatter and swish of machinery and with the fearful scents of blood and decaying offal defiling the air, has few opportunities of studying the nicer qualities of his possessions. He may be full of bullock lore and able to recite sensational and entertaining stories illustrative of the ways of the big mobs which tramp from native hills and downs to the city of the thousand deaths. He knows, perhaps, something of the individualities of his herds, and will tell how fat beasts form friendships, and how they pine when separated. Then will he register his personal regrets, counting in the measure for fat, for, refusing food, the animals fall away in condition, so that the sorrows of two fat bullocks due to parting, enforced by determined men on horseback, cracking whips and using violent and threatening language, come home to the owner in terms of pounds, shillings, and pence.

Here are few sordid considerations, for does not the full-fed and contented herd supply generously milk and cream with no apprehensions of the butcher? Perhaps on that account the sentiments of the sleek cows are more tender. At least it has been noticed that when the time comes for the flash young bulls to be banished, and they are transported, the mother's grief is loud-voiced and prolonged. Under stress of departure and all the novel excitement of a first experience of the motion of the sea, the fat calf, which has rollicked in all that makes for good temper and ease and comfort, becomes mute. Tears trickle from big, affrighted eyes, and the head is turned wistfully when terms of comfort are uttered. He is of the make of man and will not whimper. But the mother, on the discovery of her bereavement, arouses the echoes of the hills with her calls.

Accustomed to the voices of the individuals of your herd, your ears are also attuned to the significant tones of each—the low warning hum of the mother to her safely hidden new-born, the imperative command to obedience, the note of inquiry when the wandering offspring is out of sight, the anxious call when it is absent from her side unaccountably, the angry bellow when she thinks injury is being done.

The other day a lusty young bull which had been wont to treat me as a chum, and perhaps as a slightly inferior animal, was reluctantly parted from. His face displayed his emotions-astonishment, grief, resignation—and once, and only once, did he permit himself to protest vocally. But for a week his mother's sorrow has been insistent. Early on the morning following, the banishment, she led off the rest of the herd in Indian file, to search accustomed scenes. At times she hastened—perhaps she heard in fancy the loved one's voice— but more often and with rare persistency she shrewdly scrutinised every possible hiding-place, lowing plaintively and with a coaxing, wistful tone. Frequently, attended by silent, sympathising companions, she made frantic appeals to me, and then there seemed to be a note as of upbraiding, if not accusation, in her voice. Knowing her feelings, it was easy to interpret them, and her doleful mood and loud yet melodious protests against the arbitrary usage of man affected the wonted serenity of the Isle.

How many lusty, fat, sleek, good-humoured, straight-backed, frolicsome calves had she reared, and when they had come to the age when a mother's pride must be in the full, each in its turn had mysteriously disappeared. Was this not a subject of moan? Why should she not tell her grief to the responsive hills, and send it as far as her voice might carry over the irresponsive sea?

Time soothes all such pangs. She calls now when she spies me in the forest, still suspecting where responsibility rests, and mumbles as she crops the succulent herbage. A few more days and her sturdy offspring will be forgotten; but the recollection of her material woes excites the thought that human beings, in guiding the destinies of domestic animals, may not always be conscious of certain moral aspects of such incidents. Are we justified in lacerating the feelings of those creatures, which have become accustomed to our ways, which submit to our arbitrary authority with wondrous patience, which depend on us in many ways, and which trust us with unquestioning fidelity?

Against all precedent, the dairy herd was started with a bull. Though such a beginning is not to be recommended as a general precept, it must be confessed that in this particular instance developments proved its wisdom. Unjust fears were overcome while yet he was undistracted by society of his kind. Having no other company, he sought ours in frank and friendly manner. Occasionally he would accompany me on indefinite excursions in the bush, and would oft tempt me to play. With the fable of the frogs and the boys in mind, I had to decline participation in his sportful moods, for what would have proved pure frolic to him might have been fraught with disaster to me. At this period of the dairy herd, he spent most of his leisure moments in the paddock where poultry congregates, and where many of the domestic rites are performed. He was at home, and he was a gentleman, and did no one premeditated ill. Longing for something to play with, he would make hostile demonstration against the wheelbarrow, but that dull-hearted vehicle never responded except by ignominious collapse at tenderest touch of horn. One evening, when all the good little chicks had been put to bed for the night, the bull, impatient for play, overturned two coops so suddenly that two of the inmates were crushed flat. There was no sheltering mother to protest against such violation, and so the adjoining coop was visited. But for once he went wrong in strategy. The coop contained an exceptionally numerous family, the mother of which richly deserved the name of "Scotty." The coop was overturned none too politely; the squeaking chicks vanished in the grass and remained discreetly silent; the irate hen, with the valour of ignorance and all feathers on end, flew in the face of the startled bull. Though a white leghorn, she has fighting blood in her veins, and as she hurled herself—stuttering with frantic exclamations—at the violator of her home, he backed with a mirth-provoking look of surprise and dismay. He seemed to wish to say that he regretted the intrusion, and would apologise and ask permission to retire. The hen was not in the mood to accept apologies, however seemly the cringing attitude of the bull. Making herself ever so much bigger than Nature intended, she followed up her advantages, slapping her enemy's face with widespread wings until he winced again, and clawing with truly feminine extravagance and uncertainty of aim. The first round was all to the credit of the hen, and the startled poultry cackled derisively as the bull retreated. Sure of victory, the hen followed him up, skipping, flapping, clawing, and scolding as only an irate hen in transports of rage can. Still the bull backed. He was a gentleman, and genuinely afraid of female tantrums. With half-shut eyes, he submitted to the buffets of the wings, while encouraging remarks from friends and companions further excited the delirious pugnacity of "Scotty." Then it seemed to dawn on him that honour was at stake. Gallantry forbade him to do violence to a lady; honour forbade him to run away. What other recourse was open? He must treat the whole episode as a joke. So, rubbing his muzzle on the ground, he invited the hen to come on. She did so. There was a splash of outspread feathers against his front and more clatter than ever. He pawed the ground, jerking little clods over his shoulders, and, lowering his head, menaced the hen with horns that could have tossed her over the highest of the mango-trees. But there was a smile on his face the while, and the spectators knew, though "Scotty" did not, that it was all a joke. Again and again she flew in his face. Just as often he refused to take her seriously, though all the pantomime of battle was displayed. She cackled in impotent anger. He bellowed with gratification. Not a fowl in the yard saw the joke, and all the little chicks in adjacent coops strained their necks to watch the battle and their voices in shrill comments. Having made not the slightest impression on the jovial little bull, "Scotty" retired, feinting and scolding, while he, still blue mouldy for a game, coaxed her by unmistakable gesticulation to one round more. Twice during the night "Scotty" dispelled the silences with loud exclamations of wrath and defiance. She was fighting her battle again in her dreams, and though I was not there to see, I am very sure that the gentle bull beguiled his wakeful moments with smiles. There are several white hens in the yard, and whensoever one crosses his path the bull, who does not pretend to discriminate, tosses his head with an interrogative gesture. "Do you want to fight?" he says, and the hens flee—all except "Scotty."

The herd comprises a dainty little cow of most placid disposition. Nothing disturbs her placidity, incites her to hurry, or bewilders her. Cure the dove of its timidity and shrinking and you will have a good prototype of Parilla, who, taking life easily and affably, is fat and amiable. When she brought home her firstborn, mooing plaintively, he, big and fat for his age, walked into the byre as a matter of course. Here was the first evidence of heredity. It was patent that Fillo Billaroo was born with a mind like that of his sweet-tempered mother. He earned his name because of acute dissimilarity to the swiftlet which swoops about the cleared spaces, never resting save in a dark and dirty cave.

Though, apparently, entirely unselfconscious, Fillo Billaroo at once established himself as a superior sort of creature. He did not exact any rights. They were conceded with all possible grace. He enjoys privileges none other dares to imagine. When he has exhausted for the time being the maternal source of refreshment, he visits other mothers, and with such a pompous, patronising, good-humoured, thoroughly appreciative and yet gentle way, that the absurd creatures are flattered. They realise he is something quite out of the common, and give agreeably of their best. Thus he has become a favourite, and he drinks so much and has become so fat that he could not for a couple of weeks accompany his lazy-pacing mother on her daily rounds, but would be planted in shade and coolness with cautions against straying until called for late in the afternoon. Often would Parilla forget the hiding-place, or rather pretend to, and beseech in wistful tones for help in the search, and when it was successful the greetings she bestowed displayed the bigness of her heart.

Once the little mother left Fillo Billaroo in charge of Lady Clare, a much more experienced matron, who cannot bear to permit her frisky heifer out of her sight for a moment unless safely planted, and then the treasure must not be wandered from more than a hundred yards. Parilla went off for the day. Late in the afternoon, Lady Clare with her heifer and Fillo Billaroo were found far away from the mob and driven home. It had been hot, and the big calf has an enormous appetite and apparently Lady Clare had been coy. When he saw his mother and his mother saw him, he stooped with uplifting nose, sniffing; she stopped feeding and begin to sniff. He seemed to say to himself, "I do believe I know that little creature. Yes; I am certain I must have met her before. She rather resembles my own mother; but I have so many fond, kind, and obliging aunts that it is not so very easy to make sure. She has a special look. Can I be mistaken? I really hope not, for I am painfully hungry."

In the meantime Parilla was saying to herself—you could see it all plainly written in her big, round, bulging eyes, so full of inquiry, hope and longing— ! "The sight of that really fine fellow reminds me that I, too, am a mother. He is a pretty fellow; I fancy that Fillo Billaroo is not unlike him. I now recollect with dismay that I have not seen him since morning, when Lady

Clare condescended to look after him. And there's Lady Clare! Oh! if she's mislaid Fillo Billaroo! But can that fine, beautiful fellow be mine? I must inquire. Come!" And she moo'd, and Fillo Billaroo murmured "Mum," and they rushed to one another, and the look in Parilla's face was that of perfect happiness.

———————————————————————————————————

BABBLING BEACHES

"By the wisdom of Nature it has been appointed that more pleasure may be taken in small things than in great."—Ruskin.

On a breezy day, when the sun scorches the sand and the wind continuously sweeps off the dry surface, and your ears detect the musical sound accompanying the process—vague as the visible part of it is blurred and misty—then it is that you are made aware of the agencies by which time creates geographical differences. Precipitated at the apex of the spit, the sand as it sinks tints the verge of the sea, while the lighter spoil, leaves and wisps of seaweed, trip off on independent voyage. The current from the south pares the spit, preserving its shapeliness. The ebb from the bay maintains the fluent inner curve. The dry wind, the current with its northerly set, and the ebb in conjunction, push the spit to the north, and as the sand advances, vegetation consolidates the work. Then comes the season of northerly winds, when the apex of the spit is forced backwards and outwards into a brief but graceful flourish, in the bight of which small boats may nestle, though the seas roar and show white teeth a few yards away. Since the winds of the north are less in duration and persistency than those from the south and east, the tendency of the spit—in defiance of the yearly setback—is to the north. Driftwood, logs, and huge trees with bare, branchless limbs become stranded, to dry and whiten in the sun and reinforce the sand, and in their decay, with ever contributed seaweed, to make mould for vegetation. The work of encroachment and consolidation is incessant and strangely rapid, for vegetation never lacks pioneers of special character to prepare the way for the less venturesome and less hardy. Often before vegetation appears, coral chips, shells, small stones, and sharp gravel, are concreted into platter-shaped masses which seem to become the base of blocks of rough conglomerate, capable of resisting the attacks of the sea; and a few yards back, where a mangrove-bordered creek once existed, the mud and decayed fragments of wood have been transformed into a black, cheesy substance which might be mistaken for soft coal. So do these beaches lay bare their secrets.

When the mainland streams pour out their floods and the commingled volume hurries north in a mud-tinted, sharply delimited current, and whole trees are cast up on the beaches of far-away isles, vivid examples of the dispersion of animate and inanimate things by purely natural means are afforded. Weighty stones are found locked among roots which, as the wood decays, are deposited on alien sands, thereafter to invite speculation as to origin and means of transport. On one such raft voyaged a living specimen of the white and black banded snake, one of the most singular of the family, for Nature has bestowed on it a placid disposition, and provided it with an unmischievous mouth and fangs so minute that, although classed as venomous, it is not considered injurious to man. Though strange and interesting, on the plea that the family is quite sufficiently represented, the derelict was unwelcome, save as a living proof of the practicability of natural transports. By what grace, indeed, could the creature which earned the Almighty's bitter curse be accepted as "wilsam"—goods of God's mercy driven ashore, no wreck or ship being visible?

This small bay never ceases the laying of tribute at one's feet. There are seasons when the amount is less than at others; but how seldom are its sands trodden without a display of the infinite variety of productions of the ocean? When the mood of the sea is savage and the spoil from the reef is flung in ridges among the vegetation of the shore—coral in blocks and shattered masses, shells, seaweed, sponges, and other dead marine animals and driftwood, heap on heap—days of enthusiastic toil might be spent in sorting out the oversurplus of the secrets of the sea. But for months together the beach maintains its cleanly orderliness, and during these dreamy days the sea will tell of many a pretty treasure which the sands will reveal in the face of the sun.

The most famous of botanists compiled a floral almanac; the months, and in some cases the weeks, being associated with the development and flowering of significant plants. So might it be possible to ascribe to particular months the tokens with which the obliging sea bestrews the beaches. It is not proposed herein to attempt any such design, which would involve special knowledge of the science of conchology and the compilation of the records of years of patient observation. A few examples of the material on which the delightful work might be undertaken are given, so that the wealth of one brief strip of beach may be taken as typical of a vast stretch of calm waters within the Great Barrier Reef.

The ridges and furrows of the cyclone season, when the clean sand is covered and stained with weed, dead and living molluscs, coral, leaves carried from the hills by flooded streams, all fermenting in the heat, tell that Christmas is past and March not yet over. Many a year passes without such a storm as compels the groaning ocean to ravage its reefs. Then the beaches, during the first three months are not particularly fertile, nor are the shells to be found special or peculiar. In April many specimens of the mollusc known as Tapes, of which there are several species, are cast ashore, empty but fresh. In life the animal buries itself in the mud at the edge of the sand, and some disturbance of natural conditions, possibly due to the fresh water from flooded rivers, causes seasonal mortality. The most conspicuous of the species is that known as "literati," because of the erratic scribblings decorating its valves. With others of the genera, it is to be found cast away at other times of the year, but the end of the wet season seems exceptionally direful.

April is confirmed, too, but transiently, by the presence of a frail mollusc (HAMINAEA CYMBALUM) which is washed ashore attached to seaweed, soon to disappear desiccated by the sun and ground to powder. The shell is semi-transparent with a sandy tint, and in form not unlike that of a common snail. As the weather becomes cooler, a thin, delicate bivalve decorates high-water mark. It is one of the tellinas—semi-transparent, lustrous, and fragile—which occurs in muddy sand, but why the species should be more susceptible to the ills of life during a particular season is not apparent. When the fates do conspire against its welfare dozen of bright specimens may be picked up during a casual stroll, the animal having disappeared. The epidemic the beach thus announced with pink and glittering shells coincides with low night tides, which possibly leave the inefficiently protected animals exposed to the attacks of uncustomary enemies which thrive only when the muddy banks are exposed. The cause of the exhibition of the relics is not of so much concern to the unlearned observer as the relics themselves and the part they play in signifying the progress of the season. If strong winds occur during the cool months, among the wreaths of broken seaweed thrown on the beach may be found unbroken and fresh specimens of a singularly beautiful and fragile univalve known commonly and most appropriately as the "bubble shell" (HYDATINA PHYSIS), which when alive is a most lovely object, its fine spiral lines being black and faint yellow with faint purple edges, while the mantle is fringed with light blue intermingled with pale yellow. In some specimens the base colouring is fawn, the lines, of varying width, being brown and "comely crinkled," like the face of the pleasant old woman of whom a poet wrote. Such a frail shell is subject to many mischances before it reaches the beach, and a few hours of exposure to the sun tarnishes its lustre. To obtain it in perfection the beach must be patrolled every day during due season, and very rarely is the collector rewarded by the discovery of unsullied specimens.

When the chill is out of the surface the spring-time of the sea begins. Vegetable life is strenuous, so that one may chance to see a lazy turtle bearing on its back a weedy garden. The water is alive. Miles of space are belted with that plant to which Captain Cook applied a significant name, likening it in its myriads to "sea sawdust." Some dare call it "whale spawn," forgetful that the whale is not a fish. Others assert it to be none other than the "coral insect," which does not exist save in the minds of those who write odes to such creatures:

"Ye build, ye build, but ye enter not in,

Like the tribes whom the desert devoured in their sin."

It consists of minute vegetation in bundles, to be individualised under a strong microscope, though when countless billions drift on to the beaches and die and become green and grey with corruption, the fumes are by no means in proportion to the marvellous littleness of the individual plants. Then we know by the organs of scent and sight that August has come. The beaches are foul. The breakers roll in unbroken or with a muddy, froth, for the scum acts as oil, calming even troubled water.

The Red Sea is said by some authorities to derive its title from the scum formed by this plant (TRICHODESMIUM ERYTHRAEUM), which is strongly impregnated with iodine. It emits a most disagreeable odour and exhales a gas which affects the mucous membrane, causing in some individuals sneezing and inflammation of the eyes. One amateur fisherman of considerable experience and by no means susceptible to intangible irritations, and not to be diverted from his sport by trifles, has frequently been compelled to move from a favourite ground by a stream of the scum drifting to his anchored boat. The fumes gave intense smartness to the eyes, which were relieved by a gush of tears, but keen discomfort recurred when the tears were wiped away.

Following the least desirable of marine phenomena is that which is known as the "blanket weed," which floats ashore in loathsome blobs, a hand's breadth and more, the centre a grey, solidified slime, with a periphery of long, dull green, slimy, shapeless fringes Individual plants coalesce on the sand and, mingling with other weeds, cover respectable beaches with a woolly, compact mass not unlike a rough, thick blanket, but teeming with unpleasantnesses. Isolated plants cling to ropes, which become garlanded with thickened slime, from which evil-smelling mud oozes. Offensive to man afloat and ashore, the "blanket weed" is a luxury to mullet and garfish, for during its period both may be seen in shoals skimming the surface of the sea in abandonment of habitual shyness, and the stomachs of both are found to be full of the greenish-grey slime. With the compliance of the sun the impurity disappears, giving place to the graceful weed of vivid green that attaches itself to dead and whitened shells and fingers of coral covered at low water. Every flood-tide deposits a zone of shells splashed with green, while the shallows glow as a field of rich pasturage. In favourable situations, such as the upper part of a long immersed log, coated to the water-line with goose barnacles, the plant grows long and luxuriantly, falling on each side like a silken mantle.

One other season, ephemeral but universal, do the babbling but truth-telling beaches record. No rocky cove, no smooth strand, no rubbish-accumulating creek, no mangrove-fringed islet, no coral esplanade white under the tropic sun, no sand-bank with crest of windshaken bush, is free. It is Christmas. Christian and pagan alike tell it to the sea, and the sea tells it to the beaches in—corks.

Though there are grounds for the belief that some molluscs are seasonal in their appearances and disappearances, the majority are always with us, though subject to many casualties. A few months since an epidemic broke out among a certain species of sea urchins (Echinus), spherical animals with shells thickly set with spines, keen and exceedingly brittle. The beaches were strewn with thousands of the dead, no apparent exterior injury having been suffered. The particular species afflicted gathers to itself, seemingly as a disguise, but perhaps as ballast, the dead shells of cockles, which are retained by the spines. It was noticed that the dead were not encumbered.

A curious and one of the rarest of local shells is that known as the elephant's tusk (DENTALIUM APTINUM). Pure white and slightly fluted longitudinally, it typifies the marvellous extent of Nature's requirements and her fertility in design. It is especially interesting to note that the existence of the species in Australian waters has not hitherto been recorded, the nearest known locality being the Moluccas.

The DRUPA RICINUS (so specifically called because of resemblance to the prickly seeds of the castor-oil plant) has another feature almost unique—two ivory-white projections in the mouth, singularly like a baby's teeth. In the waters of Florida is a distinct curiosity in the form of an altogether different mollusc which is commonly known as the "bleeding-tooth shell," the gory stains about the base of the tooth being highly significant. The local example of the whimsicality of Nature owes its excellence to absolute purity. No fond mother crooning to her first-born ever looked on budding teeth more delightful in modelling and pearliness.

CHAMA LAXARUS belongs to the same family as the clams, the largest of living molluscs, its specific title being an allusion to the tattered raiment of the beggar of the most edifying of parables. Occasionally the china-white upper valve is decorated with a broad streak of buff. Some of the genera are attached to coral or rock indifferently by either valve, and it is exceptional to find on the beach a perfect specimen—that is, the valves united. Since on the reef the shells are frequently protectively disguised with seaweed and other growth, it is only after the violence of a cyclone that the amateur collector expects to be rewarded.

Unlike some others of the family, the cockscomb oyster, though not objecting to the near-by presence of its kind, seems to hate a crowd. Half a dozen may occupy separate areas on a rock, and solitary specimens lie embedded and strongly anchored in the sand. A typical example may weigh over seven pounds. So big and weighty a shell can scarcely be sensible of its invariable burden of parasites and other encumbrances—but the variety of such tenants never fails to excite curiosity. That which is illustrated accommodated another oyster of delicate texture, a thorny clam (which has the reputation of being poisonous), a mass of seaweed, a serpentine mollusc, two species of coral—the red organ-pipe and a mushroom—three burrowing crabs, besides a number of smaller animals, fixed and mobile, in addition to the congregation of less obvious life critical examination would undoubtedly have revealed.

Most species of univalves are wanderers, many bivalves are free, and multivalves become fixed at an early stage of existence. The goose-necked barnacle, with its five valves, comes in its myriads attached to derelict coco-nuts, floating logs, and pumice-stone. The species owes its name to the fabulous belief that it was the preliminary state of the barnacle goose of the Arctic regions, the filaments representing the plumage and the valves the wings. It has been found on shells, whales, turtles, and marine snakes.

In the mud close to the edge of the beach sand one of the most singular of marine animals exists, and often its empty, horny, flexible, semi-transparent shell, always tinted green, may be found. It is known in some works as LINGULA ANATINA, and by the natives of this Isle, by whom a certain part of it is eaten, as "Mill-ar-ing." A pinhole in the mud indicates the presence of the animal, and the hungry black boy, thrusting his hand with outspread fingers below it, closes the fingers and withdraws anything but an inviting morsel. To the tongue-shaped shell is attached a pedicle or stalk, attaining a length of ten inches, opaque and tough, which is broken off, seared over the fire, and eaten with apparent relish. It is remarkable that in localities in which this mollusc is found a seaweed occurs similar in shape and size, the chief difference in appearance being in the length of the stalk, which in the plant is thin and membranous.

The Phorous, or carrier, otherwise the mineralogist, is remarkable for its extraordinary habit of cementing to its exterior stones of irregular size, and in some cases dead shells of other species, an office performed by the use of an exceptionally long tongue. Its movements are said to be very clumsy and erratic, as if its self-imposed burden was too cumbersome for its strength. Personal observation fails to verify its staggering gait, for dead specimens only have been found. The stones are, no doubt, designedly acquired as a disguise and so represent another form of life insurance. When stationary the mineralogist successfully baffles observation; but some day, peradventure, in a moment of preoccupation, it will reveal itself lurching along over the rough country it favours. How few living things escape the "penalties of Adam." Some bear sorrows, some stones.

Among the fixed molluscs are what is known as the winged shells, to which the "pearl oysters" belong. The name is apt, for the expanded valves are not unlike the form of a bird in flight. The illustration shows a rare species, several specimens of which were found attached to the mooring-chain of a buoy by what is known as the "byssus," a bunch of tough fibres which passes through an hiatus in the margins of the valves. Like the king's daughter of the Psalmist, PTERIA PEASEI is "all glorious within," the nacreous surface, margined with lustrous black, shining like silver with a tinge of blue.

Only a very small proportion of the species of shells to be found on the shore of this bay have been enumerated. In a work of general character a complete commentary on any particular branch of natural science would be out of place, nor is it competent for one who has but a trifling knowledge of a special subject to deal with it in an enlightening manner. It would be highly interesting to ascertain by study and observation why the denizens of so many parts of the ocean meet in community in such a narrow space, though it may not be very difficult to present a fairly satisfactory theory for the continuous presence of many species by reference to existing features and prevalent conditions. Within the area of the bay the water varies in depth from a few feet to four fathoms, the rise and fall of the tide being about two fathoms. The fringing coral reef represents all stages of development and decay—live growth on the outer edge, ever encroaching on the deeper water, and comprising many varieties; dying masses on the shore-side, and a considerable extent of dead and denuded relics lying in mud. There are also weedy patches, bare sand-banks of limited extent, uncovered at low water, and muddy depressions both in the deep and shallow portions and clean sand. Strong currents race past the sand-spit and across the bay, carrying, no doubt, continual supplies of spat from elsewhere to settle in quiet places. No one who has lived on the margin of the tropic sea can be astounded at its prolific life, though it may be a matter of unceasing wonder that along a beach not more than four hundred yards in extent should be found shells representative of species existing in nearly all the warm waters of the world.

And there are other isles with other beaches. One may present a narrow strip of soft sand, cringing and squeaking under foot, almost entirely composed of finely ground coral and shells, among which polished fragments of red coral are to the beach-comber as the "colours" the gold fossicker may find in his dish—prospective of reward. They reinspire the like fervour which leads to the discovery of mountains as well as microbes, for may they not signify the existence within the bounds of the Great Barrier Reef of the precious coral of the Mediterranean and the Red Sea? Above such hopeful sands lies a band formed of stag's-horn coral, bleached snow-white, each time lying at right angles to the sea, and higher up on the strand are blocks and lumps of weather-stained coral among which vegetation is springing. A few yards further back stands a group of Pandanus palms, the van of the dense and intricate jungle covering rock and ridge.

The shore of the sister islet may at the moment be but series of steeply shelving banks of coral debris, to the base of the granite ramparts over which the luxuriant foliage falls.

Each islet has its distinguishing features, each beach its budget of news for ears attuned to "small measures," each its display of seemly things—the sweepings of the floor of the sea.

THE LOST ISLE

"Some unsuspected Isle in far-off seas."

BROWNING.

In a region of rare serenity it lay—a blue stud on a silver shield—aloof from other lands—unmapped, untarnished, pure, gleaming in the dawn of exultant day.

Emblem of perfection, its charms were imperative, partly because of remoteness from the taint of man-trodden land, mainly because, by right of discovery, it was joyfully mine. Could anything be more desirable than such a blending of jungle-clad mountains, verdurous hills, sheltered valleys, orange-tinted beaches, with the shadows of white headlands staining the sea purple?

An all-comprehending glance revealed the Isle in the shape of a five-rayed star, each ray irregularly serrated. Here was promise of many a landlocked cove to which the breathings of the sea would be foreign. Unsalted streams wound among the foothills of the central mountain, whence a spire of rose-red porphyry shot into the luminous sky from unbroken jungle, the superficies of which were soft and brilliant as sodden moss.

Some of the valleys showed in succession ever-green, flower-bedecked glades, with great trees and blossoming shrubs in scattered clumps and patches, among which sinuous ribbons of jungle denoted the courses of deep hidden streams. Others were merely precipitous depressions in the unbroken mass of foliage, variegated with aspiring palms so slender of shaft that their unceasing swaying in the still air seemed an act of unconscious affectation for the display of huge bunches of gaudy fruit, seductive and dulcet to the taste. Spider-webbed tree-ferns with furry, water-bespangled trunks stood in crowded groves on the brink of spray-creating cascades and along the margins of cool rivulets which murmured as they hurried to the sea.

Water-dripping moss padded the lintels of grottos, before which dangled translucent ferns of delicate form, yet so rich and intense with life that crozier-tipped fronds took the hue of flowers—coral-red, golden-bronze, and yellow; while golden dust clung to hairy undersides like pollen to the thighs of hive-returning bees. Deep in perpetual shadow lived a shy plant with heart-shaped leaves, so succulent and distended as to resemble green capsules, and in association with each leaf was a single semi-transparent fruit, pink with a central glow like the fire of opal, but so frail that upon touch it resolved into a dewdrop which glistened, trembled, and was gone in a moment.

In the full blaze, feather-foliaged trees crowned with gigantic red blossoms offered as a sacrifice fruit which blushed before the insistent gaze of the sun; while beneath this gay canopy vine and creeper and pliant shrub wove an undergarment which screened the moist earth and created a realm of subdued light in which all the flowers were pale of tint and tremulously fragile, though of almost forbidding magnitude of form.

Birds of painted plumage and loud and sonorous note sang and fluttered among the flowers and fruit with no ill thing to disturb them, no dissonance to compel them to silence and fear.

Whithersoever I gazed, the lone and lovely Isle denoted a paradise of unkempt vegetation, unfeared birds. No stump was there to betray the passing of the devastating axe. No footprint except that of birds—erratic, rectangular, scribbling—dented the sand. No human being had ever visited those groves perfumed by orchids, gauzy as the wings of the butterflies which poised over them and sipped the nectar stored in their slender throats.

Each bay and inlet and cove differed in delightsomeness. Unsoiled, weedless sand littered with shells floored this deep and sheltered nook, where shadow and substance blended to the complete deceit of the closest scrutiny. The next was as a garden of shrubs with living blossoms and fruit in strange shapes and gaudy colours. Many of the subaqueous plants expanded and retracted their blossoms harmoniously, as if to the strains of music audible only to the mute denizens of the sea—a measured, waving dance, fantastic and wondrously beautiful. Crystalline clearness magnified the detail of the next, the portals of which were coral, dyed extravagantly and variously according to the secret of the sea, with its inexhaustible chemicals. Fish in unimaginable shapes, fantastic hues, and sea-things harmless and educative to the sight, roamed the coral gardens, retiring at will into sapphire-blue caverns or flashing in the clearness with lightning speed and scarce visible effort. Cream and yellow, old gold, blue, pink and lavender, the corals flourished in myriad shapes. Anemones, large as plates, royal blue and greyish-green, and each bristling with thousands of independent activities, embossed snow-white blocks.

Opening out into an oval basin, the inlet was again constricted, the bottle-neck entrance to a perfect haven being guarded by huge masses of limestone, weathered grotesquely, from the crevices of which sprays of peach-coloured orchids quivered, while the flora of land and sea commingled on the lustrous surface. Beyond again, the inlet wound round the base of it cliff vocal with the fugue of birds which flew from flowery parapet to flowery parapet.

Gradually the cliffs retreated, leaving fair banks with shrubs and great trees with branches pendulous over unbroken placidity, and there, on a knoll, stood a palm, rigid and straight as a column, crowned with shimmering fronds which shielded masses of nuts, brown and green, and great sprays of straw-coloured infloresence. More palms beyond, thick-set; and beyond again an avenue in perfect alignment, each tree perfect in stately form, with one blotch of glorious purple—as high and compact as a church—to block the diminished distance.

The boat drifted to the landing never touched by foot of man. Lost in admiration of the imposing and manifold perfections of the Isle, eager to wander at will among those enticing glades, and to make festival with their genial gods, I stepped out—and into nothingness!

Can it be that never again shall be discovered in the Land of Dreams the Lost Isle?

PART II.
THE PASSING FACE

THE CORROBOREE

"No ceremony that to great ones 'longs."

SHAKESPEARE.

Summoned, invited, children, men, women, and piccaninnies assembled to participate in the duties and recreations of the moment.

Message-sticks had been carried into unfamiliar country by nervous boys. One of the organisers at ease with his pen sent to his kin formal and official invitations mingled with social and affectionate greetings. All responded.

The beach sent its silent-footed contingents trailing along the yellow sands, carrying in well-worn dilly-bags oysters and scraps of half-baked fish smeared with smoke, and gritty. All their lives had they trudged along the convenient margin of the sea, where the receding tide leaves a firm, level, springy track. They were familiar with all its moods, and took little heed of any.

The fame of a previous Parliament had spread far and wide, even to that aspect of the Dividing Range which sends its waters to the great shallow gulf to the west. Natives who, though living among the mountains but two days' journey from the coast, had never seen the sea, hastened thither in bee-line, passing through unknown but not unfriendly country. Though the age of tribal feuds was past, special weapons of defence were carried, for did not strange jungles teem with spectral denizens whom imagination endowed with appalling shape, with cunning, and with rending ferocity? Unmolested, the party arrived one evening, to gaze with mute astonishment on the sea. It was almost as incomprehensible, and therefore almost as fearsome, as the phantoms of the bush. Mysterious, vast beyond the range of vision, here grumbling on the sand, there mingling with the sky, the strangers peered at it through the screen of whimpering casuarinas and trembled. The rustle of the subsiding north-easter made for fear. They told one another that the big salt water was alive. It talked in austere tones, while their own sleepy lagoons were silent and tame. Wonderingly, they retreated to the jungle for the night, there to take counsel of the long-shoremen.

"That b-i-g fella salt water, him talk all asame?"

"Yowi! Him sing out plenty. Mak'm b-i-g fella row!"

"That fella him walk about lika that?"

"Yowi! Him walk about. Quiet little bit. Sometime run about splash'm water; mak'm boat capsize. Plenty men drown finis!"

The strangers shivered and longed to return to their cool hills; but the long-shoremen beguiled them with descriptions of the fish and the crabs and oysters the generous sea gave, and told that in the morning it would be "quiet fella" and that they need not be afraid.

With taut-strung nerves, the highlanders approached the sea, which shone in matutinal placidity. When the ripples wavered on the smooth sand and ran in caressing ripples towards their feet, they started and shrunk. The incomprehensible ocean was alive and much to be feared, for was it not so big that no one could see where it ended? They sat and watched its enticing gestures, and, gathering courage, stood tremulously while the tide splashed their feet and retreated. The boldest walked in ankle-deep and danced in daredevilry, and soon young and old were gambolling uncouthly, tasting the sea's quality, shouting and splashing. None ventured more than knee-deep; some crawled and wallowed in the wet sand, too fearful to trust their lives to so big a thing which showed itself to be alive by breathing and moving. The morning was spent in moist frolics, and when the north-easter began to work up a little sea, which spoke in menacing tones, the terrified strangers withdrew.

Late in the afternoon the corroboree began, many of the participators having spent hours in the assumption of the festive costume of the down of sulphur-crested cockatoos plastered to the skin with grease and the blood. It is not to be supposed that white down in the hands of experienced dressers is incapable of variation in style. Several original designs excited the approbation of spectators. The down was arranged in tufts following the perpendiculars of the body from shoulder to shin, or in a series of circles accurately spaced, or in intersecting spirals, while the heads of all performers and combatants were converted into white mops.

And with the clapping of hollowed hands and the clicking of boomerangs the function began. And having danced to their own satisfaction and the delight of the crowd, the warriors with ostentation and bluster recited private grievances and challenged those against whom they had real or fancied wrongs to combat. Most of the noisy declamation was ill-founded. The many had no grievances and no intentions of fighting, but out of the shouting crowd stepped two big men who sought compensation for "another Helen." Though not lovely or winsome or an heiress, she sufficed as the motive for an honourable and public strife, quite as sincere as many of the scuffles without the walls of Troy. Spears and boomerangs were thrown viciously and dodged and evaded skilfully until one of the men found a boomerang sticking fast in his leg. The wound was decisive, and with much hullabaloo the defeated warrior limped away, while the lady, whom niggardly Nature had denied the grace of blushing, passively went to the victor.

Among the strangers to the coast was an old man but a yard and a quarter high, with unkempt, grisly beard, a head which needed not the glorification of cockatoo's down, long, thin arms, huge hands, thick, stump legs, and sprawling feet. No far-reaching crab of the reef just showing its worn brown tusks off-shore was more grotesque of mien and gait. To emphasise his malignant mood, he carried a huge boomerang, which seemed to obey and embody his whims. It sprang from his powerful hands in resolute and impetuous flight, whirred threateningly overhead, and returned to foot, fluttering and purring, as if endowed with affection for its unlovable master. None so mastered the missile; but for all his weird influence over it, he was subject to the restraints of another weapon which seldom left his hands. Is there not a spiritual law which imposes checks on the bombastic tricks of crude and cultured alike, or was it by force of gravity that the point of the dwarf's long and slender spear dipped into the ground, punctuating mock martial struts with perverse irregularity? Prodigious in his own estimation, his jibes and taunts were almost as terrifying as the erratic flights of his boomerang; for the dwarf was a privileged individual, the Thersites of the campaign, and with one advantage over his prototype—he really wanted to fight. So he swaggered, heeding not the reproving spear; he fumed; he mocked; for no warrior affected to notice his vainglorious absurdities. He was as much in earnest as those who fought on account of elemental love, and far more so than any of the blusterers who talked big and looked small. He longed to fight, and for money.

Each warrior was challenged individually, and when none responded he railed against all for cowards and sent the boomerang hissing defiance against the blue sky, to fall with mutter and thud at his feet. In his rage the little man became hysterical, and the more he scolded the less important, while the swaying spear emphasised increasing agitation, but brought him neither humility nor jibe, for the race does not intentionally relieve its drama with comedy.

No more influential personage was present than "Mooty," the crafty, determined, plausible philosopher—the sagest of the counsellors, the most flowery of orators, the most weird of the wizards. Long before he had established his reputation as a medicine-man. A settler had purchased some cast-off goats in a distant town, and had employed a black boy of the district as assistant drover, and the name of the boy was Tom. Since there are many "Toms," a distinguishing surname had to be bestowed, so "Goat" was affixed, and as "Tom Goat" the stranger was known. Having no sweetheart, he made love to several dusky dames, all of whom rejected him because his absurd name made him a figure for fun. Rosey, wife of Jack, was persistently courted, and scornfully she despised her wooer. That individual, however, was not without malignant resource. Rosey complained of a sore throat, and as she got worse her boy became similarly afflicted. The faces and throats of both swelled alarmingly, so that Mooty, who had the cases in hand, gave up hope. Both were resigned, when Mooty, to his own horror and the dismay of everyone, caught the dread disease.

No such illness had ever been known in the district, and since it had not only baffled Mooty's skill, but had irreverently seized him—the only physician of credit and renown—its cause must be supernatural. Thus did he reason, as he began occult investigations. Jack and Rosey lay in their camp passively dying. Mooty prowled about, the sleeves of a discarded shirt tied under his distended jaws. No physical origin for the mysterious disease was found during the two days he devoted to methodic search and secret rite. Then an anticipated discovery rewarded him and made his name thrill among his race. To a condescending white man he told of his skill in these terms:

"Two fella him close up finis. Me bin look out camp belonga two fella. B'mbi me bin find'm little fella fork stick close up alonga groun'. Me frait. My word, me bin pick'm up easy fella. Me look out longa little fella hole. Me bin see hair, too much, belonga Tom Goat. That hair bin mak'm two fella no good. Him mak'm me fella no good. Me catch'm that fella hair along two fella stick. Tchuck'm along ribber. My word! That fella hair no good! Him go phuff! Kill'm fish, too many. B'mbi me fella go alonga camp. Me tell'm two fella, 'You no more mak'm die. Me bin find'm that fella hair belonga Tom Goat.' B'mbi two fella him get up; him no more die; he walk about."

Exasperated by such impropriety, aghast at the consequences, Mooty— doctor alike of laws, of science, and of medicine, and a man of imperative mood—sharpened his tomahawk at the Chinaman's grindstone, theatrically testing its edge with distorted thumb. Tom Goat disappeared as silently as last night's dew, for Mooty does not hesitate to summarily administer his own judgment when his professions are scorned, his family bewitched, his countenance distorted with mumps.

With feasting and fighting, with dancing and storytelling, quarrelling and reconciliations, the assemblage spent a happy week. Then the jungle reabsorbed the nervous hillmen, and beach-combers straggled along the yellow sands.

THE CANOE-MAKER

"Last scene of all, . . . Is second childishness and mere oblivion."

SHAKESPEARE.

A tottering old man, frail alike in frame and mind, squats dying in an alien camp. His teeth have almost disappeared, worn to the gums by the mastication of food in which sand has been mingled in immoderate proportion. All his life has been spent on the verge of the sea. He has never known smooth food. Before he left his mother's breast grit was on his lips, for in her sleep she snoodled naked in the sand. Hers was the age of bark rugs or none, and was ever lord of the beach who shared with his lady so rare a comfort?

Counterparts of Cassowary's babyhood are extant to this day—milk-bellied, nose-neglected, fumbling-fingered toddlers, who smash with stones almost beyond their strength infant oysters and gulp a mixture of squash and sand.

As he grew up his food, seared on a fire on the beach, was always more or less gritty. Possibly it would hardly have been relished if the accustomed condiment had been absent.

For many a long year Cassowary was a sort of king in the locality of his birth, though this rank brought him no isolation. Now he is without rank and grim in his lonesomeness. True to the sentiments of his race, the men and women who knew him when he was strong and lusty strive to make him comfortable in his dotage; but he is repellent. His surliness does not vex them. They pity and excuse and endeavour to soothe. To strangers whom Cassowary has never loved and would now assault with spear and nulla-nulla, they apologise.

"Poor fella, Cassowary. Him no good. Close up that fella finis."

Then they tell of his strange fantasies. Similar delusions have afflicted notable men of the world, and even to this day are there not apprehensive monarchs whose precautions are similar to those of the age-worn savage? He imagines that he is regarded as a useless encumbrance, and that his fellows would gladly hasten his departure to that country on the bourne of which he painfully lingers. Suspicious of plots to rob him of the poor vestiges of life, he is ever on his guard against poison, his special dread. Rather than run risk he submits to semi-starvation, for the decayed monarch of a narrow strip of shore has no servitor on whom to impose the office of taster of his dishes. A stranger may of his goodwill offer a tribute of tobacco. It is cast away with every manifestation of indignation and haste. He is sure that the one solace of existence has been drugged, and that if he indulges he must die. How marvellous the self-denial! How many of us would purchase half an hour's existence such as his at the cost of declining the one luxury of life!

Flour from his master's hands is served like the stranger's tobacco, though he may not have tasted food for days; nor does he accept a portion of the damper cooked in his presence until he has seen others eat. Then he feeds reluctantly and with extreme caution, not to gratify the palate, but to maintain life.

Was ever monarch or Roman pontiff beset by more vindictive and envious foes than this helpless old savage who possesses nothing save a grimy shirt and the fragments of a blanket?

Cassowary, an old man when I first met him, was of the sort which does not make friends with white men. Silent, resolute, reserved, a man apart, he disdained the race-shattering language his fellows hastened to acquire. His pidgin English, limited to a few words, was almost as unintelligible as his own rude tongue. Once I landed on the beach which was his favourite resort, and as the anchor slipped into the sea, smoke puffed and drifted from the camp and the lonesome man's dogs barked; but by the time the camp was reached the smell of the fire had gone, and all tracks had been obliterated as if by the efficient touch of the wind. The heat of the sand at the entrance of the dome-shaped humpy revealed the site of the covered embers, and the rest was silence.

At the back of the humpy, concealed by carelessly disposed bark and grass, was a bark canoe which Cassowary, fisherman and oyster-eater, was never without. In those days he deserved the reputation of being an unrivalled maker of canoes which, during the first few weeks of their prime, were sound, neat of appearance, quite seaworthy, though of small dimensions and exceedingly light. Others might be expert fishermen and skilful in more exacting sport of turtle and dugong catching, but all acknowledged his special superiority. Though custom had made him a king, Nature had designed him for a canoe-maker, while with that invincible irony with which she rebukes the self-esteem and baffles the ambitions of mortals, she discounted her gift by the bestowal of frank distrust of the sea. He was so impelled to the exercise of the one talent that during youth and manhood his chief occupation and never-ending delight lay therein. That which his right hand had found to do he did with all his might, his frail craft being the admiration of all, while the confidence with which others managed them proved their quality. They toyed with the sea in its placid moods, and were deferential in its ill-humour. But Cassowary never ventured beyond easy hail from the shore, however urgent the occasion or propitious the day.

Fear also restricted his wanderings in the bush, which kept him within sound of the dreaded waves. He was an unaffected beach-comber. Neither the food-bestowing sea nor the safe dry land was for him.

By instinct he seemed to be guided to the best trees for bark, generally selecting "gulgong," though others were equally pliant in his hands. Raw from the tree, he would soak the single sheet in water, and while sodden steam it over a smoky fire, and, as it softened, mould it with hand and knee. Bringing the edges of the end designed for the stem into apposition, using a device on the principle of the harness-maker's clamp, he sewed them together with strips of freshly cut cane. Two stretchers gave to the craft beam, and the necessary sheer and thwart-ship stays of twisted cane stiffness. Gunwales of cane were sewn on, the stitches being cemented with gum made plastic by frequent renderings over the fire on a flat stone, and then the canoe was complete save for the hand-paddles, spoon-bowl-shaped pieces of bark.

Each canoe sat well down by the stern when the fisherman knelt in it, crouching forward like a jockey on the withers of his mount, and sending it along by the alternate strokes.

Cassowary was wont to scan each new work with the tilted head of an artist. All the stitches were regularly spaced, and since they were burnished with smoke, the canoe became a study in brown, braided with gold, representative of something more than a means towards earning a diet of fish, and inevitable grit. It was neat and of harmonious colouring; innocent of the least touch of finery; not a scratch expended on ornament. All its lines, save those of the stretchers and stays which stood for rigidity, were fluent. It was not made to model or measurement, but developed under the maker's hard hands and tough fingers—a tribute to his artistry and skill. On the water it was as blithe as a bubble.

Often had the wish to possess one of Cassowary's masterpieces arisen. He scorned barter by abandoning his property whenever the interferer appeared. When the camp was deserted while the boat was being brought to anchor there was a strong temptation to take the canoe, leaving some adequate reward. The self-denial is almost regretted, for the old man with the thin white tuft on his chin, his shyness, his hatred of strangers, and delusions of his decrepitude, are characteristic of an age soon to be of the irrecoverable past. A canoe from such accomplished hands would have represented a complimentary record of a race deficient in the elements of history.

Several years have elapsed since Cassowary made his last canoe. He acknowledged that his fingers had lost their cunning, but the fates ordained that his ideas should blossom as his manipulatory skill withered Gradually he became feeble in mind and body, and was wont to spend his time crouched in a rough shelter dreaming prodigious dreams. He would wake not only his fellows, but a pitying neighbour of other complexion, with enthusiastic shouts announcing that a "big fella steamer" was whistling out at sea; that it was his steamer; that it carried two bags of flour, and tea and sugar and tobacco, and one "good fella trousis"; and he would demand help in the landing of his merchandise. Worn with age, sleep would soon again claim him, but never and anon his great cry, hailing the phantom steamer with her beneficent cargo, would wake the poor and squalid camp.

The time came when Cassowary could no longer obtain for himself the coarse and trivial food essential to life, and he and another outcast, blind and maimed, quartered themselves on the camp on the beach; arid in spite of fretfulnesses and suspicions, their fellows administered to their wants. Being brought face to face with facts, the State gave orders which meant an old-age pension for the outcasts. The dole was liberal enough. The mistake was that it came too late.

There was no reaction, as is oft the case with those who retire after the bustling phase to live on the bounty of the State, for Cassowary and his blind companion had never been strenuous workers or brain-compelling men. The pension represented unexampled abundance. It was real, and yet it came from a source almost as intangible as Cassowary's ship. Food and tobacco! What more could the heart of a casual relic of such a race want? Actually he wanted nothing more, save, peradventure, a blanket; but he dreamt he did, and no earthly agent could diminish the festal extravagance of the scenes among which he revelled, conducted by the enchanted sleep.

Cassowary had at last come to his kingdom. His time had always been his own. The ready-to-hand food gave him leisure. His days were all dreams. Weary of crouching over the fire before the opening of his humpy, he began to wander in the flesh as he was wont to wander in mind. He was seen a mile away from the cheerless camp, where his companions, with smoke-dried eyes, lamented his absence.

Was he searching for a tree which might provide bark for yet another canoe—his last work, a paragon? A few days passed and it became known that Cassowary was missing. His shrunken body disordered a patch of buff sand just above high water.

Had the desolate old man, in his fancy, made the best of all canoes, and for once ventured out to sea?

TWO LADIES

"To one, resolution; to another, a disposition to dance."

NELLY, THE SHREW.

As the steamer from the South enters the bay, the traveller sees ahead the fringe of houses on the low lands fronting the inlet where shipping finds safe and convenient harbourage. To the left he may be introduced to a strip of open beach between two low points of grey granite, back from which are scattered groups of modest buildings and huts which form the aboriginal settlement. The choice of the site for the settlement was influenced by the character of the country. Although but a short distance by sea from the port, it is isolated by its background of hard and inhospitable hills patched with almost impenetrable jungle. Few consigned there ever leave of their own motive, however earnest the longing may be. The home-sick realise that escape is difficult and, if successful, futile, for are not the police everywhere, and strong and compelling? Why undertake the unknown perils of unknown hills—spiritual perils more to be dreaded than physical—when capture and again banishment are certain?

Nellie Oongle-bi, among whose matrimonial experiences was Tom, of this Isle, and who since his death has gone from bad to worse, had been found under the protection of a coloured alien, sadly degenerated and saturated with opium. For her own salvation she was transported to the settlement afar off, with its frontier of sea and background of repulsive hills. She went, being in the clutches of a superior force, tractably enough, but with none of her unconquerable love of country subdued. Nelly has nothing of an attractive nature. She has a vixenish temper at times; is always on the alert for fancied slights; is by no means cleanly, unless under duress; and does not hesitate to foment subjects of quarrel. Few among her relations and friends would mourn her exile. Even her own son, Jim, was scoffingly indifferent. She was far from being so, but played her part well, being obedient, quite tame, and ever observant.

She "sat down" at the settlement, and made friends with two or three of the women there with whom she had previously been acquainted; but while she talked with apparent resignation, she scanned the hills, especially fixing in her mind a particular gully which leads up to a ridge promising an outlook to the south, upon which her hopes were fixed. Soon after dark on the second night she took to the bush, carrying a dilly-bag and a blanket. She is now one of the population of a far-distant settlement, the site of which happens to be within her own country. How she overcame the distance without food, friends, or resources, has to be told, though not altogether in her own language, for such would be unintelligible to the ordinary reader.

She was determined to run away as soon as the steamer landed her, for that part of the North was not her country, and she could not live anywhere else. Besides, she was "sorry belonga that boy Jim." During the first night of her homeward pilgrimage she never ceased walking among rocks and through the scrub, for she was fearful of being recaptured. Without pause she clambered on until well into the next day, when she slept for a little while. Then on again until dark. One big "mung-um" (mountain) stood in the hopeful direction. Thitherwards she hastened, losing count of the days and nights. Nelly has no conception of figures beyond one, two, and a great many. The climbing of the mountain occupied many days. She was bewildered, for she could not "catch'm that sal'water" which would lead her home. At last from a spur of the mountain she saw the sea—"L-o-n-g way. Too far. Me close up sing out." Though she might cry, the sight of big salt water beside which all her life had been spent was a joy and a stimulant. Pushing and worming her way through the jungle, she encountered nothing but birds, wallabies, and snakes.

Once she was startled by what seemed to be a worn narrow track. Advancing cautiously along it, she came across a huge carpet snake coiled "all a same rope alonga boat." It was asleep where an opening in the roof of vegetation made a patch of sunlight on the jungle floor, and she passed by, treading noiselessly. For food she had the fruits of the jungle, crude, harsh, and bitter. Food, indeed, was almost repugnant, for her thoughts were concentrated on her country, so she hastened down towards the now hidden sea. Far inland she heard its welcome noise—a greeting and a call from home which made her forgetful of all weariness and fret.

In course of time—a weak woman carrying a blanket and living on innutritious foods does not struggle through jungle at any remarkable speed—the foothills and then the low-lying country at the junction of two rivers were reached. Here she took off her few and bedraggled garments, and, making them into a bundle with her blanket and bag, waded through swamps, eventually emerging on a sandy beach, which she intended to follow until she regained her country, many a weary mile to the south. Providence provided an easy means of crossing the estuary of the rivers—a kindly white man, owner of a "little fella boat, little fella ingin." To him she told the story of her escape and her longing for her own country and her own people, and was ferried across. Then she picked up a camp of her race, the members of which, sympathising with her, accompanied her on her way for a couple of days. One day she woke from her sleep on the edge of the mangroves with her blanket sopping with blood which had flowed from her mouth and nose during sleep. "Me bin sorry belonga that boy Jim. Me bin sorry belonga country. That 'nother country no good belonga me. Me think me die. Me walk alonga sandy beach. Some time alonga b-i-g fella rock. Me close up tumble down altogether. Me tired. B'mbi catch'm Liberfool Crik (Liverpool Creek). Plenty fella sit down. He bin sing out, 'Hello! You come back from that place?' Me bin say 'Yes; that country no good belonga me.'"

A month or so after Nelly was again found in the service of a coloured alien, tugging away with another weak gin at what she calls a "two-fella saw." For her task of sleeper-cutting her reward would probably be a handful of rice and a dose of opium per day.

Nelly is now at her leisure within a mile or so from the place of her birth, hardly conscious of the feat represented by her solitary pilgrimage. Occasionally she has the company of her tall and indifferent boy. She enjoys the society of her relations, and indulges as oft as may be in exhilarating misunderstandings with them. Without a vehement squabble now and again life would be intolerably insipid. Anger, accompanied by fluent abuse, is to her a kind of spiritual blood-letting for the casement of her suddenly plethoric temperament. But such is of her frailty. Proof of her strength of purpose, has it not been given?

MARIA DANCES.

In her youth Maria gave promise of a rare condition among coastal blacks— tendency to width and breadth. As she grew in bulk she seemed, if not to decrease in stature, at least to remain stationary. Thus it was that her figure became perfect.

If there be one feature of animal physiology more adorable than aught else in the eyes of the lords of the soil, it is fat—fat under any and every circumstance. They admire it in animals of the chase, and the paltry, greasy relics of a feast may be smeared over the body with something of the pride and gratification derivable in other and cleaner walks of life from perfumed powder, pink and white.

Being fat and shiny as a girl, Maria had keen and ardent lovers. She was an adorable novelty.

Blacks do not gaze into the faces of their sweethearts. They have never found chaste delight in the writing of woeful ballads to their mistress's eyebrows, or to the glorification of their snubby and expansive noses. If any of Maria's admirers had been lyrical, her buxom condition would have been the theme of their idealisations. In time she became the mother of children, still retaining that charming superiority of bulk which excited the rage of sisters whose skins did not shine, whose flesh did not quiver whensoever they walked, talked, or even smiled.

No marvel that her matrimonial experiences were the comment of the camp and gave rise to many differences, but, since placidity and fat have been known among so-called civilised peoples to blend in the individual, Maria's demeanour called for no comment. It was not her fault, but the flightiness and whimsicality of Nature which had contrived to make her the belle of the camp. And why not enjoy the obvious admiration of the stalwart youths as well as the discomfort of the sisters who had not an ounce of irresistible fascination of which to boast.

For some years the form of Maria had not waddled across accustomed scenes. Quite unexpectedly it loomed up as large and buoyant as ever. The light-hearted denizens of the camp had arranged an evening's entertainment. The fires burned low, the sea babbled, making white-skirted frolic on the hard level sand, and the piping voices of the honey-seeking flying foxes among the tea-trees seemed to chide the parrots of the day for having left so little refreshment in the blossoms. Behind a screen of faded blankets the warriors of the camp were adorning themselves with white clay and feathers and long, shaggy beards of bark, while the leader of the orchestra began to tune his boomerang and fire-hardened sticks, and his attendants to squat ready to drum on thighs and lap with hollowed hand in time with his refrain and clicking music. The fires flared up, and the band emerged with thumping step and emphatic grunts to illustrate the ceremonious visit of strangers to a camp at which the nature of the reception was in doubt. One individual, in chalk for the most part, advanced, half nervously, half anxiously, to the musician, and modestly retired, and advanced again and retired, until reassured, and then the crowd came forward whirling and grunting, and, with high-waving arms in unison and swaying bodies, gave token of happiness.

ACT II.—The master of ceremonies carried to the front a big and rough sapling. The fires glowed again, the orchestra clicked and thumped, and a single boy in an ancient red handkerchief and chalks danced into the light, and, keeping time with the music, began in pantomime to fashion the sapling into a sword, using a fictitious shell, with which he scraped off imaginary bark. While absorbed in his work, his companions came from the screen in haste, skipping round him and mimicking all his actions and grunting in unison with him, while making the sand-ridge to quiver with intensity of tread. Presently all flopped down on haunches in close formation round the sword-maker, still maintaining rhythmical sway of body and limb, and while some held the sapling, others toiled strenuously towards the completion of a good and true weapon, the master of ceremonies encouraging and exhorting the workers until nature could hold out no longer, and they bounded to their feet and, with grunts and signs and with bodies reeking with perspiration, whirled away into darkness.

ACT III.—Each of the noisy players came suddenly into the glare carrying a rotund, compact bundle, and, squatting down, began with grunts and sighs the great "coco-nut" act, obviously one of the masterpieces of the corroboree. In perfect time the sham coco-nuts were beaten with hands in lieu of sticks or tomahawks, while the accompaniment became faster and faster. Ever and anon each, still rocking, would peer closely at his prize to satisfy himself as to its quality, and forthwith continue the resonant belabouring of the shell, until the meat therein was available with joyous shout.

ACT IV.—Most of the accumulated bark and leaves having by this time passed into flame and smoke, the attendants raided the nearest gunyah for fresh supplies of material for illumination. The big fires lit up the arena anew, and, marshalled by the conductor, the band rushed out of the darkness uttering grunts which rang a change on the monotony of previous vocal efforts. A masterpiece of composition, it conjured up the dimness of the jungle and the smell of damp vegetation. All squatted in a double ring, back to back. This formation was not strictly maintained, for each individual made half turns to right and left alternately, simultaneously scratching the sand with distended fingers and kicking vigorously until the sand ascended in the smoke-tinged glow, heads bowing and ducking with mechanical regularity, as the entertainers sought—and with conspicuous success—to portray a community of scrub turkeys building an incubating mound.

Then it was that the favourite and belle of the camp, the fascinating creature whose magnificent condition bestowed privileges undreamt of by other ladies, became conspicuous. Her costume had evidently been designed for a lady not divinely tall, but considerably less of flesh than the wearer. Maria did not actually overflow, though perilously near that point. Surely buttons were never designed to resist such strain. Coloured ladies generally sit meekly among the audience and chatter and maintain the drum-beats, lacking which no corroboree could be successful. During the intervals they may emboss pictures in the impressionable sand with cunning forefinger and giggle, for the subjects are often quaint. Maria, sure of her privileges, waddled out from the flame-obscuring dusk, turned an ample back upon the double ring of boys, and played her part as one of the giddy and industrious wild-fowls. Her fingers scratched the air and her feet the dust with a realism not to be excelled by the most gifted of the boys, while her half grunt, half chuckle, exactly imitative of the social garrulity of the turkey, gave artistic finish to a scene which would have been absolutely delusive if feathers had been in fashion. Maria, a fleer at mere ponderosity, skipped and whisked from left to right with fay-like airiness of foot until a thrill of delight went through the camp. The frolicsome turkeys scratched and scattered leaves that were not, and gobbled and clucked, until, panting and perspiring, all rose, and with a simultaneous shout scampered for the screen, while the master of ceremonies shouted "Finis!" The music ceased, the flames faded, and substantial Maria dissolved in the gloom.

SOOSIE

"No legend! Well, let us invent one."—SCOTT.

A crinkled fist, fumbling and twisting, protruded from a rent in a dilapidated dilly-bag. It had done so with infinite feebleness for many an hour in unavailing protest against the woes and weight of life, for faint scratch smeared with blood denoted the friction of tender skin against the broken edges of the cane-made bag.

A scarcely audible, inhuman wail—pathetically staccato—told of unceasing pain. Whomsoever the bag contained was enduring martyrdom.

"That fella, him no good. Close up finis. B'mbi me plant'm along scrub."

Thus spoke the pleasant-faced gin who passed with the dilly-bag along a narrow aisle of the jungle, intent upon ridding herself of a vexatious encumbrance, and at the same time performing the rite of unrighteous burial.

Squirming in dirt was a naked infant-black, foul, and but a few days old.

"Mother belonga that fella him dead—finis. That fella, him no good. Him sing out all a time. More better tchuck'm away."

Frail outcast—the very scum of a blacks' camp, its repulsiveness was tragic. Dirt and odour sickened, yet its appeal was irresistible. That universal language, a human cry, which everywhere and always quickened the pulse, stirred pity to its depths. I seized the stained bag (it was a desperate deed) and, breaking down its worn sides, displayed its contents—a girl in all the infamy of neglect, starvation, and dirt—a panting mummy reeking with offence.

Spreading out a handkerchief, I put the awful atom on it gingerly, while the foster-mother reiterated her counsel to "tchuck'm alonga scrub."

In the guise of a frail bundle at arm's-length was Soosie conducted to a civilised home.

Dismay tempered with pity greeted her.

"How horrible! How dirty!"

"Is it really a little girl? It looks like a wild animal."

"Do let me nurse it."

Thus was crinkled-faced Soosie welcomed.

Many successive baths did she endure, faintly wailing, until dirt soaked off and the wails ceased for the time being as Soosie sucked ravenously at a tiny sugar-bag.

What a frail little life it was—feeble beyond expression, and ugly with the ugliness of savagery. She wriggled and screwed up her skinny features with inane ferocity. A motherless wallaby would have submitted to human solace and ministrations with daintier mien; but the whole household thrilled with excitement. Could the spluttering spark of life be made to glow? That was the all-absorbing topic for days. Gradually some sort of a human rotundity became manifest, and on the occasion of the bath it was more and more apparent that instead of being impenetrably black the skin-tint was a mingling of pale brown and pink; and as regular nourishment began to be effective the features changed, losing their gross animalism.

Just because of the waif's helplessness was repugnance to her conquered. She had no other redeeming quality. In a certain sense she was fearsome; she required unremitting attention and care; her whimpering fits, in beast-like monotone, shook the nerve of the most patient of her attendants. She was a charge to keep and foster, and the duty was performed with devotion, which took little concern for self-sacrifice. Before many months had passed Soosie had been transformed into a fat roly-poly with a perpetual smile and gurgles of satisfaction, which even vocalised sleep.

All this happened years ago. In infancy Soosie had been informally adopted. She was now a bright, sensible, slender girl, whose full, melting eyes pleaded for inevitable facial defects, and whose complexion was very greatly at fault. She grew up more averse from the manners and moods of her mother than those of us who better understand the differences of race. To her a black was more abhorrent than a snake. She loathed the sight of those who came about the place, and would not defile herself by touching the cleanest—kind-hearted "Wethera," who had so nearly interred her, and to whom she was as a princess; "Wethera," who was wont to say, "That fella Tchoosie, too flash. Close up me bin tchuck'm away. Boss he bin catch'm."

Soosie evaded all possible reference to her kin, and when others spoke in sympathetic terms would say: "How can you bear to think of those horrible people who live in dirt and only half dressed in the bush? I love the scrub, and but for them would like to wander in it all day. I dare not while they are about, for some day one of them might touch me, and I would never feel clean again."

We often wondered at the irreconcilable attitude which Soosie (she was always "Miss Soosie" to all but members of the household) adopted to her own race, for she well understood where she had been born and the manner of her salvation from imminent death.

Though no special training had been hers, none of the domestic arts were unknown to her. She acquired them with ease and practised them with the air of a dignified princess and neat-handed facility. While the other children of the house stewed over lessons and rebelled against essential tasks, to Soosie everything seemed to make for holiday. She read voraciously, so that her application of English became so keen that she was the first to detect verbal dissonances. She, the youngest of two girls and a boy, would often correct their speech, not as a budding pedant, but because her ears were delicately attuned to the music of the tongue and could not, without offence, hearken to discords. She was an affected prude. Her self-chosen style of dress, her pose, her disdainful airs, her repugnance to coarse work, her inclination towards occupations and pastimes which involved isolation, showed that self-consciousness ruled her life. She lived within herself, and her life was gentle, contrasting with the boisterous playfulness of her foster sisters and brother, upon whose romps she smiled indulgently, but in which she never took part. In her own estimation she was a girl quite out of the ordinary, and one to whom the most honoured of guests must be polite, if not deferential. She exacted little niceties of demeanour from all, her equals and inferiors, for was she not treated as a daughter of the house? Often, however, in her preoccupied moods would she assume an air of detachment and jealousy towards the other children, for she could not but contrast herself with them. They were white; she was pronouncedly of the despised race. How wistfully would she scan the face of strangers! How teeming with resentment against fate her inevitable conclusions! In all save features she was white. Over her inheritance, the cruellest which fortune could bestow, she was shudderingly horrified. Not all the longings of an untainted mind could make her skin less tawny. Its stain was too deep to be blanched by the most fervent of prayers. Her outlook on life, her intensest wishes, were those of a white girl of more than decent perceptions—of actual refinement, for they tended to the avoidance of everything unpleasant and unsightly. In other respects, too, she was an absolute variant from the type, for her sensitiveness to the pain of others and of the lower animals amounted almost to a mania; for though she had a girlish horror of blood, her eagerness to solace sufferings made her so courageous that she became most apt and prompt in the administration of first aid. Her big, startled eyes showed the sincerity of her feelings, while her firm, slender fingers deftly applied bandages as she spoke in soothing tones.

The soul of a white damsel was in habitation of the body of one whose parents had been black and utterly degraded. In the days of old evil spirits were believed to be capable of taking spiteful possession of the bodies of the weak to work, in unseemlinesses and indecencies, for the mischief of the soul. Here was a good and gentle spirit which strove undemonstratively for the salvation of a being the circumstances of whose birth bordered on the infernal. It was as if the baths of infancy had purified the soul, while the permanence and perversity of blood triumphed in feature and complexion.

While the other children of the house deserved and obtained love and affection in full measure, towards Soosie were exhibited similar sentiments, with, perhaps, more consideration, for was it not plain that her life was a continual conflict—a conflict between body and soul—a body self-abhorred, a soul which needed no purification?

A creek which had its source in a ravine of the huge mountain which intercepted the rising sun and caused accustomed shadow an hour after the illumination of the western hills, ran past the lonely little house, which stood in a clearing the upright walls of which were on the sky-line scalloped with fan-palms. For many years Soosie never ventured into the jungle unaccompanied, yet she seemed to possess a sense of happenings beyond the almost solid screen of vegetation. Primal instinct contended against her affections and her love for a sheltered, clean life. Though she had always avoided association with the children of the camp, and her knowledge by imitation or precept was negative, yet was the bush an open book to her. She knew when and where to look for birds'-nests. She knew at a glance a venomous from a non-venomous snake, an edible from an inedible nut. As a child her favourite head-dress was a squat, fat mantis, the bright orange and yellow of which contrasted boldly with her fuzzy, coarse hair; and when the insect palled as an ornament it would be frizzled and slyly eaten.

Once as we strolled on the bank of the creek gazing at the lazy, red-finned fish among the swaying weeds, her wandering eyes detected a neat circular bore in the trunk of a huge silky oak. Having shrewdly scrutinised the bark, she judged the tenant to be at home. With a portion of one of the "feelers" of creeping palm stripped of all the prickles save two, she probed the tunnel and, screwing the instrument triumphantly, withdrew a huge white grub, which she ate forthwith; and then, with a grimace, assumed an air of shame and contrition, for she had astonished herself as well as others by an exhibition of untaught bush-craft and ancestral appetite.

She more than once confessed in shamefaced terms to an almost uncontrollable impulse to rush away to the mountain, that she might solace herself with the solitude and food in plenty there; but that when she conjured up the chance of meeting some "dreadful native" she thanked God for home and loving companions. How frequent and how intense was this unconfessed lust for the bush we knew not.

When Soosie was fourteen there came to the neighbourhood a hardy young fellow who began to clear a small area of jungle land; for civilisation, which had been marking time for nigh upon two decades, now marched slowly, and to no throb of drum, in our direction. Times were changing, and in some details less desirable conditions arose. The infinite privacy of the bush suffered. The little clearing was no longer our own. Soosie's demeanour became more reposeful. She had seemed to think that it might be her fate, in common with others, to become a ward of the State at some mission-station; but as settlement advanced, though still miles away, for we were the furthest out, and no interfering guardian of the peace came to enforce officialdom and insist upon obedience to the letter of the law, it was comforting to reflect that this unofficial daughter might be permitted to live out her life unhampered even by the goodwill expressed, in the first stages, by the visit of a policeman.

Her presence was necessary, not only on account of her amiable disposition and self-sacrificing ways, but for the actual load she bore of the duties of a quiet home. We had failed, however, to take into calculation the chances of another means of separation. There was now no disguising the fact that our new neighbour, Dan, was casting sheep's eyes in Soosie's direction, and to her evident dismay. It was of little avail to upbraid him as to the unseemliness of attachment to a girl who, however civilised, was of inferior race and despised colour. He frankly confessed that he wanted a wife as a companion and helpmeet; that he could not hope, in consideration of his own lowly birth and slender means and uphill task, to induce a white girl to halve his loneliness. He had studied Soosie, and was sure that she was his superior except in matter of colour. She was far better schooled and had been used to softer life.

"What," he asked, "don't you and the Missis and Miss Clare and Fan, and Bob, here, love her? You couldn't help it; and you are not ashamed. You treat her as your own child. It would be no sin for me to take her as my own wife. If she'll have me I'll marry her before the best parson in the North. What of her complexion? It's only a little more sunburnt than mine."

But Soosie was shy—more than shy. Her sensitiveness amounted to physical repulsion. She declared that, though she liked Dan, she would never marry.

"I do feel in my heart that I am nothing more than a black girl, and almost a savage. What if some day the horrible part of me got stronger, and I did go to the mountain by myself? I have heard you say that blood will tell. Often I am frightened of myself, especially when the nights are very still and I listen to the scrub hens chuckling and the flying foxes squealing, and smell the scents of the scrub. It must be very nice to live away from everybody in the very loneliest part of the big mountain, and to feel at home with actually wild things."

There was no affectation between us, so I said in comfort: "But my dear girl, you are whiter at heart than many a girl born white. It is only your skin that is dark. Perhaps if in a year or so you did marry Dan it would be the best, for a good woman, no matter what her complexion, will always earn respect.

Society may not want you, but you would not want society; and it will be very many years before society hampers life in this part of the bush."

Soosie thought for a few minutes, and then replied with delicate discretion. "I can never marry Dan. Sooner or later he would despise me. It might be all right while I was young, but—we—we—blacks get old very soon. Fancy Dan having an old gin in his house; for he won't be living in a one-roomed hut all his life!"

"You are spiteful against yourself, and that's not like you, Soosie."

"I have my feelings. How else may I restrain them?" she petulantly exclaimed. "He must never think of me. It might drive me to the mountain—just to save him from me."

Dan, good fellow, was discreet. He decided to play the laggard in love, realising that any show of impetuosity might frighten Soosie. It came to be understood that in time she might see the wisdom of accepting him, and I, knowing both, and to whom mixed marriages are abhorrent, was convinced that no girl could have been better qualified to fill the position of a bushman's wife. Modest, clever, sympathetic, healthful, none of the stains of the town had ever tarnished her mind. Her voice was that of a well-schooled white girl, and all her perceptions coincided. If the wander lust was to be suppressed for ever, it seemed to me that Soosie must marry, and marry young.

While Soosie's demeanour was still the cause of earnest solicitude, a perplexing complication arose. An old man of the camp whence she had been discarded began to do his best to attract her attention.

Gifts of birds'-nests, eggs, ferns, orchids in flower, a cassowary chick, neat dilly-bags, gay with crude Pigments, were brought to the house with messages such as this:

"That fella 'Pad-oo-byer' he bin gib'em alonga 'Ky-ee-rah.'"

"Ky-ee-rah" (the evening star) had been proclaimed to be Soosie's totemic name, and "Pad-oo-byer" we knew as "Duckbill," because of a fancied resemblance to a platypus.

The gifts were tearfully repudiated. They seemed to announce that Soosie, was regarded by her mother's kin as one of themselves, notwithstanding her civilised environment.

Though for the girl's sake, not on account of any personal repugnance or despiteful attitude, the blacks had been kept at arm's length, I was on good terms with all in the district, and took interest in their doings and folk-lore. One of their primary beliefs was that children, black and white, were actually the produce of the locality, belonging, not to chance parents, but to the very land on which they were born. The germs of life, they assumed, came from the soil; the soil assimilated all flesh after death. Infants were but phases of the life with which the soil teemed. All the neighbourhood belonged to the camp—the land and everything which sprang from it, for they were the original possessors. It was their country. They argued that such things as sweet potatoes, pumpkins and mangoes, the very roses which adorned a sprawling bush, the richly tinted crotons, the flaunting alamanda over the gateway, were, strictly speaking, common property. So, too, over those children born on the place certain proprietary rights were claimed. They were akin to them, alien to their parents. Whites and blacks born in the same district must, according to their ideas, be more closely related than folks whose birthplaces were separated by distances beyond comprehension.

Such being the general opinion, fortified by undeviating oral tradition, in Soosie's case the theory was ever so much the more arguable. She was claimed, not alone on the grounds that she was a native of their own land, but because, having been born in their own camp, she must be subject to it.

Duckbill intercepted me on the edge of the clearing one morning especially to propound the law of the land.

Soosie, he told in his pidgin English, had been given to him by her uncle. She was to be his gin now that she was grown up. "More better you hunt that fella. Him want sit down alonga camp."

The bald proposition shook me, for I could not but see the logic of it from Duckbill's standpoint. He was the "big man," a wizard—ugly, old, and villainously dirty. Here was the camp's husband for the coloured girl with the white heart. The idea was revolting, and then and there I resolved at whatever cost to save the girl from such degradation.

"Clear out!" I shouted, assuming frantic anger. "You fella chuck'm Soosie away when she little fella piccaninny. That one belonga me now. Suppose you fella kick'm up row big fella government come clear you fella out. No more let you sit down longa this country."

"Country belonga me. You no humbug. You bin catch'm that fella Tchoosie l-o-n-g time. You bin make'm good fella. Belonga me now."

The disgusting old fellow went on to explain that he intended to come up to the house that evening. "You hunt'm that fella Tchoosie, me catch'm. No good belonga you."

I was to drive the gently nurtured girl out of the house so that this foul creature might seize her as he would a struggling wallaby, and take her to live a degraded life in the camp! Explanations and threats were of no avail. Duckbill, who was unable to comprehend that he and others of the camp had by abandonment forfeited all rights to Soosie and that she was now a "white Mary," made it plain that he would forcibly abduct her if I would but give him the slight assistance of expulsion. Otherwise he would catch her himself.

Threatening the camp with the presence of the "big fella government" if he or any of them dared to interfere, I went off, while he shouted his orders to "hunt that fella close up karrie badgin!" (sunset).

Forthwith the house was put in a state of semi-siege. Soosie, with tearful eyes and tremulous hands, hysterically implored us to protect her from a fate worse than death. A message brought Dan, who first disdained to take Duckbill seriously. Told how Soosie had been wooed with gifts, and that her maternal uncle had officiously bestowed her upon the gaunt, ill-favoured king of the camp in accordance with tribal law, which regarded her as a mere chattel at the disposal of the whim and fancy of the nearest relative or at the demand of the most authoritative man, he became concerned and installed himself as Soosie's special guardian.

A few minutes after sundown Duckbill appeared, quite unconscious of offence against civilised customs, carrying a waddy with which to administer an anodyne should his capture prove the least refractory. Threats and scoldings were lost. He was incapable of comprehending why there should be a moment's hesitation about the fulfilment of his legitimate rights and demands.

Though protests were vain, the fact that Soosie did not show herself imparted some glimmering of sense of the situation to him, and he wandered off in the gloom grumbling "That fella too flash," and frankly announcing "B'mbi me catch'm."

For weeks Soosie kept within doors, or if she ventured out was accompanied by one or other well able and determined to protect her. Her nerves were at acute tension; her life that of a hunted creature; for though she thought her fate inevitable, she concentrated her mind on what seemed to others pitiably weak and inconsequent schemes for the bafflement of Duckbill.

Was it that some ineffaceable trait told her that the tribal law as expounded by Duckbill was so wise that resistance to it was vain, and that the trivial plans over which she worried were merely invented as a sort of temporary palliative? She scorned the possibility of existence in the camp, yet strove to contest it by the use of fantastical devices. She urged that Dan and I should get some fearsome masks and rush the camp in the gloom, at the same time setting off fireworks, and so create such terrifying effects that none would venture near the spot again. With bated breath, she even suggested that I should make a "death-bone" to be employed for the secret ill of Duckbill;

she thus exposed the dross of hereditary superstition which rose to the surface during mental ebullition.

It was quite in the nature of things that under stress such a nature should break down. She nestled close to Dan, promising to be his sweetheart on the condition that, rather than that Duckbill should take her away, he would shoot her. If it came about that the dreadful black man was himself driven off or disposed of by some other means and the country made safe for her, then she would marry the man who had saved her, and she hoped that she might never disgrace him.

Dan accepted the guardianship. His hut was two miles away and on the far side of the river. He saw little of it for the next few weeks.

Duckbill and his friends, as we were well aware, knew of our plans for the defeat of his proposed outrage. If Soosie could be ceremoniously married to the faithful Dan, no black in the neighbourhood would endeavour to molest her. Indeed, all, even to Duckbill, would be flattered and demonstrative of pride in the alliance.

A fortnight later Duckbill again intercepted me. Since the previous verbal encounter I had gone armed. He carried, somewhat ostentatiously, a tomahawk and a couple of nulla-nullas.

"No good you keep'm that fella Tchoosie. Me bin look out plenty. That fella belonga me. Suppose you no lat'm come, more worse b'mbi. Me want mak'm that fella all asame black fella. You gib it Clare belonga Dan."

My fingers twitched on the butt of the revolver. It was an ultimatum. That which from other lips would have been resented as complacent insolence had to be endured with apparent calmness. Threatening him with all the consequences of a visit from the "big fella government," I hurriedly left, for I was not too sure of self-control.

A stricter watch than ever was maintained, for the least relaxation of precautions might have involved results for which a lifetime of regrets would not have atoned. Though of such a low type of the human race, the North Queensland aboriginal possesses certain admirable characteristics. His mind seldom swerves from a set purpose within view of attainment. He may be rebuffed and disappointed, and may assume indifference to or forgetfulness of his purpose; but in his heart he does not accept defeat until an absolutely decisive blow is received. Invisible to us, the old man persistently waited, and watched. The dogs frequently detected his presence, if their eloquent alarms and their excursions were to be credited. Though she continued to pit her wits against the secret cunningness of the dreaded old man, Soosie was often preoccupied, seeming to regard herself as one not primarily concerned. Her calmness was preternatural, contrasting strangely with her previous petulant agitation and tragic despair. She avoided Dan, while clinging with profuse demonstrations of affection to her foster-sisters.

The reason for her change of policy and manner was revealed with distressing suddenness. At daylight one morning the door of the room in which she slept under lock and key was wide open, and on her quaintly embellished table a primly written note:

"DEAR MUM,

"That horrible man who wants to take me away is right, and the Bible is right. I belong to this country, and must go. I would rather die than go to the camp; but I must know the big mountain. The dreadful people don't go there. They are frightened of it; I love it. I shall live there by myself till I die, and Dan will never be disgraced. You and Dada and Clare and Fan and Bob have been all the world to me. You did your best to make me white at heart; but since this trouble began I have thought and thought, and found that the black in me smudges all the good out. Don't try to come after me. I shall hide. I would be too much ashamed ever to look at you again. Forget me, for I am nothing but an ungrateful little savage.

"SOOSIE."

In all haste Dan and I set out for the camp, a mile or so further in the jungle. It was situated in a natural, symmetrical clearing, a circus hemmed in by sullen vegetation, and upon which no plant save blady grass ever invaded.

The camp was deserted. Save for a few still warm spots indicative of artfully smothered fires, there were few signs to indicate recent occupation. An hour's search revealed definite tracks leading east—to the mountain.

No pains had been taken to baffle pursuers. Apparently the blacks had just wandered off aimlessly in obedience to a whim of the moment. There was nothing but conjecture to support the opinion that the decampment had anything to do with the disappearance of Soosie. Probably the blacks were aware, in advance of ourselves, that she had stolen away. If so, they would inevitably get her, having, possibly, the advantage of hours of start and being efficient in the art of tracking. Our plan was to hasten so that we might, if fortune favoured, be in time to save the distracted girl from the repulsive and obscene ceremonies to which she would be subject if she fell into the hands of Duckbill.

An hour's walk brought us to the foothills of the mountain. The tracks turned abruptly north, winding indeterminately as if no special object had been in view. It might be that while the men of the camp had been intent on following Soosie's tracks, the women and children had straggled after as if the quest was of no special concern to them.

In the broken country well in to the base of the mountain all traces of the exodus was lost, though bush instinct, supplemented by the actions of the dogs, gave sense of its direction. Blundering down into a ravine where blanched vegetation betokened complete seclusion from the sun, we clambered up the opposing steep emerging from an entanglement of jungle on a high and open ridge which commanded an unimpeded view to the west—a scene of theatrical clarity with a single theatrical smear. From a hollow far below slothful smoke filtered through the matted, sombre, dew-bespangled foliage, rose a few feet, and drifted abruptly, dissolving from diaphanous blue to nothingness. The resonant whooping of a swamp pheasant, antiphonal to a bell-voiced, crimson-crowned fruit pigeon in a giant fig-tree, the screeches of a sulphur-crested cockatoo as it tumbled in the air, evading the swoops of a grey goshawk, materialised the peace and the conflicts of a scene upon which no man had made mark.

The phantom trail of smoke betrayed the resting-place of the fugitives, though all tracks on the uneasy earth had failed. Odours of the jungle soothed my mind, contradicted the transaction of any unholy orgy, and gave assurance that the men had unravelled Soosie's wanderings until she had begun to ascend the mountain, and that, being then on strange and terrifying ground, they had abandoned the search, returning to familiar level country free from the excursions of dreaded spirits.

With light hearts we descended the ridge, and, plunging again into the dimness of the jungle, struck as direct a route as possible for the smoke-revealed camp. Crossing a narrow creek, we peered silently through the screen of ferns and banana plants, where in a secluded glade were the wanderers in happy festival.

Could any scene approach nearer the ideal? Men, women and children, mostly unclad, talking and laughing in modulated tones, while amusing themselves with trivial occupations and eating convenient food in the depths of the jungle, sanctified by distance and scene and sound! Peace smiled, propriety approved. They ate of the fruits of the earth. The fern-embowered stream gave them to drink. No sign of the white man, with his interfering and desolating ways, assailed the sight. It was as if the mist of centuries had lifted, and for once time-soiled mortals were permitted to gaze on a Garden of Eden free from danger and innocent of sin. There was none here to make the quiet folk afraid or discontented.

As I stepped out, the scene changed with pantomimic celerity. We were in the midst of a community of excitable and resentful people, who, viewing us, if not with active hostility, at least with surprise and anger, seemed embarrassed by guilty knowledge. None of the customary greetings welcomed us. None offered other than scowls.

"Where Soosie?" I demanded in authoritative tones of a boy accustomed to treat my slightest word with respect.

With averted face he sullenly said: "That fella Tchoosie he run away. He go l-o-n-g way, alonga mountain!"

"Look here! You no humbug. Where Soosie sit down? Plenty row along white man suppose Soosie no come back. That fella Soosie belonga Missis. Missis very sorry. She bin make'm Soosie all asame white Mary."

Still the face-averting boy reiterated: "That fella Soosie he bin go long way— more far. You fella make'm Soosie no good."

Others gathered round. Several carried weapons—nulla-nullas and wooden swords—and assumed hostile attitudes.

Dan became uncontrollably excited, storming for the production of Soosie, and being met with inconclusive statements and evasions. Being one who knew no fear, who deemed his questions justifiable, who felt himself more than a match for the whole camp, and was convinced that the blacks were in possession of essential information, he urged the policy of chastising the sullenness out of a couple of incommunicative boys. His attitude, and mine, hitherto, towards the blacks had been of cheery good-nature tempered with considerate authority. Present moroseness was novel, and he was eager to sweep it away with a sturdy stick, and thus to demonstrate that when a friendly white man visited a camp blacks should be deferential and alert to assist his mission.

In the mood of the men tragedy was inevitable unless both of us kept cool. What would be the ending of a fray between two white men and many armed blacks, some of whom were aching under a prolonged, however inconsequent, grievance against a white family?

"Look here, Dan. Leave those fellows alone," I said firmly but quietly. "There'll be sorrow for some if you begin a row."

"I don't care for a hundred blacks! I'd kick myself if I could not floor half a dozen single-handed! Where that Soosie?"

To distract attention from Dan, I moved off a few yards.

"What you ki-ki?" I asked of Wethera, who gnawed with concentrated satisfaction at a charred bone. "You ki-ki wallaby?"

"No wallaby! This one 'mandee' (hand) belonga Tchoosie!"

Scorched flesh and blackened bone had left their smear on the face of the kindest cannibal of them all. On the fire was a foot with charred ankle-bones;

in a dilly-bag other fragments, but in Wethera's countenance no consciousness of evil-doing.

"Come here!" I shouted.

The excited man strode to the spot.

"Soosie," I said, in the calmest tones I could command, "has been murdered. This is a cannibal feast!"

With a bound he upset the gin, who shrieked as she grovelled in the embers.

"You wretches! You kill Soosie! I kill you!"

As he drew his revolver from his belt I seized his hand, and, restraining him as best I could for a moment, spoke authoritative and soothing words, and led him away weak and tremulous.

Not for many months—long after Dan had left the district—did exact information as to the fate of the hapless girl reach our ears. Wethera told of the tragedy. Duckbill had followed her tracks from the house towards the mountain, had overtaken her, and, since she had fought frenziedly, had "killed her alonga head little bit," not intending to kill her "dead, finis." Carried to the camp, it had been found out that she was actually dead. Then all had become stricken and run away.

By her obstinacy Soosie had offended tribal law. She had suffered. In the necessitous jungle animal food is never wasted, be it beast, bird, or reptile.

It had been an edifying sacrament, too, founded on immemorial truth, for had it not been devoutly believed that Soosie's most excellent and potent personality would remain with and glorify every participant?

BLUE SHIRT

"A strong, untutored intellect, eyesight, heart; a strong, wild Man."—
CARLYLE.

Half a century ago, when hardy and adventurous men made laws unto themselves, and their somewhat hasty and inconsiderate hands began to sting the aboriginal population, there lived on this Isle a stalwart native whose force of character constituted him a captain among his fellows.

Possibly he was Tom's father. Before he passed away, Tom had often told that his father was king of this realm and a man of parts. He it was who harpooned a huge green turtle to the east. The game was so extraordinarily strong that others hastened to his aid, for the capture was beyond the capabilities of one man kneeling in a tucked-up sheet of bark. The whole fleet of canoes barely succeeded in towing the massive and reluctant creature to the nearest beach, and Tom was wont to tell that it took eight strong men to turn it on its back. It was "kummaoried" on the sand, and Tom oft pointed out the very spot as proof of the most famous feast within the range of tradition.

Let it be accepted, then, that Blue Shirt was Tom's father, since history is silent on the point, and none is left to question or authenticate it. He was a big man, and his son was like him. He was fond of colours; so, too, was his son. He was a fighter; his son's meritorious scars proved him worthy of his blood. He was a man in authority and full of territorial pride; his son's dominance was undoubted, for did he not chide the "big fella gubbermen" on its audacity in disposing of his Island—his country—even to a friendly white man?

Blue Shirt was the ruler and lawgiver of this Island when a barque strove with a cyclone which eventually shattered her to pieces and scattered her cargo of cedar-logs to the four winds. After the wreck a boat put out from a not distant port on a beach-combing cruise. The boat was known as the CAPTAIN COOK. About a hundred years before her namesake had reported that he had seen about thirty natives, all unclad, on an adjacent islet. With the captain was his mate, two other white men, a black boy, and a young gin. Many derelict logs were seen and certain wreckage, which made the boat's company inclined to the belief that some of the castaways might have landed on Dunk Island. They steered hither, anchoring in the evening.

Early the next morning three stalwart black boys put off in canoes to the CAPTAIN COOK, and, making friendly demonstrations, were invited on board. Food was given them, and to the leader the captain presented a blue shirt. No dweller of the Island had ever before possessed such a sumptuous and glorious garment. Indeed, if the absolute truth must be told, no dweller had dreamt of anything more desirable than an inadequate cloak laboriously wrought from the inner bark of a fig-tree, raiment sanctioned by the first of fashions.

Having made it known that they belonged to a neighbouring islet at the moment unfriendly to the overbearing Dunk Island tribe, Blue Shirt and his attendants mentioned that cedar-logs and other attractive flotsam bestrewed the beaches, and volunteered to conduct the strangers to the best places on the understanding that they, being alien and hostile, should remain under the protection of the rifle-carrying white men.

The captain, two men, and the black boy, followed Blue Shirt ashore; but, although he was conspicuously clad, could not find him or any other man. A few old and casual women represented the hospitable inhabitants, while Sabbath quietude brooded over the scene as they strolled along the yellow beach. By chance one of the party glanced towards the spot where they had landed, and saw half a dozen vigorous gins endeavouring to haul the boat above tideway.

How excellent the strategy!

The designing but faint-hearted women fled when the white men charged for the boat, which now was seen to be endowed with an incredible, uncanny rocking movement of its own. Looking beneath, they saw a huge cripple straining himself, Atlas-like, to heave it over. In spite of inferior legs, his brawny shoulders had almost accomplished the feat when he was unceremoniously interrupted. While he sprawled away, a mob of blacks rushed suddenly from the cover of some rocks, the leader of the assailants being Blue Shirt, who had painted his unclad parts martial red and white. The strength of the party was guessed at thirty. An exact census was not taken, for with spears and nulla-nullas and big swords, each warrior having the protection of a shield, the treacherous band swept on the deluded guests of their leader, whose hostile yells scandalised the meek phrases and friendly signs of a short hour before.

The captain, poor, outwitted man, had laid his rifle beside the boat. It was too late now to bring it into decisive action. Keeping close together, the defenders warded off the first rush with whatever came to hand. The rifle was recovered; but Blue Shirt, recognising that it represented victory, struggled for it determinedly. A spear was thrown at close quarters straight for the captain's neck, but one of the men deftly twitched it off, a feat that so enraged the warriors that they made him their special target, until at last one of their spears pierced his hand. Being rough and thready, the black palm-point made an ugly wound; but the resolute man drew it out, and, breaking the spear in twain, threw it into the boat, and as he did so, another grazed his abdomen. While he was thus defending himself against the spears and nulla-nullas of outrageous fortune, the captain made wide, sweeping movements with the butt of his rifle, and the other man and the boy, the boat being by this time afloat, tugged at the oars. The attacking party followed, the captain making good misuse of the rifle, the odd man and the boy occasionally perverting an oar to wrongful but, at the crisis, effective purpose, while the wounded suffered the hate of him who earns personal as well as racial animosity. He sustained a cut on the head from a wooden sword, yet he fought on, retaining his wits, while a kind Providence, and his own artfulness and agility protected him from hurtling spears.

The cost of the little excursion was paid in wounds and bruises and, eventually, putrefying sores, while the souls of all instantly mortified under the sight of triumphant Blue Shirt jeering and gesticulating as only an uncouth black dare, as he waved over his head a tomahawk he had abstracted from the boat during the morning's pleasant entertainment.

No one of the poor, depraved representatives of the race has any knowledge of the event in which Blue Shirt showed himself to be a successful plotter, a bold strategist, an original tactician, and a brave fighter. His son is dust. His grandson, though true in complexion, knows more about engines than he does of wooden swords and how to use them. The zest of life was with his ancestor, who during a long life had but one shirt.

THE FORGOTTEN DEAD

"Of lonely folk cut off unseen."

HOOD.

A few months ago chance bestowed the opportunity of listening to the conversation of one who for very many yearn has hung upon the skirts of civilisation. A bushman of rare resourcefulness, wide knowledge of the dry as well as the moist parts of North Queensland, a reader, and an acute and accurate observer of natural phenomena, he has often entertained me with the relation of episodes in his career which, though quite unsensational, is of the material of which the history of the bush must be compiled. He is now settled on a tidal creek, his nearest neighbours miles away. Independent of the regular assistance of blacks in the cultivation of his land, he is one of those who, while acknowledging no such thing as comradeship, and who, true to his sentiments, keeps them at arm's-length, has, albeit, acquired confidences rather unusual.

When his reading matter has become exhausted, he has sat night after night for months together absorbing the lore of the camp. To him has been disclosed many a well-guarded secret. Not unto every man who asks do the blacks tell their thoughts or impart their legends. You may study them; but they, too, are discreet students, who often keep their counsel while seeming to comply with your anxiety to learn of their ways and be wise as they are wise.

My friend is one of those undemonstrative, self-contained men in whom some of the coloured, cautious metaphysicians find a congenial soul. Therefore is he a compendium of much out-of-the-way and covert knowledge.

As we talked on the subject of the unexplained disappearances of men in the bush of Australia, he told the incidents of the forgotten dead to which these writings have special reference. I use my own words, so do not bind myself to historic exactness.

He had been away earning his own living, for his estate, fruitful as it is, did not then quite provide for his sustenance, markets being distant and far from consistent. Returning, he found the blacks who had associated themselves with his humble establishment had in the interval sought change of scene. The land that he called his had belonged to their ancestors centuries before Cook tied the ENDEAVOUR to that disputed and historic tree, and was theirs when he had first intruded. His hut, his horses, his implements, were much as he had left them. The camping-place of the blacks appeared to have been unoccupied for some time. Such was in accordance with usual happenings. Going about his lonesome work, he reflected that his dusky acquaintances would return in their own good time, and being a man of mental resource, the solitude was by no means irksome.

Within a fortnight they appeared unceremoniously, and, taking casual part in the ordinary work, the affairs of the isolated estate went on as smoothly as before. There was a stranger in the camp, a middle-aged man, timorous, and knowing little of the ways of white men. Of him scarcely any notice was taken. Yet in a few weeks it was evident that the stranger was determined to make himself pleasant. Accordingly, the white man refrained from advances, while for the love of mental exhilaration he pondered: "That boy wants to tell me something. He shall tell me all he wants to in his own way, while I will play the part of an indifferent auditor."

That the stranger had some secret on his soul was apparent. My friend resolved to receive that secret in the spirit of gracious condescension. So played he his part, and line upon line, here a little and there a little, the story was told.

Few of the tribe of the stranger had ever seen a white man. None had ever visited the coast. All were myalls, living naked among the mountains in gorges gloomy with jungle, and but rarely hunting on the foothills. One day consternation and curiosity spread through the camp. Three strange men with yellow faces and short black hair had been seen. They carried nothing in their hands, and seemed frightened. Thus the nervous couriers of the camp spoke.

Next morning the men took up the tracks, and, sneaking close up, followed, alert and unseen, the unsuspecting visitors to their country.

Bewildered in the jungle, the queer-looking men wandered aimlessly, moaning and wailing. They were lost. Suddenly the blacks appeared. Two of the strangers, glad of the company of any sort of human beings, smiled and gesticulated pleasantly, making it plain that they were hungry, tired, and frightened, and, longing to get back to the coast, would bestow upon their guides unheard-of blessings for safe-conduct thither. Strangely, the black men accepted the trust. Four each took a hand of the confiding strangers, and, pointing ahead and chattering, induced them to walk quickly in a direction in which by signs they indicated the dwelling of a white man.

The third wanderer had run away, blundering through the jungle, and the blacks had refrained from following him. Nodding gaily and jabbering volubly, but with mutual intelligibility, hosts and guests paced along a narrow track, each of the latter personally and firmly conducted by two of his newly found and most attentive friends. Others of the tribe, "like frightful fiends, did close beside them tread"; and while the escorts lured the yellow men with comforting pantomime, the frightful fiends fell on them suddenly with great wooden swords, killing them off-hand and on the very verge of the camp.

Willingly hurrying to the place of execution, the murdered men had saved the calculating blacks the trouble of carrying their carcasses.

Then four went back for the nervous escapee. He was safe, for the tracks were as obvious to them as a plough furrow to a European. Crouching beside a fallen, decaying tree, where bird's-nest ferns grew outrageously gross, they found him; and they jeered. He screamed and shouted in unknown tongue, while the brisk, stubby hair of his head stood on end. (My friend's hair-brush was alluded to in graphic illustration.) They struck him down, and, smashing in his head and seizing arms and legs, jogged back to the camp.

And the festival lasted many days, though plenty made gluttons of them all.

The forgotten dead were Javanese—deserters from a sugar-plantation; for the tragedy happened long ago, when labour was being drawn from Java and other oversupplied countries. Desertions were not uncommon, for the sanguine men of the equator endure with less philosophy than others that sickness of the heart which comes from love of one's native land when absent from it.

From Java's seething millions were the nostalgic three ever missed?

EAGLES-NEST FLOAT

"My raft was now strong enough to bear any reasonable weight."

ROBINSON CRUSOE.

Those who study primitive races, applying their wisdom and learning to the investigation of the origin of domestic and other implements and contrivances, inform us that the first boat was probably a log, on which the man sat astride, using a stick as a means of propulsion. In time the idea of hollowing the log occurred, Nature undoubtedly presenting the model and inviting the novice to squat inside. But what was the inhabitant of a certain island in the Gulf of Carpentaria to do since Nature failed to provide a tree big enough to possess the degree of buoyancy necessary for his frail frame, when he wished to cross the narrow channel separating him from a lesser island where turtle are plentiful and unsuspicious?

Being in status something above a wallaby—the largest animal other than himself of his native land which, when hunted, occasionally swam towards the opposite shore, he constructed one or other of two rafts or floats, both derivable from Nature's models. One was in the form of an eagle's nest, and not nearly so large as that in which some eaglets are reared, made by interlacing branchlets of white mangrove until the mass was sufficient to support his weight. With a double ended paddle rudely shaped from the thin buttress roots of the red mangrove, and comic in the crudeness and disproportion of its parts, he felt himself safe miles out to sea. When he approached a passing vessel he presented the illusion, not of walking, but of sitting on the water, for the float was almost completely submerged. If it became necessary for his wife to attend him on his marine excursions, she was towed behind, and used her own pedal power. Possibly this primitive raft is the pathetic expression of man's first struggle against the restrictions of the sea.

The other resource of the boatless islander was another description of float, also retrogressive from the log; the idea not transmitted to him by any high-minded bird, but forced upon his attention by elemental strife. He would have seen that the wind and the waves occasionally tore from his beaches Pandanus palms, and that the matted, fibrous roots thereof floated. Pondering in his dim way, and being sadly an hungered and aware that fat and lazy turtle were basking in the sighed-for shallows, he took a bundle of buoyant roots and light sticks and lashed it securely at one end with strips of bark. He then spread out the other end until it took the shape of a fan, and weaved the strands loosely together with beach trailers. His raft was complete. At least this description applies to that in use to-day, which represents the highest stage to which the design has been brought.

Under the influence of the peril-ignoring hunger, the hunter sat on the float with legs extended frontally. Across his thighs crouched his favourite dog, and behind him, her thin shanks outside his and her skinny arms round his slim waist, sat, uncomfortable, his cowed wife—a necessary part of his equipment. Can he be imagined half turning to his deferential spouse, and saying: "My dear, in the words of Shakespeare,

> *"On such a full sea are we now afloat*
>
> *And we must take the current when it serves*
>
> *Or lose our'—turtle"*?

Is it not edifying, too, to reflect that the timid man, encouraged by the object-lessons of Nature, given in pity of his simplicity, had contrived the only rafts the resources of his island made possible? And does not the fact that he had courage to cross the estranging deep thereon give graphic proof of the inhospitality of his native soil?

Flat and generally of sad aspect, the country of the raftsman lies remote and uncommended. The scented sandalwood is there, dwarfed, attenuated, worthless. The most fragrant of the Pandanus palms is plentiful, the fruit forming the chief part of the vegetable diet of the lean and stunted inhabitants, who find difficulty in fashioning weapons with which to obtain fish and turtle, the land failing to supply straight sticks of the length needed for spears. Each has to be spliced. The islands are expressed in the race they sustain—possibly the lowest of Australian types. Does it not bespeak much to the credit of men and women who have been used to the cities where the advantages of civilisation are at command and its comforts available, that they should abandon the society of kin and friends and isolate themselves in a drear and unfriendly tract for the sake of a few coloured folk whose mental capacities are feeble and whose habits are shockingly disgusting?

NATURE IN RETALIATION

"Red in tooth and claw."

TENNYSON.

In a mangrove creek a shoal of barramundi had been bombed with dynamite. Immediately after the explosion the white onlookers as well as the blacks dived off-hand into the stream to secure the helpless fish. One of the party seized a weighty and unconscious victim of the outrage, and to retain it thrust his fist through the gills and found himself unable to withdraw, and when the fish began to revive he realised that he was not master. With a supreme effort he did manage to get his head above water to gulp a mouthful of air, but the gallant fish promptly exerted itself, and a deadly struggle took place on the muddy bottom. Once more the fish was tugged to the surface, only to dive just as the man became conscious of the applause of the interested spectators. When they came to the surface again ill luck on the part of the fish had brought it into the shallows caused by a ridge of rocks, and the man hauled his prize ashore, frankly acknowledging that the happy chance of the rocks and not his own wits and strength had given the victory into his hands.

On another occasion heartless dynamite was used in a creek, where had assembled many blacks, who scrambled riotously in the muddy water for the spoil, among which were several huge crabs, some dismembered by the force of the explosion, some stunned, some merely agitated. Dilly Boy, the biggest and the greediest of the crowd, acquired several fish and three or four crabs, the largest of the latter of which seemed sound asleep. The dynamite had ministered an anodyne from which, apparently, there would be no awakening. It the boy disregarded, while he secured those which were more or less active. Busily engaged, he was not aware that a crab when he seems asleep may be merely plotting. This hero was hatching out a scheme whereby it might be revenged for the outrage. It watched and deliberated, and as the boy sat down grabbed him with ponderous and toothed pinchers on that part of the body which is said to be most susceptible to insult. The boy rose. Not half a plug of dynamite could have given more hearty impulse, not all the clamour of a corroboree equal his yell of surprise and anguish. He capered. The crab, which had not speculated on the caper, and to avert summary divorce, locked its claws, now guaranteed to hold to death and beyond it—to destruction. Astounded—indeed, petrified—by the high antics of the boy, none of the spectators could venture to his aid. They were fully engaged with unrestrained and joyful hysteria. The more the boy yelled and cavorted, the more frantic the fun. Blood trickled down the chocolate-coloured skin, but the valiant crab held on. It was there for a definite purpose. The hour and the crab had arrived. Vengeance for centuries of wrongs to the race and heroic self-sacrifice animated brain and inspired the claw with the dynamics of ten; while the afflicted victim imagined—he had no mirror to hold up to Nature—that he was the sport of a lusty crocodile.

Amidst his shrieks he commanded the ministration of his wife. She ran to meet him with a waddy. True to the limitations of her sex, though her intentions were admirable and dutiful, the result was disastrous. The boy got a paralysing blow on the small of the back, and flopped down. Up jumped Dilly Boy, and the gin raced after him, murderously inclined to the crab. Half her blows were misses and the other half seriously embarrassed her husband, as his tumbles testified. She belaboured him impartially and with perverted goodwill from shoulder to heel, for she aimed invariably at the crab, and where is the woman who ever hit where she designed? The crab was merely tickling; the faithful spouse, with the tenderest motives, was cruelly beating her lord and master to disablement, and it can scarcely be credited that the echo of his remarks has yet subsided. In his fervour the boy made an exceptionally vicious threat against the gin, and in response she missed him and hit the crab. Under such forceful compulsion the crab parted with its claw. It was ponderous and toothed, be it remembered, and well and truly locked, and retained its grip. The target being smaller, the aims of the gin went more and more astray. The back of the boy, owing to the incessant misses of the waddy, changed from brown to purple, and a red ribbon wavered down his thigh. Still he ran, and the devoted gin coursed after him with the energy of a half-back, the fury of a disappointed politician, and the riot of three-dozen cockatoos scared from a corn-field. Almost worn out, the boy sprang round, and, seizing the waddy, began to chastise the gin, whose screams blended with his unwholesome threats. But the claws held on—not like grim death; they were grim death. Every second blow was directed aft— one blow forward, which generally severely disagreed with the gin; one blow astern, which afforded neither mental relief nor physical comfort. The gin fled from the infuriated boy; the boy from the fearsome relic of the crab, and called louder as he ran. When in full flight, the gin tripped over a mangrove root, and, spread-eagled, fell. The boy came tumbling after, but the remnants of the crab—the bony bud of a tail—stood erect and firm. Then the pitying spectators seized Dilly Boy, and, holding him, unlocked the pinchers. He rolled over—it was the only easeful attitude—as he cursed all gins, crabs, and dynamiters with wondrous fluency. And may the potency of those coloured curses rest upon the latter!

"STAR RUN ABOUT"

'It is the stars,

The stars above us, govern our conditions."

SHAKESPEARE.

Primitive folk have ever looked up to the heavens for signs of good and ill. Celestial appearances have fought for them terrestrial battles, or have weakened their arms by prognostications of impending disaster.

Appeals have been made to passionless planets for justice against mundane decrees, and when coincidences have been favourable the devout student of the skies has loudly proclaimed them as proof of supernatural interest in trivial, transient occurrences. In accordance with the degree of poetry in the fibre of the people, so, in a certain degree, has the belief in stellar influence been manifest.

The blacks of North Queensland, being, possibly, the least of the races in a poetic sense, have but slight regard for the interference of the stars in their poor little affairs, and in this respect are saner than many a nation which has given abundant proof of wisdom. One of their beliefs is that meteors are baleful, though under given conditions they derive from such phenomena longed-for assurance. A meteor is described as "Star run about." "That fella no good; him kill'em man!" Yet in circumstances to be mentioned they find in a meteor a sign that life has been restored to an individual whom they have done to death. It is the opinion of men who have studied the customs of the blacks that they—and to their honour be it said—were never among themselves premeditated, gluttonous cannibals. Human flesh was eaten, if not with solemnity, at least with ceremony, for the belief exists to this day that the moral and physical excellencies of the victim are assimilated by those who partake of his flesh.

Reincarnation is prompt and practical, and unaccompanied by wasteful and delusive hope. Herein lies the explanation of many a deliberate and confessed killing, while to the meteor have the perpetrators looked for absolution and remission of their sin. That which in the eyes of the white man is regarded as an atrocious murder has not been, in their semi-religious code, in any sense criminal, but a rite from which many if not all the camp must inevitably benefit.

In one respect the killing of a boy is the highest compliment which may be paid him, for it is proof that he has personal qualities which are the envy and admiration of others, and for general welfare should be shared by all. The boy who so dies is an unconscious patriot. This is proved sufficiently by the fact that only what are considered to be the more vitalising portions of the boy's body are eaten, whereas if gluttony were the impulse of the deed the whole of the body would be consumed.

An illustrative incident has been told me by one who has gained the confidence of the blacks, and to whom other facts connected with it were personally known. Not many years ago a boy from from a distant locality visited a certain district in company with his master. He was tall, well favoured, a good rider, quite an athlete, an accomplished performer with the mouth-organ and concertina; ready and persuasive of tongue. These qualities provoked unaffected admiration; for the natives of the place are undersized, ill-looking, and deficient generally in the arts of pleasing. Before the master left, Caesar was persuaded by his envious fellow-countrymen to remain with them to be flattered and courted.

To evade trouble, the whole camp took to the hills for a while. In the meantime Caesar's master departed, thinking, no doubt, that the boy would follow him to his own "more better country." After several weeks the local blacks returned, but Caesar was not of the party, and it did not occur to any of the white residents to ask questions concerning him. In accordance with the love of notoriety which affects humanity irrespective of complexion, one of the boys began to boast of being as good as Caesar, and to prove his contentions by aping the manners of his absent friend. It was not long before he blurted out the secret by which he had become superfine—he had participated with others in a cannibal rite after Caesar had been good-naturedly killed.

Rumours of the tragedy came to the ears of the police. The ringleaders of the assassins were arrested, and one at least endured a term of imprisonment as punishment. Caesar had been lured away and killed because he was a good fellow and strong, and because his murderers wanted to be good and strong like him. Certain parts of his body were eaten, without relish, but with fervent hope. A remarkable circumstance in connection with the sacrifice and ceremonial rite for the general welfare is that the perpetrators console and comfort themselves with the belief that should a meteor appear it is a sign that the victim did not actually die, or if he died under their hands, that he has come to life again. Those who were concerned in the killing and who had partaken of the flesh sat together for several evenings gazing with expectation into the sky. A meteor flashed across it, and it was hailed as a sign that Caesar was alive and had gone to his own country. The contrary evidence of relics of the dead was waved away before the imperious and disinterested testimony of the falling star. "No matter. That fella him no dead—finish. Him walk about 'nother country. Him good fella. That fella star run about bin tell 'em."

They felt themselves to have benefited materially and spiritually by participation in the rite, and were calm in their belief that the victim was none the worse for the temporary misfortune from which he suffered.

In another locality a meteor signifies the death of an individual, and is referred to as "Tee-go-binah." When a death cannot be directly attributed to it locally, the phenomenon is referred to with such rustic logic as this: "Some fella dead alonga 'nother camp. Might be longa way." The ancients felt "the sweet influences of the Pleiades." One of the two intimacies of the blacks of North Queensland with stellar phenomena which has come to my knowledge is associated with reincarnation after a deed of blood. Their faith is as absolute, perhaps, as was that of the men of old.

BLACKS AS FISHERMEN

"For I tell you, scholar, fishing is an art, or at least it is an art to catch fish."—
IZAAK WALTON.

Along the coast of North Queensland evidence may still be obtained, though it ever becomes more difficult to secure practical demonstration, of several novel methods of killing fish in vogue among the blacks prior to the advent of civilisation. In many parts, indeed, the presence of the white man has swept away not only the use of decent, if trivial, pursuits and handicrafts, but the knowledge also that they ever existed.

The few facts here presented are, with some slight reservations, drawn from actual observation. No doubt the well-informed on such subjects will have plenary reasons—if ever these lines are honoured by perusal of the class— for the accusation that there is nothing in them having the virtue of newness or novelty. But I am not a professor with a mind like a warehouse, rich with the spoils of time, but a mere peddler, conscious of the janglings of an ill-sorted, ill-packed knapsack of unconsidered trifles.

Some pioneers know more about the acts of the past than the best informed of the younger blacks, who look with wonder and unconstrained doubt when shown articles similar to those which their grandfathers must have used almost every day.

Though the blacks of the past had but casual knowledge of the cruel little barb that the resourceful white fisherman finds essential to sport, and had neither neat tackle, nor reels, nor creels; though they were denied the solace of tobacco, and every other accessory, they were adepts at fishing. They had at command a stock of accumulated lore so graphically transmitted that the babe and suckling must have seemed to acquire it almost intuitively. They knew much of the habits of fish. Their methods of laying under tribute the harvest of the sea were so varied and unconventional that when one expedient failed, others, equally free from the ethics of sport, were available at the shortest notice. Fishing was not a pastime, but a serious occupation in which nearly everyone was proficient.

Times are changing; but still the mouths of smaller creeks are sometimes dammed, save for certain sluices and by-washes where puzzling pockets are set. Weirs formed by stakes driven into the sand and interwoven with twigs guide incoming fish into ingenious traps, whence they are scooped up in dilly-bags. Occasionally the whole camp, dogs and piccaninnies included, take part in a raid upon the sea. Men in deeper water, women and boys and girls forming wings at right angles to the beach, enclose a prescribed area in the ever shifting, mobile fence. Certain of the men have huge dilly-bags made of strips of lawyer-cane, and shaped like a ninepin with a funnel for a head. The tactics of the party combine to drive the fish towards the silent men having charge of the dilly-bags, who manipulate what certainly has the appearance of being a very awkward utensil in the water with great skill and alertness. Hurried to frenzy by the shouting and splashing of the crowd, and the flurrying of the surface with bushes, the fish dart hither and thither until most of them have found their way into the bags, at the only spots where, for the time being, peace and quietude prevail. At other times a somewhat similar design of basket is used for trapping eels.

Men armed with spears surround and exterminate a shoal detected in shallow water; and the boomerang and the nulla-nulla as well as the spear form the weapons of the solitary fisherman. On one of the islands of the Gulf of Carpentaria the boomerang (I am told) alone is used, the blacks being so expert that little is left to chance.

Though the wommera, or, as it is known locally, the yellamun, is common in the neighbourhood of Dunk Island, it is not employed as an accessory in the spearing of fish. Further north it is so almost universally, a combination of boomerang and wommera being the most popular form. This dual-purpose weapon is merely a boomerang to one of the ends of which is fitted a spur, which engages the socket in the butt of the spear. While on this subject, it is interesting to note that, though the common form of the implement for increasing the velocity and range of the spear is generally considered to be peculiar to Australia, its principle is embodied in a contrivance which was used for a similar purpose in the New Hebrides in Captain Cook's day.

Describing some of the arts of the inhabitants of Tanna, Cook ("Voyages of Captain Cook round the World," vol. i., chapter vi.) says that in the throwing of darts "they make use of the becket, that is, a piece of stiff plaited cord, about six inches long, with an eye in one end and a knot in the other. The eye is fixed on the forefinger of the right hand, and the other end is hitched round the dart where it is nearly on an equipoise. They hold the dart between the thumb and the remaining finger, which serve only to give direction, the velocity being communicated by the becket and forefinger. The former flies off from the dart the instant its velocity becomes greater than that of the hand, but it remains on the finger ready to be used again."

It is obvious that the Australian implement is much the more reliable and effective. Cook mentions that with the dart the Tanna Islanders "are sure of hitting a mark within the compass of the crown of a hat at a distance of eight or ten yards; but at double that distance it is chance if they hit a mark the size of a man's body, though they will throw the weapon sixty or seventy yards." Such a standard of marksmanship would be regarded with contempt by the average black of North Queensland. The use of this becket (introduced very many years ago by the Kanaka) is a fairly common accomplishment among coastal blacks.

In shallow water, too, fish are chased until they become so exhausted and nerve-shaken that they partially bury themselves in the sand, or endeavour to elude observation by concealing themselves beneath stone or coral, or by remaining passive among seaweed, trusting, no doubt, to protective tints and assimilation with their surroundings. Few of these stratagems of the fish are of avail when once a hungry black is on its track. The science of war, we are bidden to believe, is not designed for the slaughter of mankind, but so to impress the enemy with a demonstration of overwhelming power, force, and majesty, that he may become mentally unable or unwilling to offer resistance, because of its obvious futility. So it is with the black in pursuit of a fish or turtle in shallow water. By noise and bluster he works on the senses of the fish until it becomes semi-paralysed. Then he proceeds callously to the killing, which, in the case of fish, if his right hand is encumbered, he generally accomplishes by a crunching bite into the back-bone at the shoulders.

At rare intervals the black varies his tactics by a night attack, which is often highly demoralising. When the moon is on the other side of the world, with spears and flaring torches of paper-bark, he rushes in a band to raid the reef, to the dismay of startled and bewildered fish. Substitute for the gurgling cadences of semi-submerged coral and muteness and universal dimness instant noise and splashing, and dazzling lights here and there and everywhere, and it is not to be considered strange that the fish—tipsy with panic and confusion—fail to exercise their habitual alertness.

At a certain season of the year—November and December in the neighbourhood of Dunk Island—myriads of fish, about the size of a sardine, appear in shoals, an acre or so in area, or encircle the islands with a living, bluish-grey frill yards broad. The blacks bestow on this godsend, popularly known as "sprats"—HARENGULA STEREOLEPIS (Ogilby)—the name of "Oon-gnahr."

How skilfully does Nature dovetail her designs! This great multitude of fish appears when it is most needed. The terns (sea-swallows) are rearing their families, and ever need fresh food in unstinted quantities. The small fry come to an excited and enthusiastic market. Slim, silvery kingfish, grey sharks, and blue bonito, harry the shoals, ripping through them with steel-like flashes, and as the little fish ruffle the surface of sea or emerge therefrom in living silvery spray, in frantic efforts to escape, the terns take all they want, screaming with satisfaction. Then, too, the blacks join in the work of destruction. When the frill of fish lies limp on the beach, they fabricate a seine net, cheap, but admirably suited for the purpose. Long strands of beach trailers and grass and slender twigs are rolled and twisted up—apparently without the slightest art—into a huge loose cable eight inches in diameter. The men run out the cable into the water at right angles to the beach while still the gins, with nervous haste, are adding to its length. If it breaks, a few twists and pokes suffice to repair it. The men at the lead curve in towards the beach, and the gins and piccaninnies wade out in line to meet them. Gradually the cable, shocking in its frailty, is worked in, enclosing a patch of the fish in a perilous coffer dam. Tumult and commotion are almost as necessary contributories to the success of the stratagem as is the cable. But before they realise what has happened, they are in such close company that escape is impossible; dilly-bags are filled in a single dip, and it may take half an hour to pick out those "meshed" in the cable. It is all the work of a few minutes, and the haul often amounts in quantity to a surfeit for the whole camp.

One of these rude seines which was overhauled was composed largely of the long, leafless, twine-like branches of the leafless parasite CASSYTHA FILIFORMIS (which the blacks term "Bungoonno"), IPOMEA PESCAPRAE ("Koree"), Blady-grass ("Jin-dagi"), and the tough sprawling branches of BLAINVILLEA LATIFOLIA ("Gallan-jarrah"), the whole being reinforced with withes of CLERODENDRON IMERME ("Missim"), all of which plants grow on the verge of the sea.

Vast as is the congregation of small fry, it gradually fritters away, martyred to fish, flesh, and fowl. By the time the little terns are thrown upon their own resources the violet frill of the sweet islands is frayed and ragged, and drifts loosely in shabby remnants.

For large fish—groper, the giant perch, king, bonito, rhoombah, sweet-lips, parrot-fish, sea-mullet, and the sting-rays (brown and grey)—a harpoon and long line are used. When iron is not available a point is made of one of the black palms, the barb being strapped on with fibre, the binding being made impervious to water by a liberal coating of a pitch-like substance prepared from the resinous gum of the arral-tree (EVODIA ACCEDENS).

The point is eight or ten inches long, the barbless end being swathed in fibre so that it may fit easily into the socket of the eight or ten feet shaft. A long line is tied to a point above the swathing, and, being drawn taut along the shaft, is secured to the end by a series of clove-hitches. When the fish is struck the point is drawn from the socket, while the shaft acts as a cheek on, and an indicator of, its course when just below the surface. Such harpoons and lines are also used for the capture of dugong and turtle, the line being made of the inner bark (the bast layer) of one of the fig-trees, and is of two strands only. Occasionally the HIBISCUS TILLIACEUS is laid under tribute for ropes and lines, which, however, are not considered as durable as those from the fig. Nets, set and hand, are also made with twine from the fig or hibiscus.

When, at low spring tides, the coral reef is uncovered, small rock-cod, slim eels, parrot-fish, perch, soles, the lovely blue-spotted sting-ray, catfish, flathead, etc., are poked out unceremoniously with spears or sharp-pointed sticks from labyrinthine mazes, or from the concealment afforded by the flabby folds and fringes of the skeleton-less coral (ALCYONARIA), or from among the weeds and stones—a kind of additional sense leading the black to the discovery of fish in places that a white man would never dream of investigating. At this opportune time, too, huge, defiantly armed and brilliantly coloured crayfish are exposed to capture. A statement was published recently that this was the speediest of all marine animals. The assertion is much to be questioned, but there can be no doubt that the crayfish is a wonderful sprinter. Familiar with its lack of staying power, blacks race after it uproariously as it flees face to foe, all the graduated blades of its turbine apparatus beating under high pressure. Two or three rushes and the crayfish pauses, and then the agile black breaks its long, exquisitely sensitive and brittle antennae, deprived of which it becomes less capable of taking care of itself; or it may find its gorgeous armour-plates smashed with a stone or penetrated by a spear. For the most part, however, the crayfish lurks in coral caves, sweeping a considerable frontal radius with ever-shifting antennae— not in pride or conceit of their beautiful tints and wonderful mechanism, but with a pitiful apprehension of danger, for the admirers of the creature are many and ever so much in earnest—the earnestness of unceasing voracity.

Having a decided partiality for eels, the blacks of North Queensland have devised several means of capture, one of which does not call for the exercise of the least skill on the part of the individual whose longing for the dainty becomes imperative. His placid perseverance, too, is of no avail, unless luck favours. Wading in a shallow, mangrove-bordered creek, he blindly probes the bottom with a six-feet length of fencing wire, the modern substitute for the black palm spear. Frequently he trifles thus with coy Fortune for hours, an inch or so separating each prod; and again, in a spasm of indignant impatience, he stabs determinedly into the mud at random. Non-success does not make shipwreck of his faith in the existence of the much-desired food in the black mud, for as far back as his own experience and the camp's traditions go, substantial reason for that faith has been plentifully revealed. He returns to the monotonous occupation until an unlucky eel is impaled, and then it is given no chance of escape.

Pushing his spear a couple of feet through, the boy grips the prize with both hands, or bends the wire into the form of a hook. Fortune may continue to smile, and the boy takes several during the afternoon.

Many boys enhance the charms of solitude by ingeniously tricking eels, Nature presenting them with an efficient engine of deceit and destruction, so designed that neither the agitations of art nor the invention of science could much improve it. About two feet of the thong or lorum of one of the creeping palms (CALAMUS OBSTRUENS) is all that is necessary. These lora are armed with definitely spaced whorls of recurved hooks, keen as needles, true as steel, about one-eighth of an inch long. Three or four of the whorls are removed to provide an unfretful but firm grip. The pot-holes and shallow pools and gullies and trickling creeks are populated by nervous, yet inquisitive, semi-transparent prawns, upon which eels liberally diet. So silent and steady of movement is the boy that even the alert prawns are unaware of, or become accustomed to, his presence; and what is there to warn the eel, enjoying its comfort among the dead leaves in the gloomiest corner of the pool, of danger? Could any but a black boy detect the difference between the brown sodden leaves and the half-inch of body which the eel has unwittingly exposed? The "pig-gee" (as some term the lorum) is used with almost surgical delicacy of touch to hook away two or three of the leaves. Then it is placed parallel to whatever increased length has thus been made visible, and with a decisive twitch the eel is torn from its retreat and killed off-hand.

Even the shy, long-armed little prawns (PALAEMON AUSTRALIS) do not escape special means for their destruction. A pliant rod about four feet long is improvised from the midrib of the creeping palm before mentioned, to the end of which is fastened a slender thread of the same material, split off by using the nails of the thumb and second finger. This strand, which is about four inches long, is delicately noosed. Standing a few feet away from the water-hole, the black so manipulates the line that the noose encircles the tail of the prawn, which, making a retrogressive dart upon alarm, finds itself fatally snared. The prawns are not, as a rule, eaten, being reserved for bait.

In creeks and lagoons thin, hollow logs are submerged. Eels naturally seek such refuges, and in due course the boy dives, and, sealing the ends with his hands, brings log and eel to land. Dr. W. E. Roth mentions that crayfish and a certain fish resembling the rock-cod are similarly captured, and remarks that the log is lifted at an angle, with one hand closing the lower aperture, in which position it is brought to and held above the surface, when the water trickles out between the fingers of the sealing hand.

Yet another method (analogous to "bobbing") is practised for securing eels. Huge worms, found under decaying logs, are threaded by means of a needle formed of a thin strip of cane on a line from ten to twelve feet long until several feet of bait are available. The line is merely doubled, the ends made fast to a stout pole, and the loop dangled in the water. The boy fishes patiently, nor does he strike at the first nibble, but permits the eel to swallow slowly what might be considered an undue proportion of the bait, when it is landed and compelled to disgorge for the benefit of the next comer.

Among coastal blacks—all of whom may be said to be fishermen—some are ardent devotees to the sea. Others of the same camp restrict themselves to unsensational creeks and lagoons. The frog in the well knows nothing of the salt sea, and its aboriginal prototype contents himself with milder and generally less remunerative kind of sport than that in which his bolder cousins revel. Such a man, however, may possess aquatic lore of which the other is admittedly ignorant, and be apt in devices towards which the attitude of the salt-water man is adverse, if not contemptuous. The fresh-water man is skilful in the use of a net shaped something like the secondary wings of a certain species of moth, and expanding and closing similarly. It is made of fine twine (one-inch mesh), preferably from the bark of one of the fig-trees or the brown kurrajong, tightly stretched on two pieces of lawyer-cane each bent to form the half of an irregular ellipse. This net ("moorgaroo") is manipulated by two men working in concert, principally for the capture of eels. They do not wait for the eel to come to them, but by shrewd scrutiny discover its whereabouts under the bank of the creek or among the weeds and roots. Then one silent man holds the net widespread, or adroitly dodges it into intercepting positions, while the other beats the luckless fish in its direction with more or less fluster. The persistency with which the creeks are patrolled by men with spears, netted and poisoned, invites one to marvel that any fish escape, and yet once again quite a haul is made.

That great philosopher, Herbert Spencer, once in his life made a joke and confessed to it, with apologies for its littleness. Lunching at a tavern in the Isle of Wight, he asked: "Oh, is not this a very large chop for such a small island?" Similarly, I have been astonished at the apparent disproportion between the size of the eel and the insignificance of the creek whence the exultant black has hauled it.

An instance of the poor part which the slimmest eel plays when pitted against the Smartness and resourcefulness of the black may be related. A large eel, in a moment of indiscretion, showed itself in a fairly deep creek. Bewailing the absence of his wing-net, or "moorgaroo," the boy hunted the elusive fish hither and thither with cunning determination. At last it disappeared under a log. In most of his activities the black boy sniffs at conventions. Hastily stripping, the boy dived and when he reappeared the eel was vainly squirming in one of the legs of his trousers which had been knotted below the knee.

Another boy, a stranger, brought with him traditions which he successfully materialised in favour of the employment of several light darts instead of a single heavy spear for fishing. The subject was frequently debated, but none of the camp adopted George's theories. His favourite weapons were the dried stems of an all too common weed, which generally grows straight and true. Into the thick end he would insert a four-inch length of No. 10 fencing wire, sharpened to a delicate point, and with a battery of eight or ten of these he would sally forth. His bag averaged high. Often he treated me to practical demonstrations of the success of his methods. A big flathead reposed in two feet of water, half buried in the sand. George had one of his darts fast in a twinkling, and the fish flashed away, the tip indicating its movement. In a few minutes the hapless flathead was carrying no less than six darts, and as such a handicap was absurd it abandoned the race for life.

On another occasion he struck a big sting-ray so full of his impish darts that it resembled an animated pincushion of monstrous proportions. It, too, realised the futility of kicking against so many pricks. On the other hand, Tom, with his heavy shaft and barbed point, relied on a single weapon. It seldom failed, for his right arm was strong and disciplined to a nicety.

On a shallow tidal creek a settler had made a corduroy crossing of the fibrous trunks of the Pandanus palms, which the blacks of the neighbourhood turned to account in the capture of fish. A few frail sticks, artlessly interwoven with grass, formed a primitive weir at the down-stream end of the crossing. Fish which went up with the tide frequently found themselves stranded on the way down, for the water passed freely between the palm-tree trunks without affording them right of way, and the rude weir often stopped for ever belated bream, mullet, and barramundi. This simple trap, though it does not appear to be put into use on the coast generally, seems almost to indicate an instinctive knowledge of a studied design described to me by an observant friend who has travelled into many an odd nook and corner of Queensland. On a deep but narrow tributary of the Georgina River a permanent trap on a large scale was wont to be maintained. A tree had been felled across the stream so that each end of the trunk was supported by the respective bank. Straight stakes were driven firmly into the bed of the creek as closely together as possible, the heads resting against the horizontal tree-trunk. This palisading formed the base of an embankment of packed grass and rubbish, sufficiently tight to raise the level of the stream about three feet. In the middle of the embankment, and about one foot below water-level, a hole about one foot square had been cut. A platform about ten feet long by three feet wide, having a fall of about one foot and formed of a number of straight saplings laid parallel with the stream, and supported by a couple of transverse bearers on four stout forked sticks, received the escape from the sluice. At the lower end of the platform was a rough weir of twisted grass, which was continued up each side for about half its length. Water passed with little hindrance through the platform, while jew-fish, yellow-tail, and bream, were retained in considerable numbers.

Many years have elapsed—peradventure centuries—since the blacks of Missionary Bay, Hinchinbrook Island, built a weir of blocks and boulders of granite which oysters cemented here and there. On the fulness of spring tides fish frolicked over and among the boulders. Those which delayed their exit found themselves in an enclosed pool which at certain seasons of the year runs dry. To this day the sea continues to pay tribute, though the blacks of the locality have passed away, and there is none but the red-backed sea-eagle or the heavy-flighted osprey and a rare and casual white man, to receive it. Among the few emblems of the vanishing race, this persistent weir-taking toll of the fish month after month, year after Year, for the benefit of successive generations of eagles and ospreys, appeals vividly to the imagination.

HOOKS.

From what can be ascertained at this late date, pearl shell hooks were very sure and killing, but seem to have been used principally for smaller fish—whiting, perch, bream, flathead, etc.—the occurrence of large hooks being exceedingly rare. Mullet (if tradition is to be credited) were seldom caught by hook and line, but were speared among the mangroves at high tide—a practice which prevails to this day. The Dunk Island examples have a resemblance to one of the forms of pearl-shell hooks used by the Tahitians in Captain Cook's day.

Tortoise-shell hooks capable of holding large kingfish and fair sized sharks are common among the natives of Darnley Island, Torres Straits. During the process of cutting and paring the hooks to the size and design required, the shell is frequently immersed in boiling water, which temporarily overcomes its inherent toughness. Incidentally, it may be pointed out that the evidence derivable from these fish-hooks does not afford proof of Papuan influence on the mind of the Australian aboriginal, except at the extreme north of Cape York Peninsula and a few miles down the eastern coast of the Gulf of Carpentaria. This default seems the more remarkable in face of the fact that outrigger canoes, doubtless of Papuan or Malayan origin, were known as far south as the Johnstone River.

To say that the coastal blacks of North Queensland had no knowledge of the use of barbed hooks is misleading. In sheer desperation, when the supply of pearl-shell hooks was exhausted, they were wont to attach bait to their harpoon-points, and they used such unpropitious means successfully, and occasionally made a miniature hook by tying a sharp spur to a thin, straight stick. Recent proof has been obtained of the use of the lorum of one of the creeping palms, from which all the spurs save three at the thicker end were scraped off. With the knowledge of the efficacy of the barb under extraordinary circumstances, is it not the more remarkable that they failed to employ it systematically? Dr. W. E. Roth describes crescentic hooks of coco-nut shell and wooden hooks with bone barb, and also barbs improvised from one of the spines of the catfish. He also mentions as "the most primitive form of hook" the dried tendril of HUGONIA JENKENSII ("pattel-pattel" of the Dunk Island blacks). To anyone familiar with the crescent pearl-shell hooks, the use of the singular tendrils of the Hugonia would immediately be suggested; but my observation, inquiries, and opinion do not support the theory. The shape of the tendril is all that can be said in its favour. It is neither sharp nor tough enough for actual use.

With these barbless hooks the bait was not impaled, but strapped on with shreds of bark.

NARCOTICS AND POISONS.

It is said of the great Mogul Emperor Babur that he boasted of being able to make fish drunk so that he might haul them in shoals, and when "Carathis" pronounced her "barbarous incantations" the fish with one accord thrust forth their heads from the water. Is it generally known that the North Queensland blacks also are expert in the use of narcotics and indifferent to the ethics of sport? The most commonly used of the fish poisons on the coast of North Queensland is likewise employed by the natives of Zambesi Land for a similar purpose. The plant is known botanically as "Derris." Two varieties, "scandens" and "uligijiosa," are known in this State. The aboriginal titles vary in different localities, but "Paggarra" will suit the present purpose. Some blacks are so offensively civilised that they know the plant by the name of "Wild Dynamite." Possibly it owes its popularity among fish poisons to the fact that it is the handiest of all. It trails over the rocks, just out of touch of high-water mark, but not beyond the reach of the spray of surges. With roots investigating inclement crevices, and salt air damping its leaves, the plant flourishes, and flowers prettily in graceful racemes. In the semi-obscurity of the crevices the flowers put on a tinge of pink, literally blushing unseen. The heartless blacks tear up the plant, branches, leaves, flowers and all, coarsely bundle them together, and, wading into an enclosed pool where fish are observed, beat the mass (after dipping it into the water and while held in the left hand) with a nulla-nulla. The action is repeated until the bark and leaves are macerated, and then the bundle is thrown into the pool. In a few minutes the fish rise to the surface, gasping and making extraordinary efforts to get out of the infected water. Death ensues rapidly, but the fish are quite wholesome as food.

Another of the vegetable poisons is known as "Raroo" (CAREYA AUSTRALIS). The bark at the base of the trunk and of the roots contains an effective principle, which is released in a somewhat similar fashion to that employed with "Paggarra."

The fruit of the handsome, shrubby tree known botanically as DIOSPYROS HEBECARPA is also a most effective fish poison. It is oval-shaped, red when ripe, and, as the name implies, covered with soft, fine hair. For all its lofty title and attractive appearance, the fruit is deceptive, for it bites and blisters the lips and tongue like caustic, and on being bruised and thrown into a pool on the reef, all fish are killed outright.

A different and, for a black, singularly complicated process is employed for the extraction of the noxious principle residing in the plant known as "Koie-yan" (FARADAYA SPLENDIDA). This is one of the most rampant and ambitious of the many vines of the jungle.

It combines exceeding vigour with rare gracefulness. The leaves are a light glossy green, ovate, and often a foot long, while the flowers are pure white (resembling slightly the azalea, but free from its fragility), large, and with an elusive scent, sweet and yet indefinite. The fruit, smooth and of porcelain whiteness, varies in size and shape, and is said to be edible, though blacks ignore it. A large marble and an undersized hen's egg may dangle together, or in company with others, from the topmost branches of some tall tree, which has acted as host to the clinging vine. The handsome but inconsiderate plant is turned from its purpose of lending fictitious and fugitive charms to quite commonplace but passive trees to the office of stupefying uncomplaining fish. But the element which holds such deadly enmity to the sense of the fish is not obtainable by the simple primary means successful with other plants. Indeed, the process is quite elaborate, and goes to prove that the Australian aboriginal has to his credit as a chemist the results of successful original research, and that he is also a herbalist from whom it is no condescension to learn. In this detail, at any rate, he is distinctly an accomplished person. Portions of the vine are cut into foot lengths; the outer layer of bark is removed and rejected, the middle layer alone being preserved. This is carefully scraped off and made up into shapely little piles on fresh green leaves. One might imagine that a black boy preparing the deadly "Koie-yan" was really playing at chemist's shop with neat-handed scrupulousness. When a sufficiency is obtained it is rubbed on to stones previously heated by fire. The stones then being thrown into a creek or a little lagoon left by the receding tide, the poison becomes disseminated, with fatal effect to all fish and other marine animals.

It is pointed out, however, by Dr. Hamlyn-Harris that the nature of the active principle of the "Koie yan" does not permit of elaboration by such means. The heating of the shredded bark would, therefore, appear to fall into line with the gibberish of ancient alchemists. It would bewilder the uninitiated without enhancing results.

Many other plants supply the means of killing small fish wholesale, or of reducing them to palsied cripples. The three described are fairly common, and have, therefore, been selected to point a moral. Poisoning fish is a poor sort of sport, perhaps, but there are two classes of fishermen—the hungry and the artistic. The latter use flimsy tackle and complicated gear, and play the game, giving the victims to their wiles a sporting chance. Though not the only representative of the hungry class, the black boy generally fishes on an empty stomach, and his demeanour coincides. No slobbering sentiment affects him. Yet he is not so cruel as the mean white who throws a plug of dynamite into the river while the fish are enjoying their crowded hour, though he will with as little taint upon his conscience poison a pool full of fish as drag with hooked stick a reluctant crab piecemeal from its burrow among the mangrove roots. But then he is responding to the appeals of a clamant and not over-particular stomach, while your dynamitard is occasionally a well-fed barbarian with a queasy palate.

FLY-FISHING.

The neatest and most artistic method by which the blacks kill fish necessitates the employment of a particular species of spider known to the learned as NEPHILA MACULATA PISCATORUM. This spider was discovered on Dunk Island by Macgillivray, the naturalist of the expedition of H.M.S. RATTLESNAKE in 1848. It has a large ovate abdomen of olive-green bespangled with golden dust; black thorax, with coral-red mandibles; and long, slender legs, glossy black, and tricked out at the joints with golden touches. A fine creature, gentle and stately in demeanour, it spins a large web, strong enough to hold the biggest of beetles and other insects, and, to harmonise with the superior air of the manufacturer, the gossamer is of golden-green. The great spider at the focus of the resplendent web is a frequent and conspicuous ornament to the edges of the jungle, and having no fear, and no indocility of temper, it undergoes the ordeal of admiration with an assumption of disdainful coquettism. The local name of this comely creature is "Karan-jamara." Shameless polyandrist, she maintains several consorts—from three to five seems to be the average number—and they, semi-transparent, feeble, meek, subdued little fellows, maintain precarious isolated existences in the outskirts of the web.

Though my own experience is negative, direct incontrovertible evidence is extant to the effect that birds often meet their fate by blundering into the web, to be devoured by the nimble and gaily decorated owner. I have frequently seen karan-jamara disposing of hard-shelled beetles as big in bulk as some birds, and the strongest of butterflies, once entangled, is powerless. The long-legged spider leaps on the struggling prey and stills its beating wings with one pinch of powerful red mandibles. March flies form the most frequent diet. One has been observed to dispose of fourteen of the great stupid flies in a single evening, and if the flies could reason they might, while whimpering because of the existence of such voracious spiders, acknowledge that they design their webs in a very perplexing and masterly manner.

In pursuance of inquiries—the results of which are herein recorded—a casual black boy, a stranger to these parts, and therefore unfamiliar with the local name and the special purpose to which the spider is put, was cross-examined. At first he failed to recognise the photograph, but when it was explained by the pointed allusion to a living Maltese-cross spider close at hand, a gleam of intelligence brightened his bewildered face, and he delivered a self-satisfied dissertation on the order Arachnida that is worth quoting:

"That fella Oo-boo-boo. That fella mammy belonga 'nother fella altogether. You no savee, come close up—that fella ply way. You no savee, come close up, that fella no good; that fella vite."

And the boy looked gravely sagacious and smiled the wide, wise smile betokening proud superiority of information. Had Macgillivray but known that the "Oo-boo-boo" was the parent of all the many species, and that it belongs to the discreetly valorous class that "vites" and flies away, and lives to "vite" another day, he might have achieved renown of a more popular kind than is the reward of the unromantic naturalist who discovers merely a superior spider.

This spider is used on some of the rivers as a lure, virtues almost irresistible being ascribed to it. Experiments in salt water, though not absolutely negative in their results, have not afforded any specially exciting sport; but possibly the fascination of the lure is more efficient in fresh than in salt water, and is influential over the habitual caution throughout a certain species of fish only. The trick is worked in the following manner:

The angler takes a light, thin switch and entangles one end in the web, which, by dexterous waving action, is converted (without being touched with the fingers) into a strand about two feet long. The spider is secured and squashed, and the end of the line moistened in the juices of the body, some of the fragments of which are reserved for bait, and also to be thrown into the water as a preliminary charm. These buoyant titbits attract shoals of small fish, among which the line, with its extract of spider, is delicately trailed; a fish rises to the lure, the gossamer becomes entangled in its teeth, and it is landed by a brisk yet easy movement of the wrist. A great angler recently said that throwing a fly is an act of feeling or instinct rather than reason. So the black boy with a careless flourish fills his dilly-bag, while he smiles at the serious attempts of the white man to imitate his skill.

Owing to the brevity and the frailness of the line, the catch is limited to fish under the recognised standard as to size. Tests prove that the breaking strain of the line is nearly three-quarters of a pound, but the weight of the individual is of no great consideration, since numbers are caught quickly. The gossamer is singularly sticky. The viscid substance with which it is coated is not readily dissolvable in water; indeed, water seems to have the effect of hardening it, so that the line' wears longer than might be expected. Piquant morsels of the spider are entangled in the frayed end of the line as its original potency becomes non-effective.

A friend for whose edification this novel method was demonstrated thus writes it:

"It did not take the boy long to get ready. They simply broke a switch about three feet long and attached a portion of the web about six inches long to the end; squeezed out on to a leaf the fluid internals of the spider, into which they dipped the end of the line, started a rather melodious chant, and put the line in shallow water. I was only a few feet away and could see no fish at first, but they came very soon. They were very small, about one and a half inches long. They fasten their teeth in the web, and are lifted out quite slowly. Some require to be pulled off the line after being landed. I watched for about ten minutes, during which time seventeen were caught."

Sir William Macgreggor, ex-Governor of Queensland, has described the Papuan art of fishing by means of kites, the lure being a tassel of the web of a spider of the Nephila species. No doubt the blacks here made an independent and original discovery, and in their simplicity applied it in a different, but none the less effective, style from that of the advanced Papuan.

Thus, to use the web and the fragments of a spider for fly-fishing is certainly meting out poetic justice to the spider on account of the many ensnared flies; and the black angler never pauses to reflect whether the comminuted remains of a spider can possibly be construed into a fair fly.

PART III
MISCELLANEA

PEARLS

WHAT IS A PEARL?

What is a pearl? The substance of a sensation—the consolidation of discomfort on the part of an oyster or other nacre-secreting mollusc. It is a globular deposit of carbonate of lime, with a very small proportion of water, generally enclosing a trifle which is its cause and core and, so to speak, is a waste product of the body's chemistry. In the restricted, scientific sense, "true pearls are bodies consisting of calcareous material with an organic basis." Similar bodies having cores of sand grains or other foreign substance are known as "blisters."

Science, which peers and probes into the innermost affairs of oysters, and speaks of them in terms of uneasy familiarity, asserts that pearls are frequently caused by a parasite to which they are subject.

It would ill become one who has no scientific pretensions to suggest other definitions, though he may claim to be among the few who have been privileged to observe a pearl in the making, or, rather, to watch Nature's finishing touches.

In the case of the oyster the radical home cure for the living irritant or insoluble substance which had gained entrance between its valves is an encasement of pearl-film. If this encasement is globular or pear-shaped, or takes the form of a button and is lucid, lustrous, flawless, and of large size, it may be of almost inestimable worth.

Does the proud beauty who glories in the possession of a pearl condescend to imagine that she flaunts on her bosom just so many tombs containing the dust of the germs of a parasite? Does she not rather love to think of the gems as emblems of almost celestial purity, and to dwell on the fable of the Persians rather than the audacious modern fact?

Addison has set the fable in imperishable gold: A drop of water fell out of a cloud into the sea, and finding herself lost in such immensity of fluid matter, broke out into the following reflection: "Alas! What an inconsiderable creature am I in this prodigious ocean of waters; my existence is of no concern to the universe; I am reduced to a kind of nothing, and am less than the least of the works of God." It so happened that an oyster which lay in the neighbourhood chanced to gape and swallow it up in the midst of this its humble soliloquy. The drop, says the fable, lay a great while hardening in the shell, until by degrees it was ripened into a pearl, which, falling into the hands of a diver after a long series of adventures, is at present that famous pearl which is affixed on the top of the Persian diadem.

Though one may count his pearls by the score, the hoard may be valueless. Upon such examples entertaining, if not valuable, experiments may be made without affectation or giving hostages to fortune. In all the little deformed specimens thus dissected the core has been found to consist of a foreign substance, generally what seemed under a microscope of limited power a speck of dirt. The heart of one was a blob of mud, which gave off a most baleful vapour. This was the result of the house-cleaning of a common, edible rock oyster, and the pearl, dirty green and lustreless, merely a thin casket, for the noisome mud had not solidified. The care with which the impurity had been rendered innocuous demonstrated the correct ideas of the oyster on sanitation. No doubt the germ of the special form of tape-worm which troubles oysters, irritates to pearl-making, and passes through other transformations in other hosts, and completes its cycle in the body of a shark, would be too minute for inexpert detection. The fact that molluscs do intern foreign and obnoxious substances is testimony to their decency and love of cleanliness, and so may the pearl be still accepted as the embodiment of purity. Though all its little soul be dirt, the pearl is pure, and but for the dirt or the germ of a filthy ailment it would not be pearl.

So many molluscs produce pearls that it would be absurd for the great oyster family to set up exclusive rights. They do not, for your oyster is ever humble even when tenanted with a rivalless pearl. On the coast of North Queensland, within the Great Barrier Reef, pinnas of at least two species are among the producing agents, which, covering a wide range, seem to meet in two distinct genera, far apart in appearance and habit. There is the frail, flat, translucent "window-shell" (Placuna), the valves of which fit so closely that the poor little inhabitant is squeezed to a wafer, a film, a fragment of muscle. Yet in some localities nearly every individual has a pearl, pretty in tint, but too minute to be of value. An allied species is common on the coast of China, where the pearls are collected for export to India, to be reduced to lime by calcination for the use of luxurious betel-nut chewers. These almost microscopic pearls are also burnt in the mouths of the dead who have been influential and wealthy.

Coal-black pearls occur in one of the pinnas, the interior of which is sooty, shot with iridescent purple, and since the pearl, whether produced by oyster, mussel, pinna, or window-shell, is generally more brilliant than the containing shell, that of the black pinna, with the high lights of its environment concentrated, may be a gem of surpassing novelty and beauty. But the habitual product of this pinna is small, dull, mud-tinted or brown, and of no value whatever. Another of the genera grows "seed" of excellent lustre, corresponding with the azure brightness of the shell.

The chief source of orient pearls on the coast of North Queensland is the gold-lip mother-of-pearl PINCTADA MAXIMA, while the black lip

PINCTADA MARGARITIFERA occasionally yields fine and flawless specimens of a silvery lustre. One which is still lovingly remembered was of pale blue and wonderfully lighted. The commonest of the giant clams TRIDACNA GIGAS sometimes betrays evidence of past internal trouble by the presence of a concretion of porcelain whiteness and of porcellaneous texture, but such are not to be described as pearls and to be prized as rarities only.

That some huge molluscs produced pearls before man, with his faculty for admiration, came on the scene is proved by their existence as fossils in chalk. Hemispherical specimens have been found on the inner surface of a shell which has no living representative—viz., the Inoceramus (some of which attained a length of two feet)—and spherical ones of the same prismatical structure occur detached in the chalk. It were curious to let the imagination run over the fact that the hosts of these uncommended gems died ages before the advent of man. The best of modern prizes may be puny in comparison with those which caused distress to the giant molluscs of the age when the Ichthyosaurus, Plesiosaurus, and Pterodactylus were the aristocrats of the animal world. Such gems have gone for ever, and even during this age of insatiable and adventurous search man does not secure a tithe of the ocean's tribute, for, since a pearl is a source of discomfort to its host, the unceasing effort of the animal is towards expulsion. The greatest and possibly the most magnificent are cast out as rubbish on the ocean floor, or are retained within the valves when the animal dies of old age.

So-called pearls have been found in elephants' tusks and semi-adherent to the bones of fish, and concretions—hard, smooth, and round, and of the flat hue of skimmed milk—in coconuts and in the cavities of bamboos; but in the production of the real gem neither oyster nor mussel nor pinna need fear the rivalry of anything on the earth's surface. The pearl belongs to the sea.

Completely spherical pearls can be formed only loose in the mantle or soft parts of the body of the animal; but intrusions incite a deposit of nacre in the form of a projection on the interior, which projection, often a mere bubble, but sometimes semi-detached, may take the shape and dimensions of the foreign substance. Or an inoffensive mollusc may be goaded by the piercing of its shell from the exterior to create that for which men venture into the depths of the sea. If a pearl-secreting oyster be inherently robust, its defence against assault from without may consist of the strengthening of the interior at the point of attack by deposits of nacre. Thus, a slight protuberance arises which becomes the base of a blister or button or the starting-point of a pear-shaped gem. Many a lovely gem is, therefore, nothing more than the imperishable record of aggression on the part of a flabby sponge on a resourceful oyster. Occasionally valuable pearls are found within huge blisters. Such pearls originate, no doubt, in the ordinary way, but, becoming an intolerable nuisance on account of increasing size, are confined in nacre.

One of the accompanying illustrations shows the fate which befell an infant chiton upon intrusion on a small black-lip oyster, and coincidentally the origin of a blister. The chiton family being notorious for stolidity, the infant could not have realised the risks of its trespass until the strait-jacket made its retirement impossible. The nacre has reproduced the details of the chiton's exterior with the fidelity of a casting, and further reveals the fact that it was alive when entombed, for its struggles to escape are solidified.

This deliberate act of the oyster may not stand comparison with the stone of Pyrrhus's ring, which had the figure of Apollo and the nine Muses in the veins of it produced by the spontaneous handiwork of Nature without any help from art. The marvellous stone belonged to the fabulous past; the imprisoned chiton to the prosaic present.

Another illustration is that of an accumulation of nacre which has assumed accidental resemblance to a miniature shark. It was found in a gold-lip pearl shell in Torres Straits. The like quantity in globular shape would represent a pearl of great value.

A PEARL IN THE MAKING.

On a calm and luminous day I waded, disrobed, in shallow water as limpid as the fictitious stream which legend says King Solomon improvised at the foot of his throne when the Queen of Sheba attended his court. Lifting her robes—for she imagined the crossing of the water to be a ceremonial device—the gorgeous Queen displayed her shapely calves. The water resting on the verge of the lovely Isle was as delusively clear, but was not deceptive.

It revealed living coral, good to avoid by the barefooted; clams with patterned mantles of various tints—grey, slate-blue, sea-green, brown, and buff; anemones in many shapes, some like spikes of lavender, and irritant and repellent to the touch; some platter-shaped and cobalt-blue; some as living vases with the opalescent tints of Venetian glass, which, abhorring the hand of man, retreat into the sand until only an inconspicuous fringe of neutral tint is visible. Sea-slugs in almost endless form and variety of hue, and many other strange sea things, were among the inhabitants of the reef—a closely packed arena of never-ceasing slaughter.

In the middle of a clump of brown seaweed, which had fallen apart like the neatly dressed hair of a woman, was a black streak, signifying the gape of a wedge-shaped mollusc known as a pinna. The gape was about as long as the parting of a woman's hair and about thrice as wide. As I crouched to note the functions of the animal, my shadow intervened and the caution of the creature was roused, the valves closing so that no sign of the presence of the shell was distinguishable among the slightly wavering, minute particles of alga. Changing my position, so that the pinna might not be deprived of its share of the rays of the sun, the valves soon furtively opened. A slight movement on my part and they closed again, without having revealed any hidden charms.

After a few minutes, a certain confidence being established between us, the pinna emerged from its retirement, in so far as such creatures are permitted by Nature. The mantle of this particular species is shown as a delicate fringe of lace in old gold and black. It ripples along the upper edges of the confining valves, which are intensely black with a pearly lustre. The pretty movements of the mantle—like the swinging of the skirts of a well-apparelled damsel—attracted admiration, and on peering into the shell a glimpse of something precious was obtained.

Tossed and twirled about just below the old gold fringe was a black pearl about the size of a pea. The prize was safe. Without risk of loss it could be watched in its unceasing revolutions. It seemed as if the animal, with automatic perseverance, attempted to eject the incubus, the weight of which kept it about an inch below the aperture of the valves. Such motion would naturally tend to perfection. Whatsoever its lustre, it would certainly be a sphere. Besides, it was a pearl in the making. As long as it remained within the pinna and it could not be voluntarily rejected, its size would inevitably increase. It was the rolling stone to which time and the secretions of the animal would add weight and, peradventure, beauty.

Was mortal ever before privileged to watch over the growth of a black pearl? The activities of the mantle, a blending of enticing colour and poetic motion, were slow, free, and light-attracting. The ancients believed that some pearls were constituted by flashes of lightning playing on bubbles within the oyster. A relative of the family here seemed to be wooing the tropic sun of its beams, if not to vitalise, at least to burnish its treasure.

Close scrutiny showed that the pearl was not absolutely free. It was enclosed in a transparent membrane, the merest film, which confined it to a particular position in the mantle, while it seemed to possess independent actions—vertical and revolutionary. Perhaps the rays of light which fell unequally on it through the water created the illusion of revolutions, but it is certain that the pearl seemed to be playing a game of hide-and-seek.

Was it possible for human nature to deny itself so easily gotten and pretty a prize? I confess, though the possibility of the pearl increasing in size and loveliness was obvious, that the fact that pinnas are subject to ills, chances, and mishaps, was also recognised. Left to be slowly tossed about, the pearl would become greater; but size, though an important feature, is not the only desirable quality. And while it grew might not another barefooted beach-comber discover it? Or might not one of the many unintelligent admirers of the pinna itself find entrance by drilling or by the violent crushing of the valves, and, ignoring the treasure, destroy the organs and the substance by and from which it was being delicately elaborated? Suppose, I argued, I remove the gaping shell, I shall no longer be able to enjoy the rare, the unique pleasure of presiding over the gradual perfection of a pearl, an aesthetic advantage to which I alone had been made free. Could present possession of a little sphere of carbonate of lime, polished and sooty black, compensate for the continuance of the chaste joy of watching one of the most covert and intimate processes of Nature? Balancing the immediate material gain against the inevitable moral loss, I was almost persuaded to self-denial, when, with a sudden impulse, begot of the consciousness of rightful acquisition, the pinna was forcibly yet carefully drawn out of the sand in which it was deeply embedded and in which it was anchored by toughened byssus. Directly the valves were prised apart the pearl fell into my hand. Never before had I seen one so loosely retained within its shell. Generally, in the case of the pinna, pearls are embedded in the muscles or soft parts, and are not primarily discernible, but have to be sought for by passing the "meat" through the fingers. On this occasion all previous experience had been set at naught, so that it might seem that the prize had been presented by the animal as its perfect and most opulent work.

STRANGE PEARLS.

The engaging theory of the ancients that pearls were made of glutinous dewdrops condensed by the sun's heat does not take into account the fact that some of the rarest, though not the most valuable, have assumed contrary and fantastic shape. Fish, crabs, and marine insects have proved a common origin of pearly developments while they have been regarded by some as almost miraculous conceptions on the part of the afflicted mollusc.

Hamed of Jeddah, the stubby Arab who deals in fish and oysters, and who professes to have groped over in his youth a considerable extent of the Red Sea for coral and pearls, relates many experiences in which the popular gem takes pride of place. Oriental that he is, he loves exaggeration, and while lending a propitious car to the stories in which he enshrines his prime, when he could dive deep and long, and when the precious red coral was "thick" and every shell contained a pearl, it is discreet to disregard obvious breaks and bulges along the prim path of truth. The very crudeness of his embellishments invests with kind of comic relief some of his fables, which end invariably with insipid uniformity. All the pearls which have slipped through Hamed's rough hands have been valued at five hundred pounds, never more or less. It is not for me to rub the gilt off the innocent inventions of the emotional Arab, but merely to relate one of his time-beguiling tales, and one which, probably, is of clean-cut truth.

A huge gold-lip, found four fathoms deep, where the sea grass sways indolently long, contained a tinted pearl like:

"That fella sitting down along a tree and sing out along night time."

"Flying fox?" I guessed grimly.

"No!" snapped Hamed indignantly. "'Nother fella."

"That bird which says 'chump, chump, chump?'" I meekly asked.

Again Hamed sneered ironically. "No bird. No bird carn get along oyster. Little fella-green like leaf. Sing out 'Ko-rog, ko-rog, ko-rog!'"

"Oh! Frog!"

"Yes. Like frog. Me call him 'ghouk' along my country. That fella inside gold-lip. One inch long. Leg, hand, mouth, eyes all asame. I bin get five hundred pounds for that fella."

Azure pearls in the similitude of tiny fish can be vouched for by people far more careful of their facts than Hamed—fish which have intruded themselves on the oysters and have been encased in nacre. Probably the rarity which fell into Hamed's hands was the pearly presentment of a crustacean, for marine frogs are infinitely rarer than pearls. Several molluscs admit tenants, one particular species a rotund crab; but in the case in point the wrong mansion was entered and, so to speak, the obtruder was transformed.

A common and neat industry in China is the production of fraudulent pearls, pretty and in accordance with submitted design, in which the co-operation of the obedient but frail mussel is necessary. If a round pearl is desired, a naked shot is introduced between the valves so much to the discomfort of the animal that it proceeds to cover it decently with layer after layer of pearl-film, the bulk of which depends upon the length of life granted to the mussel. Sometimes little josses are stamped out in thin uncorrosive metal, which, being presented to the mussel, are faithfully modelled, the thrifty Chinese obtaining in course of time quaint pearly gods—as potent as the best—without money and without price.

Not so long as a quarter of a century ago a spirit-bottle full of pearls—buttons, blisters, and chips of all sorts, sizes, and shapes—was purchased in North Queensland by one who had but the crudest ideas as to the value of such gems. The vendor was a whity-brown man, thin, and thinly clad in cotton. The complexion of the buyer was ruddier than the cherry, for the tropic sun had beamed ardently on his peachy Scotch skin, proclaiming him a new-chum, a bright and shining new-chum. Because he was new he was alert to the value of money. Had he not come, as all new-chums do, to Tom Tiddler's ground to pick up gold and silver? Hence, when the hatless, spare, whity-brown man in soiled cotton offered for sale the odd-shaped beads in a besmeared whisky-bottle for five pounds, his national trait expressed itself in a scoff.

The whity-brown man's seriousness, his confidentiality, his keen desire to sell, his mysticism and misty English, the ruddy young man interpreted as manifestations of the arts and wiles by means of which innocent strangers from far away lands are tempted into bankruptcy bargains. The seller, anxious to dispossess himself of ill-gotten gains prejudicial to his love of liberty, pursued the Scotch youth almost tearfully, until the bottle changed hands, but at a considerable reduction on the price originally demanded. Shortly after a friend enlightened the youth as to the probable value of the collection, and gave him some cheap advice, especially on the desirableness of secrecy. The youth accepted the advice so literally that the story ends. No one ever knew how, when, where, and for what consideration, he disposed of his embarrassments. Fresh from the land of his birth, and with the text of Burns's poetic letter in his mind, he kept that something to himself.

The days of such sensational deals are past. The primal crop has long since been harvested. Science is now bidden to stimulate the docile oyster, for the rage for pearls is as the rage of the heathen. Is it not the wish of every woman, old and young, to possess pearls? And while subject man, flushed with hope, ventures to the "utmost port, washed by the furthest sea," for such merchandise at the caprice of woman, Science plods sedately after man, beguiling him with the hope of some less risky and laborious means of acquiring the gems, while at the same time she soothes the irrepressible passion of every damsel with strings of artistic counterfeits manufactured from the scales of silvery fish, and as pleasant to glance at as many an orient.

The Spaniards say that a paper cigarette, a glass of water, and the kiss of a pretty girl, will sustain a man for a day without eating. But what is a man to do who has no tobacco, only stale water, who is separated from the nearest girl by seventy miles of perilous seas forlorn, and whose appetite sickens at the sight of the coarse fare of a béche-de-mer boat? There is but one resource for such a martyr. He must do "a perisher." That is precisely what the master of a lonely boat in an odd angle of the Coral Sea was doing when a joyful sail appeared—a dove-like messenger from civilisation and shops. It was a pitiable famine. No one had had a smoke for a week. The black boys had broken up their nicotine-saturated clay pipes and masticated them to pulp, and still treasured the quids, while the "Boss" pondered cigars during the day and dreamt them at night. But relief was at hand. The master of the strange craft, though well stocked, was not disposed to be generous, until tempted by the sight of a lovely yellow pearl, about the size of a small marble and of satiny lustre—sweet to look upon, sweeter still to possess. Aware of the other man's agonising needs, he drove a hard bargain, and the gem became his at the cost of a box of tobacco. He hugged himself for joy, and after a decent lapse, during which he acted the part of the virtuous who had relieved another's necessities out of sheer goodwill (for the pearl was only a curio, was it not?), he set sail for the nearest port.

Certain that fortune had at last beamed upon him, he laid up his lugger, wound up his affairs, and hurried off to Sydney, secretly, to dispose of his prize first-hand. An expert weighed the treasure, scrutinised it shrewdly through a microscope, and handed it back with a casual remark that it was a pretty curio, but that its market value was about half a crown. "It has been exposed to great heat, and may crumble to pieces at a change of temperature. Get me one like that uncooked and I'll give you twelve hundred pounds."

Some time after, the grasping man discovered that the pearl had been found in the "meat" of a "helmet" shell which had been roasted by a hungry and tobaccoless boy.

Without appearing to suggest anything beyond a trifling blemish in this story, replete as it is with edifying illustrations of the frailties of human nature, it would be well to remember that the helmet shell (CASSIS FLAMMEA) is not nacreous and could not therefore produce a true pearl, but merely g porcellaneous concretion, which, however, might possess a most attractive tint, possibly pale salmon or orange. Such a gem might be valuable.

Great pearls are not generally found on shallow reefs. He who would search for them systematically must dive, and if he does not possess the proper costume and accessories his trips below are but brief, and not always profitable. When a diver boasts that he can remain under water two or three minutes—and the boast is very common—he has gauged his endurance by his sensations, not by the clock. Once an expert was timed, a coloured gentleman who had great repute among his companions, all capable divers. He made a special and supreme effort, and though the watch recorded barely seventy seconds, he was much distressed. Recovery was, however, speedy; of ten subsequent minutes he spent more than half out of sight. It is not argued that human beings cannot remain voluntarily under water more than seventy seconds, but the feat is so rare that those who accomplish it are not usually pearl-divers.

The natives of some parts of Borneo declare that the valves of the oysters containing the largest pearls are always open, and that by peering into the water the pearls may be seen. They tell a story of a gigantic pearl which was thus discovered by the men of old and actually brought while within the oyster into a canoe, but had slipped from the fingers of a careless holder into deep water.

Spencer St. John, author of "Life in the Forests of the Far East," had among his friends a chief who ventured most of his possessions in a pearling cruise. Disaster attended the enterprise, but without subduing his faith in luck; mortgaging everything, even to his wife and child, he went out to woo fortune again. His slave-boy was preparing to dive one day when he started back, touched his master's hand, and with signs of great emotion pointed into the water. The chief looked, and there, seven fathoms below, lay an oyster with an enormous pearl distinctly visible. Without a moment's reflection he plunged in, and, diving with skill and speed, reached the shell before it closed, his fingers being caught between the valves. He quickly rose to the surface, and was helped into the boat by his anxious follower. Upon the oyster being forced open, a pearl, unsurpassed in size and of extraordinary beauty, was revealed. Returning to his native village, the chief sold all his smaller pearls, and having redeemed his wife and child, set sail for Manila, where lived an English friend who advanced him money, to whom he said: "Take this pearl, clear off my debt, give me what you like in return. I shall be satisfied." The author adds: "The merchant took the pearl, gave him what he considered its value—at all events enough to make Sulu ring with his generosity—and sent the pearl to China; but what became of it afterwards I could never distinctly trace; but I learned that a pearl in Bengal called 'The Mermaid' originally came from China, and as the one found in Sulu was said to be shaped like a woman's bust, it is probably the same."

Possibly the golden age of the pearl is passing as the golden age of the reptile has passed, for can it not be imagined that, in those far-back days when oysters attained a length of two feet and better deserved the title of Tridacna (three bites) than the present clams, pearls of corresponding magnificence of size were produced? Or are robust pearlless oysters to be accepted as the type of the strong era, and small oysters and pearls merely as signs of degeneracy? The largest of modern pearls measured two inches long by a circumference of four inches and weighed eighteen hundred grains. The containing shell may have been big only in comparison with its contemporaries. A very small man has been known to be afflicted with a disproportioned goitre, and there are some who argue that the goitre may be but the prototype of the pearl.

Is fact or fable to claim the most glorious of pearl stories? Some verily believe that Cleopatra did quaff the costliest beverage the world has ever known. The incident is so faithful to the character of "that rare Egyptian" that all sober record shall not discount delight in its transcendent sumptuousness. Though the pearl may have been worth eighty thousand pounds of our money, though Cleopatra was gay, though her extravagance was impious, she was a glorious woman, and she had at least one glorious, if nauseating, drink. The pearl decoction was merely an episode in her policy, which was to fascinate Antony—Antony who had called her to account for having aided his enemies in their war against him. And what was an eighty thousand pound bauble in the high affairs of State? "She was at the age when a woman's beauty is at its prime, and she was also of the best judgment. So she furnished herself with a world of gifts, stores of gold and silver, and of riches and other sumptuous ornaments as is credible she might bring from so great a house and from so wealthy and rich a realm as Egypt. But yet she carried nothing with her wherein she trusted more than herself, and in the charms and enchantment of her surpassing beauty and grace."

And then the supper following the magnificent pageant! Anything less than an eighty thousand pound pearl would have been an anti-climax, a mean and clumsy culmination of a "gaudy night." That soul-delighting gem which vanished in foam told of a superb Cleopatra's "calm felicity and power."

Some say that, the jewel—cast away so majestically was one of a pair which Cleopatra wore as ear-rings, and that when Antony restrained his hostess from a repetition of the draught, she presented the now matchless pearl to him. Another version implies that the ear-ring had been originally one monster pearl, which Cleopatra had caused to be sawn in two to gratify her lust for unique and lavish ornament.

It is said, too, that the pearl was dissolved in wine. By a simple practical test and at the sacrifice of a small quantity of baroque, proof was obtained that ordinary culinary vinegar is a solvent of pearls. The experiment also yielded these notable conclusions—that either the wine of Cleopatra's age was much more corrosive than the vinegar of ours, or that the costly beverage was prepared beforehand, or that the stately banquet was long-drawn-out while the inestimable gem spluttered and simmered in the goblet. The dissolution of such a large pearl must have been slow, and the product far from nice, but it was one of the effects by which a sovereign woman conquered the "most courteous lord" of his day.

A curious superstition prevails in some parts of the East Indies, it being believed that if gold and pearls are placed by themselves in a packet they will certainly decrease in quantity or number, and in the end totally disappear; but, if a few grains of rice are added, the treasure is safe. Rice is thought not only to preserve the original number of pearls, but to actually cause increase.

Tarnished pearls are occasionally submitted to the process of "skinning"— the removal with fine steel files under a magnifying glass of the outer 'layer, on the chance of the existence of a better underneath. The ancients treated lustreless gems differently, placing them before doves, under the belief that they could be polished by being pecked and played with by the gentle birds.

In some respects pearls are superior to all other gems. They are emblematic of serenity, and serenity is often power in the highest manifestation. None ever said an unkind word of pearls; no dubious legend clings to them, making the timid afraid. They come to us perfectly fashioned. No coarse handiwork has touched them, no soulless machine ground them to conventional pattern. The last diamond may be, the last pearl never, until the sea gives up more than its dead, its very being. Pearls may begin and end in foam; but the beginning is now and always, and the ending rare, for the Cleopatras are gone. Emblems of purity, refinement, and peace, they are truly the gems for woman. Queenly or demure, they become her, and she bestows on them a quality hard to define, but singularly sweet and acceptable. Gold and precious stones may occupy billions of years in the making, or may be the product of—

"The war of elements,

The wrecks of matter, and the crash of worlds."

Once we find these hard, cold things and take hold of and seize them, we know that we have, to use a homely simile, eaten our cake. The supply of pearls is continuous, and under the control of the cruel ingenuity of man they grow to an ordinary size in less than a decade.

Many years ago an opinion was expressed that the increasing knowledge 'of the mollusc and its habits would enable man literally to sow the sea with pearls as he sows a field with grain, and that the harvest would be certain. Under natural conditions not one oyster in a hundred is troubled with a pearl, and not one pearl in the hundred is of any real value. It is demanded that unsuspecting oysters shall be inflicted with a kind of plague, so that there shall be not one but several pearls in every suffering individual, and in the greater number chance will contrive a larger proportion of orients. Every oyster has its potentialities; Science seeks to convert potentialities into certainties.

PEARLS AND HIGH TRAGEDY.

Such merchandise has ever provoked the spirit of adventure in hardy, healthy men, and pearls have claimed the lives of the best among them. The health and figure of the friend who beguiled many an evening were sacrificed to the lustrous gem so prized of women. A model of stalwart manhood of the Viking strain, he died early, worn out with the stress with which he sought the most serene of personal adornments. There may have been some slight exaggeration in the popular belief that he had walked along the bottom of the sea from one end of the Great Barrier Reef to the other, a stretch of over one thousand miles; but that he had accomplished more than that distance in the aggregate of his submarine wanderings may be quite credible. Probably there was no human being who possessed such intimate knowledge of the character of the ocean floor within the living bounds of the Great Barrier; and since he was silent, reserved, and self-contained to all save friends of long standing, was never guilty of boasting, and ever reluctant to tell of his adventures, the world is little the wiser from his work, though at the best time of his life most of his days were spent under water in fairyland-like scenes. It may seem absurd to associate fairyland with the depths of the sea; but the shy explorer of many a coral grove has been heard to say that the scenes fulfilled his ideals of what the realms of the fairies might be like.

Pearl-divers are more susceptible to the charms of wayward Fortune than those who have not realised the thrill of expectancy with which a huge goldlip, encrusted with coral and swathed with seaweed, is seized. It may contain a gem worth a king's ransom, or but an animal which, though it may be crossed in love, is not engaging in appearance or in any feature or quality commendable. There is the chance; and it appeals to most rational men. Secretive Fortune lures on, promising the bubble pearl 'and proffering that which satisfieth not, until the stress and perils of the avocation tell on the enthusiast, who finds himself not exuberant as wont; that Fortune has been tricking him; that in the pursuit of pearls Chance is oft repellent; and that the prize which seemed impossible to avoid has eluded the most devoted seekers.

It may be that my captain did not seek his pearls with zeal beyond that which is common to the calling the world over; but that his enthusiasm beguiled him into remote and odd parts of the Barrier, that he became familiar with rare scenes (denied to all save submarine adventurers in tropical waters), that he was oft in peril of his life, and that he could pause in the midst of strenuous, nerve-racking work to watch the never-ceasing hostilities of the denizens of the sea, may not be questioned.

Not long before he passed away he told of one of his adventures in a few hurried words, after the manner of one who loves not to dwell on personal reminiscences, save as a text for the rectification of popular error in respect of sensational happenings. The story is here repeated, for it throws light on an incident which sent one ship of warfare on dubious patrol, and reveals the manner of the men who sought pearls in the old days.

"Have you found that pearl?" he asked smilingly; for we had often talked of the possibility of being rewarded with a fortune-bestowing gem.

"Yes, indeed, I have; and a real beauty. I very much doubt if you, for all your experience, ever saw such perfect shape and fine lustre. Here is an instance of the perversity of Chance. You, tied up in a rubber bag, rake the floor of the Barrier, fighting sharks and being hustled by turtle, and never find anything out of the way. I stroll about the beaches, and see what Fortune bestows!"

The size of a small marble, it lay swathed in white wadding. Minute furrows sculptured the surface in radiating lines from pole to pole, enhancing rare radiance.

The captain took the little casket in his hand that he might gloat over the treasure, as, his eyes shining, he said:

"You lucky fellow! Where did you get it? I never saw a finer pearl, and I have seen a few in my days. Fair numbers have passed through my hands; but— you fraud!"

He lifted it, revealing a counterfeit, which had once ornamented a hatpin.

In good-humour he settled down on a lounge and gradually drifted into reminiscences.

"About two years before what I am going to tell you happened, I heard of a patch of shell off an island Sud-Est way; I kept the tip to myself, determined to work the spot on my own account if ever I got the chance. I waited till I saved a few pounds, and, taking in a mate, fitted out a craft, and with a crew of very fair boys sailed away. I found the spot all right; but—my usual luck— someone had been there before me. Strange to say, the spot was by no means worked out, though it was fairly good ground and easy working, and the shell large. We did good business for a while, until one day I got a proper start. The life-line fouled on something, and I found that it had taken a turn round the bowsprit of a wreck. I got on top pretty quick, and, having had a talk with my mate, went down again. Very soon I knew the boat. It was the ——, and she had belonged to a man I had known very well. The strange part about the business was that the boat had been burned. Her deck was gone; she had burned to the water's edge and had sunk, and there she rested on her keel. I knew that the owner had left port some months before on a secret cruise. Someone must have given him the tip, too. He was well known and liked, and generally did good business. My mate and I talked over the business. We wanted to clean up that patch, so decided to remain a few days longer before clearing out to report. I was convinced that murder had been committed-that the natives of the island had massacred the party and had sunk the lugger.

"While I was below next day an urgent message came down. I bobbed up pretty quickly. A boat was sneaking out from the beach, apparently with the plan of cutting us off from our lugger, which was anchored some distance off, with only a couple of boys on board. You bet, we got up steam pretty quickly. When we got on board we reached for our rifles, and then felt safe.

"The boat was then making straight for us, and it appeared to be crowded with darkies. We had been off the island for four days, and had not seen the sight of a native. I knew there were plenty, and the fact that they had kept away had made me a bit suspicious. As the boat came along I was sure they meant mischief, and was determined, no matter how friendly they wanted to be, not to let one of the beggars on deck.

"About half a mile away we saw one of them, who appeared to be a bit lighter in colour than the rest, stand up in the bow and wave a kind of message. He kept one arm going like a semaphore. Then we saw that he carried under the other arm a basket—a peace-offering of yams and fruit, no doubt. He had only a shirt on, and still he kept his right arm working. When he got within hailing distance, the man in the bows shouted my name. He was a brawny chap. I thought to myself that if it came to a row I would pot him first, for he was ringleader.

"All the rest were naked. His scanty uniform marked him out. Probably he got that shirt from the owner of the sunken lugger. I wetted my lips with my tongue as I thought it might be my duty to wipe him out. Then my name was shouted out again, and, recognising the voice, I discovered the man in the shirt to be a well-known character who goes under the name of ———.

"'I've got something nice for you, captain! Don't look so nasty with that rifle to an old friend!'

"Still keeping our rifles ready, we let the boat come alongside and the tinted man passed up the basket, It was native-made, and all the top was covered with green leaves. Thinking of fresh yams and fruit, I pulled off the leaves, and there—poof!—the head of a man-an old man who must have died a violent death about two days before.

"The man in the shirt laughed loud and long at the disgust in my face, and, coming on board, soon told of the tragedy of which the awful head was a symbol of retaliation.

"The owner of the sunken lugger had fitted her out with unusual care. His crew consisted of natives of the island off which we were lying. As a special inducement to one of the boys, whose name was Massai, he had promised a rifle, but designedly withheld the gift until towards the end of the term of agreement. Massai had persistently begged for the rifle, and it having become necessary for the Boss' to take a trip to the port, he had definitely, promised to bring it with him. Again he designedly forgot. Massai became morose. Things went on calmly enough until one day, when the mate was below, the 'Boss' was suddenly thrown overboard. As he floundered on the surface one of the boys struck at him with a tomahawk, and then he must have realised that his life was at stake.

"Diving until well clear of the boat, he swam off to the lugger, about a quarter of a mile away. As his master came up, Massai leaned over the side, his master's rifle in his hand.

"'Don't shoot me, Massai,' he shouted. 'I give you good rifle belonga yourself.'

"Massai shouted back, 'Me catch 'em plenty riple! You no good!' and fired. The bullet splashed over the man's head. The next struck him fair in the forehead, and he sank.

"In the meantime Massai's confederates were sporting with the diver, hauling him up to the surface, pumping sufficient air to keep him alive, shutting it off until he must have been nearly suffocated, reviving him with fresh supplies, and with joy prolonging life until the fun of the thing ceased; then they had cut the pipe so that he might drown.

"The lugger having been ransacked, she was fired, and she had sunk at her anchorage.

"A few days after the man with the shirt arrived at the island, and since these simple children of Nature cannot keep their doings to themselves, he very soon was made a confidant, learning the whole details of the tragedy by pidgin English and expressive pantomime, and obtaining as proof the coat of the reckless man who had made a promise to Massai which, possibly, he had never intended to fulfil. The plot of the revenge and murder had been hatched out ashore at the instigation of Massai's mother.

"Fortified with full information, he sailed away to a neighbouring port, where he exhibited the coat of the murdered 'Boss.' Being impressed, the official representing the majesty of the law gave some vague commission to the man, who now wears other clothes than a shirt, and he sailed away for ports unknown.

"Interpreting his commission to make further inquiries very broadly, he appeared off the island, and received a cordial welcome, for he was 'Hail fellow well met' with the inhabitants of many a remote isle. He made himself very friendly, and the frank natives rather gloried than otherwise in the recitation of evidence which condemned them.

"Then he made plans for unauthorised punishment. Having disarmed suspicion—just as the boat's crew had done in the case of his friend—he waited, and one dark night surrounded the village with a well-armed, hostile force. These Papuan villages are fortified in a certain sense. Some of the exits are set with traps and spring spears, and none but those in the secret dares venture along a track when the village has been made secure for the night.

"The man with the shirt posted his forces so that the exits were commanded, and waited for dawn, his instructions being that no demonstration was to be made until he gave the signal. Before the designed time a shot was fired, and the conscience-stricken community fled, all save one old man and infant, who met their fate.

"The village was spoiled and fired, and thus retributive justice done to those who had wantonly murdered two white men and destroyed their property.

"Once again," said the captain, "my luck was out. Goodness knows! There might have been a big pearl in that patch. We didn't wait to find it!"

SNAKE AND FROG PRATTLE

"Surely, then, it interests us to know the lot of other animal creatures. However far below us, they are still the sole created things which share with us the capability of pleasure and the susceptibility to pain."—HUXLEY.

It may be edifying to confess a particular interest in man's first enemy-not such interest as the man of science displays when he seeks to add to the knowledge of the world, but a kind of social concern. None of us is likely to forget that on the authority of Holy Writ the serpent became familiar with mankind very shortly after his appearance on earth, and whispered injurious secrets into guileless ears. Ever since the scene in the Garden of Eden, war between man and the serpent has prevailed, and now, if we are to credit the sayings of the wise, the end of all reptiles, if not actually in view, cannot be long postponed. Is it not mete, therefore, to take fair opportunity of studying the characteristics and qualities of an animal, closely associated with us by fable and in fact, which is doomed to extinction by the ruthless strides of civilisation, which is regarded by some as cleanly and decent, and by others as repulsive and direful? Plain, unromantic, unsensational statements make for the acquirement of knowledge illustrative of the habits and faculties of the creature against which the hand of the average man is raised with a mixture of wrath, vengeance, and fear.

By study and observation one may come to understand the higher principles of Nature, and so learn how to withstand influences inimical to his interests without upsetting laws which tend to his welfare.

Occasionally quite casual happenings and bare and slight matters of fact show that those who study natural history first-hand acquire information not to be obtained from authoritative works. Let one instance concerning the varied diet of the death adder be quoted, since it confounds the experience of one of the most learned men in Australia on the subject. On the beach just at high-water mark, beneath an overhanging shrub, several birds sounded an alarm, notifying by peculiar and persistent screeching the presence of an enemy. After a few minutes' search, for the strained attitudes of the birds indicated the direction, a death adder was seen gliding among thickly strewn brown leaves with a limp bird between its jaws. It was quickly killed, and then the bird, a dusky honey-eater, was seen to be dead. Dusky honey-eaters generally spend their days among the topmost sprays of flowering trees and shrubs, while death adders habitually seek the seclusion of the shadiest places on the surface of the soil. In this case the adder was small, so small that it seemed to be a vain if not impossible feat for it to swallow the bird.

Hitherto the food of the adder had been deemed to be frogs, lizards, beetles, and such game of the ground. Was it curiosity which brought the sun-loving bird within reach of the shade-loving snake? Upon the incident being referred to Mr. Dudley Le Souef, who has quite an uneasy familiarity with Australian snakes, dating from the days of ardent youth, when he was wont to carry some species about with him in his pockets, that authority wrote: "I did not know that death adders ever killed birds; I did not think they were active enough, their usual prey being frogs, lizards, etc. The honey-eater must have been taken unawares."

Though scientifically regarded as "the most dangerous and probably the most deadly" of Australian snakes, the death adder has to its credit many everyday proofs to the contrary: so many, indeed, that some are inclined to class it as comparatively harmless, the reasons for such opinion being—(1) the small size of the creature, reducing the risks of its being interfered with inadvertently; (2) its amiability; (3) the fact that unless the sensitive membrane at the end of the tail, to which the curved spine is the culminating-point, is trodden on or otherwise insulted, the chances are that there will be, no active resentment. While adopting all precautions, accepting no risks, and being very eager to reduce the number by all and every possible means, it is well to avoid overexcitement; for though the reptilian age is passing away, those who live in the bush are too often reminded that snakes are still numerous, and some of them decidedly vicious.

To disappoint the snake and at the same time to discredit its reputation, calmness on the part of the individual who may happen to be bitten is counselled. He should behave as a neighbour who one dark night stepped off his verandah barefooted on to nearly cleared land. As he strode along the scarcely distinguishable track, he trod on something other than a half-burnt stick. Almost instantaneously the Scripture was fulfilled—the serpent had bruised the man's heel. Now, this man has been in many strange, not to say fear-provoking, situations, and has listened to more than one close call without spoiling the occasion by anticipatory and hideous outcry. He does not smoke or drink whisky or give way to any nerve-affecting habit. He lives within hearing of the soothing lullaby of the sea. When his heel was gripped he did not jump or offend the air with unmanly plaint and ineffectual clamour, or otherwise fluster his heart with pernicious apprehension. With calm deliberation he put his hand into his pocket and drew forth—no! not a razor-edged knife, with which to slash the region of the punctures, but a box of matches, so that the scene might temporarily be surveyed. He saw, not the expected death adder, not a deadly copper head, not the venomous black which flattens and distends the neck like a cobra when its passions are roused, not the great red pugnacious beast which has been known to kill off-hand a big horse, but a shame-faced carpet snake, which, though innocent and inoffensive, will, like the worm, turn if rudely trodden on. The snake was quite ready to apologise for impulsive and graceless misbehaviour; but it seemed fascinated by the sudden light—how little of brightness bewilders such lovers of darkness—and maintained its repentant attitude until the sacred law was finally vindicated by the fatal bruising of its head.

Many years ago a locality a few miles away suffered from a raid by bush rats, which congregated in great numbers. Similar plagues have often been recorded from the western downs; but the coastal visitation was singular, for it was associated with death adders, which seemed to be on good terms with the rats. One of the settlers was growing sweet-potatoes on a fairly large scale for pig food, the plough being used for the harvesting of the crop. Seldom was a furrow run for the full length of the field without turning up both adders and rats. Suddenly the rats migrated, and then the death adders disappeared, few of either being seen for a decade, when the association between them was again sensationally illustrated. The daughter of a settler rose at dawn, and with others ran off to the vegetable garden for salads for breakfast. While she was looking for a seemly cucumber, a rat was disturbed, and almost immediately after she was bitten by a death adder which had lain inert at the very spot whence the rat had fled. The child recovered, while the deceptive snake, which will not submit to have its tail saluted even by the airiest of treads, was killed. Not only have we here another proof of the non-fatal character of the bite of an adder, but a singular instance of association between an adder and a rat. Why and for what purpose does this apparent amicability exist?

Sometimes mankind is startled by the unexpected appearance of a snake. Will credit be given to an almost magic disappearance? Those who hearken to the voices of birds learn to discriminate between the language of content and happiness and love and that of dismay and terror. A number of loud and pleasant-noted fasciating honey-eaters suddenly changed their tune to that indicative of fear. They were, gathered on a thick-leaved tree on the edge of the jungle in a crude circle, with heads pointing to a common centre. It was simplicity to conclude that a snake was present, but not at all easy to see it, for the flustered birds began to change their manoeuvres directly help was at hand. Eventually a thin brown snake was seen doubled up and apparently sound asleep among the branchlets The gun was called for, and two others hastened to the scene, each of whom distinctly saw the snake. When the shot was fired, a peephole was made through dense leafage just where the snake had reposed, but with the report it had 'disappeared. Fragments of twigs and leaves came to Mother Earth, but even a smart black tracker failed to find a trace of the snake, though the force of the explosion must have carried portions out into the open. The point of this artless narrative is that the black boy formed the firm opinion that that which he and two others had concluded to be a snake must have been "'Nother kind. Him no good. Close up 'debil-debil!'" To him a visible snake was quite commonplace; but one that vanished under the impulse of a charge of shot represented a mystery which called for caution and hasty departure, and the boy strode away with the suggestion of hot bricks below. But the tell-tale birds, suspicious of the material only, returned, stared at the vacancy, and fluttered off with—was it?—a note of thankfulness.

The serpent has one infallible, perhaps because it is automatic, regard for its own comfort and well-being—it cannot be induced to tie itself into a knot. It is in mind that once in the old country a very long and very cold lethargic boa constrictor became benumbed and forgot the primal instinct of the family, and paid for its absent-mindedness with its life. But the ordinary snake under extraordinary conditions, whatsoever its length, is most careful to disentangle itself even when knots are designed for the special purpose of embarrassing it. Though the head of a snake be battered until all apparent sense is obliterated, the lithe body will cleverly evade attempts to cause it to disregard the great law. However tight the corner into which it may squeeze or narrow the quarters into which it may be driven, and though head and tail may be close together and in the midst of a complication of coils, and the twisting and writhing may appear to be without method, yet the snake emerges a triumph of single purpose.

A complication was presented to a 6 foot 8 inch specimen, and truth bids me say that the snake did not seem in the least bewildered. From a nest of eggs six had disappeared in one night. The loss was debited to a snake, and it being calculated that the meal would suffice for several days, no particular zeal was displayed in tracing out the thief. Experience has taught that snakes do not wander very far when good and nutritious food is to be obtained by intrusion on the cosy quarters of a pet hen., Three days were permitted to pass, and then in the nest a rat trap was placed baited with two eggs, the door being secured with wire. The bait proved to be irresistible and the trap effective. In the morning the trap was crowded with snake, which had thrust its head between the wires, swallowed the eggs, and was a prisoner until they were dissolved by the processes of digestion or the door was unbolted. The natural process was not complete when the discovery was made, but the snake had managed to make itself as comfortable as possible in its temporary habitation. The trap seemed almost suffocatingly full, and when the occupant thrust its head and more than half its length between the bars, only to be checked by the hard-hearted eggs, it was thought that possibly, in its confusion, the snake might entangle itself; but invariably it retired into the trap without putting itself into any false position. It was killed, the executioner justly reflecting that a snake has mental limitations. Nothing could induce it to tie itself into a knot, and yet, wilfully and with its eyes open, it had entered a trap from which there was no possibility of escape until in the course of nature it had digested the bait.

Is it generally known that a snake does everything with its eyes open—that it is denied the privilege of closing its eyes? Such is the indisputable fact. 'But without presuming to trespass on the preserves of men of science, the belief may be expressed that some species, if not in possession of a movable eyelid, have some means of suspending the faculty of sight. Indeed, there is evidence in support of the view that one species has a membranous eyelid similar to, but slighter than, that of a bird. It is not to be doubted that another reptile— the green turtle—is thus endowed, and that the "winking membrane" is found in many animals at the inner angle or beneath the lower lid of the eye. This membrane is represented in animals by a rudiment only. In the eyes of human beings the small reddish patch in the corner corresponds to the winking membrane—indeed, is the vestige of it. In monkeys, and in most mammals below them, there is present in this vestige a small piece of cartilage, and this is found occasionally in man. In white races it is very rare, occurring, as far as observations have shown, in less than one per cent. Recent investigations by Dr. Paul Bartels show that in twenty-five South African natives whom he had examined it occurred in twelve. Another investigation found it five times in twenty-five Japanese. It is curious to find that vestige more common in certain races, as it shows that in this small point they are less advanced than the white race.

This quotation from a forgotten source supplies important links in the chain of evidence in favour of the theory that certain species of snakes may have the winking muscle, which exists in marine reptiles and is present in some human beings. Apart from theory, it has been my good-fortune to see a sleeping snake the eyes of which were obscured by a greyish film, giving it the appearance of being "wall-eyed." Being satisfied that it was blind, for it betrayed no uneasiness at a threatening demonstration, a determination was made to preserve it for critical examination. As soon as the snake was touched the cloudy veils were withdrawn, and the eyes flashed with the fire of malignity. It appeared to be spiteful because it had been caught napping. The specimen was not preserved, although it was bottled.

The blacks of this district are more nervous about adders than any other snake, with the exception of that known to them as the "Wat-tam" (pronounce the "a" as in cat), and believed to belong to the same genus as the brown snake. This is a large snake, reddish-brown in colour, the underside, for about half the length, being bright orange, the tint gradually subsiding to pale yellow towards the tail. Post-mortem examination of the first specimen detected on this Island cleared up a bush tragedy. A nest had been built in a conspicuous spot by a pair of shrike thrushes, which the blacks, according to locality, know as "Moorgoody" and "Too-dring." The birds are the sweetest-voiced of all natives, and become wondrous tame and confiding. After the big spotted and blotched eggs were hatched, the hen would perch on the side of the nest within a foot of admirers, accepting compliments with tilted head and bright and twinkling eyes. One night the brood disappeared, and desperate things were held in store if ever a snake were found in the neighbourhood. Two days after, the alert dog gave tongue, his language demanding urgency and extreme caution. Within twenty yards of the site of the violated nest he was found "setting" at a big snake, which had raised the forepart of its body and appeared to be concentrating its strength and agility on one fatal and perfidious spring. But the faithful dog was watchful too, and agile, as he crouched fearlessly across the track of man's first enemy, with its crafty pose and glittering eyes. The black boys stood afar off, for the "Wat-tam" is so arrogant and pugnacious that it does not hesitate to attack a man, invariably with fatal results if great vigilance be not exercised—at least, such is their belief. Science, however, shows that though the snake has poison fangs, they are located so far back in the jaws as to be practically ineffective. Its fierce demeanour is probably, therefore, assumed for the purposes of intimidation. The gun speedily put the wicked-looking snake out of action, and a bulge in the body indicated the site of the last meal—the confiding thrush and her fledgeless brood. The incident illustrates another favourite theory—viz., that venomous snakes have a specific, distinctive odour, which warns animals likely to be attacked of their presence. The dog kills green tree, ordinary whip snakes, and the black, white-bellied species fond of reposing in the mounds of scrub hens, without ceremony and with all the zest and enthusiasm of a good sport; but in the case of venomous species so far he has not failed to call for help, but if assistance be delayed he takes the law into his own hands.

Be it far from me to cast doubt on the truth of that which follows. The record is found in "Memoirs of the Queensland Museum," vol. ii., page 43: "Although the scientific worker is hopelessly handicapped by the vividly imaginative journalist when snake stories are told, yet occasionally there are noticed incidents startling enough in their way. During the cooler months a young and lithe DIEMENIA PSAMMOPHIS, Schleg, popularly known as a 'whip snake,' usually retired under a piece of bark placed in its case, and it was only to be tempted out on warm and sunny days. On one occasion a small skink lizard was introduced, and the snake commenced a lively chase. The lizard ran under the bark, and on reaching the other side scampered back over the top, closely pursued by the snake. Again the lizard entered the bark tunnel, through which the tail of the snake was rapidly disappearing, making a spurt to keep up with the main body. The snake darted for the lizard, missed it, and then seized its own retreating tail about two inches from the tip. With characteristic pertinacity it held on, and apparently the classic episode of a snake swallowing itself was to be attempted. It was not until the snake was taken, out of the case and forcibly handled that it let go, there being apparently no distinction to the ophidian palate between its own flesh and that of its favourite lizard." The only comment that an unversed student of Nature may presume to make on this incident is that, possibly, the snake retained its tail because it could not do otherwise. Are not the jaws and teeth of some snakes so constructed, that the privilege of rejection is denied? The interests alike of science and the speculative world demanded that in the circumstances Nature should not have been balked. Why deprive the serpent of having its own blundering way with its own tail?

There is no doubt that man does directly benefit by the conflicts which rage continuously between living things lower in the scale of life than himself; but the common slaughter is at times so cruel and so inexplicable that it is not given the average intellect to discover good and sufficient cause, though he may observe the more obvious habits and appetites of frogs and snakes. The former oft implore aid against the attacks of green tree snakes and of a big light brown lizard, fond of sleeping in hollow logs, and since one does not understand from the beseeching tones of the frog whether it is being molested by the universal enemy or not, he often hastens to the rescue, laboriously cuts down to the scene, to find, instead of a snake, a lizard, perhaps more useful in the harmony of Nature than a frog, and certainly more endearing, since it possesses the habit of silence. Unless the frog is past recovery it has become a practice to scare the lizard, and to suggest to the frog the sanctuary of another hollow.

But frogs are not always considerate of other and gayer creatures. A friend who possessed a pet canary noticed that one morning in the cage of his pet there sat a panting frog, blinking in the sunlight. Thinking that the intruder had entered the cage to assuage his thirst, he did not eject it. It was the habit of the canary to hail the smiling morn with cheerful carol. In a few minutes unaccustomed silence prevailed, and then it was noticed that the frog was distended to a degree which must have caused it infinite satisfaction, while the canary had vanished. The conclusion was obvious and damning. Being accustomed to post mortems, my friend settled the point forthwith, the warm canary being revealed, with but slightly disarrayed feathers.

A further illustration of the capacious and criminal appetite of the frog may be quoted. The wet season had been generous and prolonged, the crop of frogs prolific. The verge of a lagoon was crowded with active and lusty creatures, belonging, if colour was to be accepted as evidence, to different species, in fairly equal numbers. A casual glance inspired the thought that the occasion was nothing more than a vast assembly of greys and greens enjoying the pastime which boys imitate. All round were leaping frogs engaged in contests—greys against greens. Suspecting no evil intent, it was interesting thus to note the derivation of the game we have all played in sportful youth;

but closer inspection proved that, instead of a friendly tournament on the grand scale, the rival frogs were indulging in shocking cannibalism. A grey frog would approach a green, when each would appear to become fascinated by the appearance of the other. Thus would they squat for several minutes, contemplating each other's proportions and perfections. Then both would leap high with mouths agape, and that which timed the feat to the best advantage, or had the widest gape, seized the less fortunate, and slowly and with much straining and little apparent joy swallowed it. Often the rivals would not meet in mid air, and the lapse provided the delusion of innocent play. There were hundreds of examples of absorption of the least fit by the fittest to survive, and the chronicling of the cannibal feast would be incomplete if a singular detail were unrelated. The participators seemed of like size. Complexion alone varied and foppish discrimination was exercised, for since dog does not in a general way eat dog, greys did not eat greys or greens greens. With unswerving decision, greys swallowed greens and greens greys, and extreme corpulency was the inevitable result. Does this not smack of the snake story? It certainly does, but it has the virtue of being unexaggerated, and why shrink from the telling of the plain truth?

An unwitnessed tragedy may be told in a very few words. About twenty-five feet above high-water mark was the shaft of a white sand-crab. The site was not common, for the crabs are in the habit of burrowing well within the range of the tide. For two or three days—for the spot was at the back of the boat-shed and under daily observation—the alert creature was oft disturbed by my coming and going. One morning it remained motionless on the verge of its retreat. It seemed to be on guard, and as a companionable feeling had been aroused, I was careful as I passed not to unduly affright it. The statuesque position being abnormally retained, I stooped down, to find the crab dead, with the froth still on the complicated lips, while beside it was a huge wolf spider, "tremendous still in death," with head crushed to pulp. One may theorise that the spider invaded the crab's burrow and was promptly evicted; a fight took place for possession of the retreat, resulting in untoned tragedy. Venom and ponderous weapon each had done its work. Each participant had been victorious, each a victim.

A still more singular bush conflict was witnessed by a friend. He heard, and not without concern, the pleading of a frog from the assaults of an enemy, but having far too many of them about the premises decided on noninterference, thinking that the hungry snake would soon silence the clamour. But the cries becoming shriller and more piteous, he investigated, finding among the leaves of a creeper on the verandah a large green Mantis—religiosa, too—voraciously making a meal off the hind-leg of a little green frog, which it grasped firmly. Almost the whole of the flesh of the limb had been eaten, and the observer was of opinion from the rapacity of the insect that there would have been little left of the screaming frog if he had not interfered.

THE BUSH TRACK

"They trade with Nature and the earth—a trade by which all that breathe upon the earth live."—RALEIGH.

It has no beginning. It ends—who shall say where Every high tide smooths away the footprints of those who use it now, just as it did the erratic tramplings of the host of the past. In those free, unregulated days piccaninnies sprawled and scampered hard, glistening beach; young men and girls there; men lazed and fought on its convenient spaces; women wandered on the serious business of food-getting. The camps stood a pace or two above high-water mark in the meagre shelter of sighing casuarinas, and were often changed, for there were six miles of gently curving, ripple-embroidered shore on which to rest. To this day most of the traffic is regulated by the tide. High water drives the wayfarer to the loose, impeding sand, over which the great convolvulus sends its tireless tentacles, to be thrown back twisted and burnt by salt surges.

The ebb discovers a broad space, firm and wellnigh unimpresslonable. The barefooted traveller may walk for miles and be trackless, so tough and elastic the moist sand. It is not an officious thoroughfare, made formal and precise by coarse hands working to plans correct to a hair, but subject to economic deviations of some soulless contractor. It was not laid with the foundation of the earth, and compacted by heat and stress. It is still in the making, and sand, coral, and shell-grit ground to pollen-like fineness and certain chemicals from the reef outside are among its component parts. One other element invokes perpetual thanksgiving—the flaked mica, which glistens delusively with hues of silver and gold, and gives to the tide-swept track that singular pliancy which resists the stamp of passing generations.

Midway between high and low water is a zone sensible to the airiest tread, being fitted for such temporary effect by a mechanical operation. Millions of the smallest of crabs, sand-tinted, delicate, apprehensive and alert, possess this area, working out their destiny by digging circular shafts. Obedient agents in the execution of the imperative ordinances of Nature, they have the quality of compacting the almost fluid spoil and carrying it to the surface in pellets complementary to the size of the individual, and such pellets retain their rotundity. They are scattered about, not without design, as may be seen if the industrious workers are closely observed, and in such profusion that the feet of the user of a crab-infested zone must press them flat. Then it is that the track becomes visible as far as the eyes reach. But the incoming wavelets, babbling in unison, dissolve the myriads of laboriously lifted pellets, effacing the record of the passing of man. As the tides ebb, the crabs begin their work again, preparing for the next-coming wayfarer. There is something almost incomprehensively great in the tireless activities of the nervous crabs, for not only do they carry compacted sand from their burrows, but they seem to spend odd moments in forming similar globes from material gathered from the surface. Digging, furrowing the surface in stellate patterns, moulding pellets which to the tenderest ripple are but the plaything of a moment, so are the lives of the shy crustaceans spent. What may be the motive for the perpetual labour, as useless, apparently, as the rolling of Sisyphus's stone? For part of the year the beach is the resort of the red-necked sandpiper, which has an enormous appetite for the small, live things of the sea's margin. To bewilder the birds and so reduce the risk to life, Nature imposes the task upon the crabs of forming replicas of themselves not readily distinguishable in size and tint, which represent labour unconsciously expended as life insurance, and serve the subsidiary purpose of detecting the passing of man.

What material has been left by the wayside for the history, not to be altogether despised because of its rusticity, of the unstable ways of one of the ancient peoples of the world, now few in numbers, forgetful of the past, estranged from the customs of their fathers, and dying without mourners and without records? Search the sites of camps the track passes, and there is naught to tell of the manner of those who recently occupied them save a tomahawk or a rare domestic implement of stone, and such stones do not preach thrilling but distinctive sermons. Why hurry along this pleasant way? Is not the one domestic appliance of the long-deserted camps worthy of passing notice? There it rests, half buried in the sand—a worn stone, with two others complementary to it to be had for the searching. It is meet that the most primitive of mills should be examined, and that one of the several and slow processes by which a poisonous, repugnant, and intractable nut was wont to be converted into food should be cited to the credit of the economic forethought of the most thriftless of people.

On adjacent flats and slopes grow survivals from one of the most ancient of all plants—a Cycad, that botanical paradox, combining some of the characteristics of the lie palm and of the pine with the appearance of a tree-fern, while being of distinctive order, which flourished during the age when the Iguanodon and the Polacanthus and other monstrous and ungainly reptiles roamed the land.

Let us rest awhile reviewing the earlier operations by which its nuts were rendered innocuous, and while the ghosts of the past make and bake their bread.

The fresh nuts of the plant (CYCAS MEDIA) known as Kim-alo, were roasted, and while hot bruised between two stones, the upper (Ookara) a sphere flattened at the poles into which the use of ages wore thumb and finger indentations, the nether (Diban) flat with a saucerlike depression.

Fragments of the husks were carefully eliminated. The coarse meal was put into a dilly-bag and placed in running water below a slight fall, from the lip of which fluming, improvised from the leaf of native ginger, conducted a gentle stream. Two days were sufficient to leach the poisonous principle; but if the initial process of roasting the nuts was omitted—as in some districts—the meal was submitted to the purification of water for as long as two months, when it would be tasteless. It was then ground on the nether stone by the Moo-ki (almost a perfect sphere), used with a rotary action, until reduced to flour-like fineness, when it was made into flat or sausage-shaped cakes, wrapped in green leaves and baked. The intractability of the Cycad is such that if cattle eat the leaves they die or become permanently afflicted with a disease of the nature of rickets. To the human palate the fresh nuts-are inflammatory, and are said to cause intense pain ending with death. That the blacks discovered the means of converting such a substance into desirable food proves that they were often enterprisingly, daringly hungry.

Let us push on, there is far to go. Chance rather than principle, it has been said, turned the paths of old England into roads. Here may be studied the germ of the primal path worn by the tread of the least reflective and least mobile of human beings, the causes of its erratic course, and the transitions by which, with amendments due to the irrefutable facts of topography, it becomes formal and authoritative—a highway for the usurping race.

Leaving the shore, one branch of the track crosses the high-water fold, follows the bend of a mangrove creek, through which it Makes a muddy ford, and is firmly impressed through forest country where every tree is orchid-encumbered, and where the eager soil produces its own varieties. It wriggles up and along a ridge, with the glaucous spathes of grass trees standing like spears on each hand, and where wattle and tough she-oaks grow leanly out of hard soil, thickly strewn with buckshot gravel, rust-coloured.

Soon it descends into a low valley and through a belt of fan-palms and jungle bordering an ever-flowering stream the banks of which are knee-deep in fat, rich loam. Huge tea-trees stand in the water, where the fibrous roots are matted like peat.

Out of the moist coolness the track abruptly ascends to a pleasant forest, and thence drops almost imperceptibly to tea-tree flats intersected by Pandanus creeks, which bulge here and there into sedge-margined lagoons. In this "devil-devil" country it is barely the width of the foot, and it wanders sinuously like the trail of a lazy snake. Sometimes it is barely more discernible than such a trail, and again in the soft places it broadens and deepens, for the man with boots has taken the place of the original soft-footed traveller, and horses and cattle are ever fond of the short-cuts which their owners design.

Here a distinct branch is made towards a river, across which Nature, the first of bridge-builders, many a generation ago afforded an easy, dry passage by throwing down a huge tree. It spans from bank to bank, and the wood is worn to slippery smoothness by the passing of shoeless feet. Thence it leads through forest and jungle and mangrove belts to another river, and away south.

The western branch keeps to forest and jungle, following, generally, the ridges, for in the wet season the grass lands are flooded, when the track is but a silvery grey ribbon on a carpet of green. With careless indecision it trends west, with here an angle and there a curve, dipping and twisting, crossing gullies and creeping up slopes. The men whose feet made it in ancient days knew all the landmarks. Mostly it keeps to sound ground, albeit its wanderings perpetuate wayward impulses.

Imagination may follow the blacks of bygone days as they swung past, a fallen tree; where sportful youths wandered a few yards to throw grass-tree spears at white-ants' nests on bloodwood-trees; where they turned aside for a drink from the palm creek. Possibly the track deviated to follow the run of a scrub turkey, or because the boys knew of a scrub hen's mound, where the rich pink eggs were raked out by the gins. It was gin's work to overhaul the mounds; the boys did not like to do the digging with their hands, for often little snakes bedded themselves in the warm compost—snakes, though they bite not to the death, make one's hands big and sore. Why incur any risk when there was a well-disciplined woman to take it? There was a turn off (which was officially followed) leading to a huge tree where in the hollow bees had hived; and another straggled up the creek to the pool where eels secrete themselves in the moist, decaying leaves.

Six or seven miles from the beach, where the scarcely discernible crabs, with persistency as eternal as the sea, are strewing the way with millions of tell-tale pellets, the track, skirting swamps, following the bends of a river, passing through forest and jungle, is lost in vagueness and indecision.

When it was ordained that roads should be defined in the interests of settlers, it was natural that the original track as it then existed—broadened and amended and bridged by the good bushmen who had used it for practical purposes—should be followed. On the plan the formal road runs a strangely erratic course, for in many places it is faithful to the footpad. Some of the zigzags of the long past, some of its elbows and angles, its stringent lines and curves, have been copied and confirmed, for the bush track is one of the fundamental things, bearing the stamp of Nature, and no more to be obliterated by the trivialities of art than is the sand of the shore and the illimitable crabs.

THE LITTLE BROWN MAN

"Care, that troubles all the world, was forgotten in his composition."—
CHARLES LAMB.

If you chance to visit the Chief Protector of Aborigines on board his yacht
the MELBIDIR, one of the first to greet you, be you an old acquaintance or
a stranger, may be "Jimmy," the cook.

He is a little brown man who wears blue shoes, which are also socks, and a
perpetual smile. The shoes, which are of some soft material, have a separate
compartment for the great-toe, and hook down the heel. The Chief Protector
has a similar pair of combination shoes—a gift from "Jimmy"—and is given
to smiling; but he does not pretend to compete with his cook in that quality.
"Jimmy's" smile is almost a fixture. It is set, yet not professional. It is the
smile of a happy man, and of one who is a diplomat as well as a ship's cook.
His customary costume is of holland. When on duty he wears an exaggerated
bib, and "Jimmy" without his bib would be as little conceivable as "Jimmy"
without his smile. He may discard it when he puts on his sky-blue pyjamas
for the night, but that he smiles in his sleep is sure. The honourable wrinkles
on his mahogany-hued face forbid him to relax the appearance of unceasing
good-humour, and who would suggest that his serenity is artificial?

When he takes a hand with the whole of the ship's company to get up sail or
hoist the dinghy on board, he whistles as well as smiles, and then the black
boys laugh, and life on the trim ship is more buoyant than ever. He goes
down into the doll's-house galley backwards, smiling. Now, it is no smiling
matter to be jambed up against a hot stove on a hot day when the seas run
high and the yacht digs her crescent nose into the blue and washes her own
decks with Neptune's suds. But "Jimmy" will bob up again in due season
with a plate of hot cakes or, perhaps, even cool cakes—and the smile. He has
been smiling to the oven, which is inclined to gymnastics, only it is restrained
by effectual bolts. "Jimmy" is a gymnast, and his free great-toes enable him
to cook under circumstances and conditions which others not so equipped
would profane.

Smiles are his antidote for all injurious mental ferments, and how many
diseases of the mind are there which are not to be alleviated by such apt
physic?

It has been said that "Jimmy" is a diplomat. He certainly is. The MELBIDIR
had run within hailing distance of another yacht, the owner and commander
of which is an old friend of the Protector and "Jimmy." When we did hail, a
silvery head and a sunburnt pair of shoulders popped up from below, and
with a comprehensive wave of sunburnt arms—the red type—vanished.

Soon the same head and the same shoulders, decently but loosely clad in blue and followed by the rest of the hearty body, emerged, and in a few minutes friends were gripping each other's hands and talking furiously about a particular island, pilots, pearls, and Torres Straits "Jimmy" passed, and the florid man in blue said, nudging his friend, "I seem to know that boy."

"Of course you do," replied the Protector; "that's 'Jimmy' from T. I."

When "Jimmy" next appeared he had a jug of water in his hand and a bigger smile than ever.

"Well, 'Jimmy,' you haven't forgotten me?" suggested the big man in blue.

"No. You capitain! My word, you young fellow now!"

And we all laughed, for though the years had been tender to the man in blue, still, they had come and gone by the decade since the previous meeting. "Jimmy's" smiles became vocal. Professional diplomats use the great gift of speech, it is said, to delude the enemies of their country. "Jimmy's" adroit compliment was the more delicate in that it was not official and he cannot possess an enemy.

When he puckers his lips to whistle, "Jimmy's" smiles are singularly infectious. The Protector's yacht is not a missionary, but merely, as her name signifies, a messenger; but the Protector does not forbid the hymnal. "Jimmy" has one, and as he studies the pious poems, for he reads fluently, whistles appropriately. While we lolled on deck, familiar tunes wooed my wandering thoughts. "Jesu, Lover of my Soul," came line after line, verse after verse, precisely, though the tone was soft. Was the black boy thus accompanying his work at the pump? No; for the strokes were not in time, and the boy occasionally chatted with his chum. I asked, and was told that "'Jimmy' mak'm good fellow corroboree." Presently he came up—smiling, and with the last notes of "Abide with Me" on his lips. Then I questioned him, and for a space we discussed our favourite hymns and hummed them, or rather I did, for "Jimmy" was too shy to do more than nod in time before a stranger. He confided, almost in a whisper, that when he was alone he learned the words of the hymns, and afterwards picked up the tunes. Is it not pretty to think of the wrinkled Japanese in bunk beside the hot and clamorous engine conning hymnal—a trifle blotched with grease here and there—and whistling softly those endearing tunes on which so many of us were brought up?

Long may "Jimmy" cook and wear blue shoes a modestly supplicate "For those in Peril on the Sea"! That he may smile to the last would be a superfluous prayer. He cannot do else.

UP AND AWAY

"Man is the merriest species of creation; all above and below him are serious."—ADDISON.

"Let's up and away, Bill," said Breezy Jim, as he started to his feet. "I'm dog tired of this game. We're just working for tucker for the boys and nothing— not even a smoke—for ourselves."

"Don't be in such a flurry. We might drop on a patch yet. I vote we stay for another week. The anchorage is all right, and the season's young. The little bit of fish we've got ain't too stinking. It'll pay expenses." Placid and patient, the half-caste Solomon Islander, Billy Boolah, kept cheek on his impetuous partner, whose restless disposition forbade him to continue long in one stay unless circumstances were essentially favourable.

Certainly fish were not too plentiful, but the aboriginal crew worked well, and were lighthearted almost to a fault. They had had no credit to pledge for the season's stores. They had merely to pick up inert and unresisting béche-de-mer from among the coral five fathoms down, where the deceptive sea looked no more than ten feet deep under the squalid flatties; to smoke and jabber in idle moments; to eat and to sleep, and to listen to Mammerroo's version of the opening phrases of "The Last Rose of Summer" on a mouth-organ worn with inveterate usage to the bold brass. The tune was not quite beyond recognition, and no musician was ever more in earnest, ever more soul-tied to an elusive, unwritten air than the black boy who wore little else than his own unwashed complexion and a strip of red Turkey twill. For long months he had pursued it with all the fervour of his simple soul, and though it said him nay, still did he hope and woo. Out of his scanty earnings he bought mouth-organs by the dozen, for he believed that owing to some defect on the part of such instruments the tune was impossible save to one. Would he ever obtain that prize? The organ which could play that tune as he had once heard it when his boss took him to a concert at Cairns had to be discovered, and to earn money to buy it Mammerroo shipped on these detestable béche-de-mer cruises. In the meantime he would play with all his energies and with endless repetition the halting, nerve-disturbing notes he knew to be incorrect.

"That boy will drive me mad. He bought ten mouth-organs at Cooktown, and he hasn't got the one that plays the tune yet. Does this smell like 'The Last Rose of Summer'? Why, you can hear those fish of yours humming! What with hardly any fish, the stink of the whole boat, and that maddening mouth-organ, I feel almost inclined to jump overboard and marry a mermaid. Let's chuck it."

"It's you as got the bad breath, Jim. Every man when he gets nasty temper he gets bad breath. That tune it's little bit close up. He can play right up to the 'left blooming alone' sometimes."

"He's taken four months to get up to the 'left blooming alone'! At that rate it will be years before he gets to the finish. I'll be mad if he stays on this hooker another month. I'll chuck the three of them—organ, boy, and tune—overboard."

"If you make yourself a fool like that, no more work from that boy. Don't be a fool and spoil this game. We're out till November. Let's make the best of it."

It was not clean work. The reek of the fish-raw, cooked, smoked, and drying in the sun-saturated everything, even the damper. The brown, shrivelled things were scattered in orderly profusion wherever the sun could catch them to top them off prior to bagging. The bitter, eye-searing smoke from the red mangrove fire in the hold, where the meagre catch of yesterday was lying on a couple of trays, stung the nostrils. The odour was as interminable as the half-accomplished tune, and Breezy Bill writhed. He was not new to the game, but bad luck had been the portion of the ship from the start, and small things irritated him, rasping his far from sensitive soul.

"I think you are going to catch fever, Jim. That's what's the matter with you. At the mission I used to read about that bird you call the brain-fever bird. It just keeps on whistling the same old thing, and white men go mad. That 'Last Rose of Summer,' it's got hold of you. Don't be a fool! It's only a good tune half done. It won't kill anybody—at any rate, a tough old shell-back like you!"

"Oh, bother! Stinks and rotten 'Last Rose of Summer' are driving me mad. I could stand lots of both if we were doing well. They might be forty overproof and played by forty bands, and every darned piccolo of them out of tune, if only we were making money. Come, let's up stick and away. We can't do worse and we might do better on that bit of 'reef Mammerroo talks about. Here, Mammerroo, stop that blasted corroboree! Come and tell us where that little fella reef sit down."

Mammerroo shuffled down to the hatchway covering and traced a chart of the locality with a grimy forefinger.

"That fella reef sit down 'nother side Red Hill alongside mainlan'. No deep water. Plenty mangrove—my word full up pigeon. Reef him little fella. Full up tit fish, calla-calla, mainlan' black. Fill'um up boat. Take'm alonga Thors'dilan'. Come back. Fill'm up one time more. Too much. Full up."

"The same old yarn. I've been all over that ground. There's no reef there, and if there had been it would have been found and skinned years ago," said dogmatic Billy, with a sneer.

"I see," said Jim; "the season's over as far as you are concerned. You can go where you like. I'm sick of it now."

TROPIC DAYS

The next morning saw the NAUTILUS scudding before a strong south-east breeze, Jim, true to his name, sulky as a toad-fish. The good wind harped on the rigging as Mammerroo tirelessly lagged after the ever evasive tune. Jim heard him not. Billy, in a rage, was inclined to bundle the boy and his battered instrument overboard, for he saw in the race north nothing but a waste of time.

Three days later the NAUTILUS anchored to the north of Red Hill under the lee of a low mangrove island uproarious with nutmeg pigeons.

All hands turned out to prospect, with Mammerroo as pilot. He was not long in locating the reef—a forgotten and neglected patch that teemed with fish. Béche-de-mer lay in shallow water, thick and big, by the ton.. The reef, with its clear sandy patches, seemed to be the gathering-ground, the metropolis, the parliament of the curious creature which makes feeble eddies with its distended gills, moves with infinite and mysterious deliberation, and which, though it may be two feet long and three inches thick, can pass through a half-inch space, constricting its bulging body during the progress.

The mangroves of the islet provided the best of fuels for the preservative smoke. The fortnightly steamer passed not so very far out, so that it would be possible to send away a couple of tons at a time without leaving the locality or suspending work for more than an hour or two.

With cheerfulness and enthusiastic haste all started to work. No irritating odour, no vexing tune, was perceptible or audible. Boys brought in such quantities of fish that the mates could hardly cook and cure them. Money was being coined, and the making of money begat dreams. Seamen do not invariably build castles in the air. They devise aerial fleets. They build bigger, better, and faster boats to sail on bluer seas into more prosperous and happy havens than belong to this too substantial world. Each sketches out the boat of his desire, and fits her with wondrous comfort and conveniences. He glances, approving head thrown back, up her tall, tapering, well-oiled masts, silver-topped with golden trucks. He paints her in rival colours, rigs her with silken sails, names her after a sweetheart, and sails away to lands fairer than any of the isles of the Pacific—those isles of dreams where in coral groves the gold-lip is embarrassed with pearls of ineffable lustre and of excessive size.

As they day-dreamed they gathered in actual riches, for the lazy fish were big and almost overlying each other in their crowded spaces.

Never was there a happier béche-de-mer cruise, for the prospects of good wages soon and a quick return to accustomed camps overladen with the spoils of the Cooktown stores made each boy as joyful as a cherub and as industrious as a scrub hen. Mammerroo saw visions of mouth-organs, one of which was sure to contain the coveted tune. Little deaf Antony thought of tobacco unlimited, a silver-mounted pipe, and plenty of unforbidden rum. Indeed, most of the boys contented themselves with these ingredients to fill the cup of happiness. But big lazy Johnnie's fancy went to a small jockey's cap of red and yellow, to be worn with a football jersey of orange and green in stripes, and blue trousers. This gorgeous costume was to compensate for present pains and humiliation, for he had nothing but a scanty and dirty loin-cloth, a necklace of grass beads, and a chip of lustrous black-lip pearl-shell stuck in one ear. As they worked they let their fancies range, and thus was the toil eased and the bags of dried fish safely stowed in the hold. With twenty-eight bags in prime condition, the NAULITUS sailed out to intercept the steamer—the LAVA KAVA. The honest stuff was sent off to the agent at the Island post, and back the stout little vessel went to the reef.

"As good as a gold-mine," said Breezy Jim, who every day became breezier, so that he threatened to develop into a gale of good humour.

"Better than splitting coco-nuts at the Mission Station," said Billy Boolah.

"Do you ever feel like chucking Mammerroo overboard now?"

Another fortnight saw another big load on the way to the agents. Mammerroo poured out his soul in fervency over the limping phrases of his besetting tune, and even Boisterous Jim applauded his persistency.

"That boy will catch 'The Last Rose of Summer' some day if the mouth-organ market holds out. I'll give him the best to be got in Cooktown, and I'm bothered if I don't teach him the tune!"

Late one afternoon a strange sail came into view. Slowly the big cutter made for the anchorage, for the wind, busy elsewhere, could spare only a few idle puffs for her business.

"That's a dago, I bet," said Bill. "And I know who it is! Why, it's that humbug, Black Charley!"

"We'll have to be pretty spry, or he'll have some of this patch. We'll head him off, and ship what we've got to-morrow."

A flattie slid over the side of the cutter and plopped into the water, and Black Charley, with a couple of downcast boys, came alongside the NAUTILUS.

"Hullo, Bill! Hullo, Jim! How's yous getting on? Yous drop on good place. I see yous boys picking up fish like a hen picking up corn."

"Not much," replied Jim. "It was pretty thick, but it was only a small patch, and we've pretty well cleaned it up. Sent away half a dozen bags, mostly mainlan' black. Too close in to be much good."

"Well, I suppose you'se no objection to me anchoring here for a bit and 'seeing what I can do with the leavings?" said Black Charley.

"We found the patch, and it's too small for two boats. We'd be better friends if you cleared off and left it to us," replied Jim. "But if you're up to dirty tricks stay where you are. We don't want sneaks on board this craft."

"It's no good being nasty. All the fish on the Barrier don't belong to yous. I got a ton and more on board now, and I'm going to run out with it to-morrow."

"So are we. Come on board and have a drink"

It was late in the afternoon when the smoke of the LAVA KAVA showed south-east. Both boats were waiting as she slowed down in her course, and while they made fast transhipment began. Then she steamed slowly ahead.

"Better send you'se boys back with the NAUTILUS," suggested Black Charley, "and me and my mate will take yous back when we've had a drink and a bit to eat. It's a long time since I've had a decent feed, and Captain Andrews, he won't mind."

Breezy Jim and Bill agreeing, the NAUTILUS cast off, with instructions to anchor at the old spot and to work until the bosses returned.

There was more than one drink as the steamer forged ahead, with Black Charley's cutter romping and curtseying behind. Then tea-time came, and the captain asked his guests to remain. Black Charley had had so many refreshments that he was scarcely fit company for the saloon, so he offered his excuses and they were accepted with politely veiled relief.

The mates told of their bad luck down at the Barnards and the Palms; how they had been driven away by the unmusical black boy in desperate pursuit of "The Last Rose of Summer," and of their great stroke of luck on the reef of which he had told.

"There's plenty more fish on it yet. We'll be troubling you to stop for a couple of months yet."

"You won't be making a very early start to-morrow if we jerk your boat much further," remarked Captain Andrews, with a smile.

"Come," urged Bill. "We'll hunt up Charley and cut away back."

The well-contented partners strolled on deck, anticipating a very tipsy Charley, whom neither steward nor bo'sun could discover.

The sun had just set. A bewildering blank astern excited a wide and comprehensive survey, and there in the blue-grey of the south-east Black Charley's big white-winged cutter was fast fading from view.

When the partners got back to the reef, via Thursday Island and Cooktown, a fortnight later, the boys were there, looking somewhat jaded. The NAUTILUS was as trim as ever, for which the owners were sufficiently thankful; but cute Black Charley, working both crews day and night like galley slaves, had mopped up the patch as clean as the floor of a hospital ward.

"We've bin had proper, Bill, old fellow. Let's up and away for Cooktown. Mammerroo moans for that mouth-organ!"

And the Christian in Billy Boolah smiled as he hummed "Left blooming Alone."

"PASSETH ALL UNDERSTANDING"

"Whence has the man the balm that brightens all?"

BROWNING.

Though not popular, perhaps Tsing Hi was the best known of his contemporaries on the tableland through which the Palmer River wanders a hundred miles from the Gulf of Carpentaria. Short, slimly made as a fourteen-year-old boy, nimble, fussy, plausible, he stood out from among his countrymen as one having authority, while he posed among the Europeans as a kind of diplomatic agent, explaining away misunderstandings, conciliating grievances, and generally comporting himself as the chartered representative of the horde of yellow new-chums which invaded the most sensational of all Australian goldfields. He appeared to have cousins among every fresh shipload from China, as well as among the hundreds who ferreted in the gullies. There was not a white man, from the Police Magistrate to Frank Deester's off-sider, with whom he was not on terms of easy familiarity.

Had he not often confidentially consulted the Warden when a cousin had blundered into the hands of the police, embarrassing that flustered official with torrents of half intelligible speech, the purport of which generally was to flout the proceedings with evidence of indubitable alibi? All this he translated to his countrymen as proof of personal influence with court authorities, and, what was more to the point, made them pay for it.

No case in which a Chinaman was concerned as the accused, or plaintiff, or disinterested witness, but Tsing Hi took, if not an official, an officious part. Every new-comer from the Flowery Land passed through his hands. He knew what personal property each possessed, and the value of the gold of the lucky departing ones. That he prospered exceedingly was evident. The fact was expressed in his costume. Beyond the court fees as interpreter, the merry, chirping little fellow had really no lawful, visible means of support. Yet he glistened and gleamed with emblems of riches. He was a dandy from the soles of his shiny elastic-side boots to the crown of his jaunty hard-hitter. Across a yellow waistcoat hung a very aggressive chain, from which dangled a huge masonic jewel in gold-and-blue enamel, and the frequently consulted watch—a big, bold-faced lever—ticked with snappy determination. Tsing Hi had much more to live up to than the huge watch, the chain, and the emblem; but they seemed to constitute special and peculiar insignia. They were always to the front. He was one of the men of his day and scene—to be admired, feared, and to be conciliated by his fellow-countrymen all along the traffic-torn road.

The dust from that tortuous road rose in an earth adhering cloud from out which honest, clean-souled men came like pain-distorted spectres, wearing grey tear stained masks with pink-rimmed eyeholes and mud edged mouths. But the dust was less distressing than that which Tsing Hi threw in the eyes of bewildered mankind by this burst and gusts of speech.

In the heyday of his fame and prosperity Tsing Hi disappeared. His absences were customary, for did he not flit here, there, and everywhere? The police were not troubled to make inquiries. They knew where he was, and the reason for his sudden retirement from accustomed scenes. The next day all Byerstown knew also.

Tsing Hi, within the rough-hewn walls of the lock-up, was sad and silent. He had been arrested for gold-stealing.

It was a clear case. Hundreds of complaints had been made. Dozens of suspects had been shadowed, until a quick-witted detective intuitively fastened the responsibility on the court interpreter, who, on the instant of arrest, had become dumb.

The ransacking of his hut revealed a magazine of riches, the earthen floor beneath the bunk being honeycombed with pits containing easily portable but valuable property. In a jam-tin were several nuggets, among them the very specimen which Bill Haddon had given to Mrs. Sinclair, landlady of the Carriers' Arms—a plane of crystal from which rose a wonderfully true pyramid of gold. It had been admired by hundreds, and could be sworn to by everyone who had seen it. There was the white sapphire, with a tell-tale flaw running down the middle, which had been found in the hopperings at Revolver Point (where fighting Cameron made his pile) by Sam Kickford, and likewise bestowed on Mrs. Sinclair as a "curio," and because that bounteous lady had mothered the unlucky Sam and nursed him through the fever which took him to the very gates of a filthy hell. Dozens could swear to it, but ever so many more were capable of bearing witness against Tsing Hi on account of the specimen which Sam's mate, who had died of the fever, had given to Mrs. Sinclair, having picked it out from the face of his drive. It was a slug of rough gold in the shape of a tiny canoe, with an upright splinter of white quartz at each end. Sam's mate had intended it for a girl down at Ballarat, and she eventually got it—an emblem of what might have been. Dozens of fancy slugs were brought to light, in addition to two hundred ounces of fine gold against which no one could make good claim.

Another tin held six rings, two of decidedly suspicious metal, the others genuine and with good stones. A fine pearl was wrapped in a fragment of silk. A pale green jade amulet, with three sets of. Chinese toilet contrivances—ear-cleaners, tongue-scrapers, back-scratchers—in ivory, were in a box with two rolls of gold-embroidered silk illustrated with weirdly indecent scenes. Three gold watches wrapped in silk handkerchiefs were stuffed into a ginger-jar. The sordid hut was a mine of wealth, and the buzzing town became furious. It had accepted Tsing Hi as a character, but not as a bad one. Being deceived, it swerved from tolerance to righteous indignation and absolute wrath. The quaking thief, not too comfortable, for the bloodwood slabs seemed too frail a partition against the virtuous anger of the crowd, was condemned forthwith.

All the identifiable gold and other property was handed over to those who successfully established claims, and Tsing Hi, limp and dejected, passed into the custody of Tim Mullane for escort to Cooktown.

Tim was rough and raw, teeming with good-nature and blessed with a brogue as thick as the soles of the massive boots made for him by his cousin Terence at misty Ballinrobe. The once perky Tsing Hi slunk alongside the far-striding Tim, and Tim looked down at him and was half ashamed of such a "wee scrap of a Chinkee" as his first prisoner.

"Come away wid ye, me little fella—come away. Doan give me trouble, and ye'll fin' me gintle wid ye. Thry to maake a fool af me, and be the Holy Saints ye'll have occasion to be sorrowful." And he picked Tsing Hi up with one hand and set him down again with as big a jolt as such a fag-end of humanity could expect to produce. Tsing Hi remained meek. The crowd was unanimously against him. Big Tim might jolt him again and again rather than he would take the risk of venturing among his recent friends, for tales of his thieving, his acceptance of bribes, and imposition of levies, were coming in so fast and thick that the crowd would have relished adding something on its own account.

Before daylight next morning Tim left with his disconsolate captive, who wore handcuffs and was manacled to the "D's" in the saddle of the horse which he bestrode manifestly ill at case. In front of him was a huge swag containing the unidentifiable gold, three watches, three rings, silk stuffs, three pairs of elastic-side boots., several pairs of puce-coloured socks, flash neckties, four hats, three suits of clothes, and other clothing., All this was his own, to be handed over at the expiration of the sentence. Tim merely held the inventory. There was some sort of gratification for ill-doing, for the swag contained a fortune. He savagely reflected that six months would soon pass. He would then vanish from "Qee'lan," to enjoy himself for the rest of his days. The sadness which had stagnated during the past week began to dissolve. He sought to make a friend of his escort.

"I tink we cam' harp way to-ni', Tim."

"Shut up, you implicating tadpole! Wasn't I ordhered to hold converse wid me prisoner? Spake win Ye're spoke ter and be civil, Or I'll jolt the teeth troo your hat!"

Tim jogged on, and the led horse bearing Tsing Hi jogged after. Tsing Hi bumped until he was fain to lean heavily on his precious swag, trying to discover by sensation an' unbruised part of his body on which to jolt.

"Hi! hi!" he shouted. "Horsey, him no goo'! You l'me walk!"

Tim whistled and jogged. Tsing Hi jolted and whimpered. The hot miles wriggled slowly past. Dust lay a foot deep on the track. It was a windless day. Tsing Hi, gripping with fearful intensity his swag, could not lift a finger to wipe the stains which stood for many tears and coursed down his cheeks in tiny rivulets, making puddles on his cramped hands. He, the dandy, smothered in dust, weeping, sore in every bone, blistered and scalded, pondered over his petty sins, moaned continuously, and longed for the hard floor of the gaol.

He, a disciple of Confucius, found no present relief in the tags of the master's philosophy that he could call to mind. Tears made him a grim spectacle. The beautiful yellow waistcoat was indistinguishable beneath dirt and dust. His carefully tended queue shook out in disordered loops, and finally dangled, dust-soiled, behind. His trousers worked and wrinkled up to the knees, chafed his unaccustomed skin, and still Tim in a cloud of dust jogged on singing:

> *"Until that day, plase God, I'll shtick*
>
> *To the wearin' o' the green."*

It was a poor little prisoner, but his first and his own, and Tim was elated, and when a true Irishman is happy he becomes poetically patriotic. But happy though he undoubtedly was, even Tim was not sorry when the chance came of stretching his legs and incidentally sluicing down the dust. The halfway house looked cool and clean to him. In fact it was neither. It must have appeared a celestial scene to moaning Tsing Hi. The rough upright slabs (once rich yellow, now dingy) promised some sort of refuge from the dust, and the narrow strip of verandah a thin slice of shade. The mound of broken bottles at the rear betokened the drinks of the past, while the mind dwelt lovingly on those of the present. Three panting goats, all aslant, but tressed themselves determinedly against the end of the house, and two boys, long since dust immune, occasionally hunted the goats into the sun and away among the ant-hills. But when Tsing Hi slid from the horse and into the shade, he felt like a saint in bliss. They gave him water, and he wailed until

Tim silenced him with threats of jolts and locked the manacles round the middle post.

Tim sighed profoundly as he scented beer. "I do belave I'm dhry, Jerry. Give's a long un. I've swallowed mud by the bucket. Give the wee little divil outside a pannikin o' tay. Maybe it'll revoive, him!"

Tim drank long and well.

"I've heard about the case," Jerry said, as he filled the thick glass a third time. "Fancy the little beggar, an' him commin' and goin' as flash as ye make 'em, and pickin' and thavin' all the time. Maybe he got the ear-rings the missis is after missin'."

"Nawthin' o' the sort's in the swag we took with the raskil."

A bit of dinner in the back room waited, for Jerry believed in keeping well in with the force. Tim fed heartily, and, in spite of dust, heat, and the chatter of the children, dozed, to wake with a start.

"Me sowl to glory! It's aslape I've bin! Let's hav' a look at the little fella and be off."

The horses stood limply, as much out of the shade as in, the big swag leaned against the wall, the handcuffs lay half buried in the dust, but Tsing Hi had vanished.

"Me sowl to glory! The little divil's scooted! It's a ruined man I am! In the name of the Saints, why is blasted Chinkees made with han's an' 'em like a 'possum? Look at the wee han's on 'em to slip out of darbies like the same. He's slipped out as aisily as meself out of a horse-collar, and the face a' him as bould and as big as the hill o' hope! I'm the ruined man, I am!"

"Off after him," advised Jerry. "There's his tracks."

"Just none o' your blasted interfarances! Lave 'm to me. He's away back to hell, an' I'll folly him! How much does I owe yer, Jerry!"

"Nothing at all, sure, Tim. 'Tis little ye've had, and yer welcome as posies in May, though it's little we see of 'em here. And good luck. Shall I tell him away, back to look out V'

"Say nothing and be damned to yer! Keep your mout closed and lave me to do the bizinis me own road," shouted Tim as he disappeared in the dust, led horse, swag and all.

A mile and a half back and a bit off the road lay the narrow, sheltered flat between two forbiddingly barren ridges which Hu Dra, the gardener, had converted into an oasis. Thin-leaved tea-trees fringed the little dam whence the industrious fellow hauled water for his vegetables. Drought-stricken, broad, blue-leaved, scented ironbarks stood in envious array on the steep sides of the ridges, and grass-trees, blackened at the butts, struggled with loose boulders for foothold. The muddy water which the forethought of Hu Dra had conserved created the green patch which insulted the aridity of the ridge. He was a proud and happy man, a follower of the healing Buddha, a new-churn with scarce a word of English, and a gardener. He had a way with vegetables. They prospered under his hands, and he also prospered, for next to gold, vegetables were highly prized in that dry, almost verdureless country. Just now he swayed along with a pair of heavy baskets slung on a bamboo all the way from Wu Shu, as the pilgrim under his load of sin, and as he swayed he sang in a weak falsetto a ditty which sounded like—

"Nam mo pen shih shih chia

Man tan lai lei tsun fo;

Hu fa chu t'ien p'u sa,

An fu ssu, Li she tzn."

His baskets, each screened with languid gum-leaves, held the week's output of his garden, representing in money value at least two pounds. It wag not likely to yield half as much, for, being a new-chum, he was fair game, and it was considered smart to impose on his good-nature. He also paid through an agent a weekly levy to Tsing Hi, which he understood purchased the tolerance, if not goodwill, under all and every circumstance of the dreaded police and the populace generally. It was a tax; but Hu Dra was patient under such exactions, as all his ancestors had been. They were unavoidable, inevitable, a part of the mystery of life, and consequently to be endured, if not with complacency, at least without murmur. His profits for the week might total one pound, a princely sum considering the scene and circumstances of his birth and upbringing in far Li-Chiang, where his father had reared a large family in a shed over a sewer, and had never possessed property or estate worth more than five shillings. Soon, if this money-making business continued to thrive, he would return thither. He might—for had he not been reared to the art of living in such places?—resume the sewer habit; but with three hundred pounds in good English gold what sewer in Li-Chiang could not be transformed into Paradise?

One basket contained a huge fruit which he understood his white customers to term "plonkn"; with it was a broad-bladed knife, with which he would slice off slabs according to demand. That one item might bring him in more money than his revered father's fortune. Wrapped in day-dreams, he hummed again his chant, dwelling on the refrain with lyrical gladness—

"Li she tzu."

Perhaps it was the name of the maiden he proposed to ask to share his fortune and his portion of the sewer, and so he repeated—

—"Li she t——!"

A big, strong, authoritative hand had gripped him by the shoulder.

He screamed. The baskets sat down plump.

"Come away wid ye! I've cotched yer! I'll tache ye to escape from lawful custody!"

"No savee! No savee!" screamed Hu Dra.

"I'll tache ye, thin V' shouted Tim, and Hu Dra reeled under the severity of the first lesson—a back-hander across the face.

"Wha' for?" asked Hu Dra, still staggering.

"Come on! You know wha' for! I'll stan' none o' yer wha' for's!"

Hu Dra clung to the basket-stick threateningly.

"Fwhat! Resisting the pollis in the execution of dooty. Me bhoy, ye're a new-chum or yer niver wad be so bould. It is sarious bizinis." The stick flew out of Hu Dra's hands, and, as if by magic, he found his hands clamped in iron bands, which pinched his wrists excruciatingly.

He yelled with vexation, fear, and pain.

"Ye can holler as much as ye have the moind ter. Be jabers, the next haythen Chinkee that gits out of the darbies I clap on'm 'll be a slippery, slathery eel, and meself after fergittin' to maake a knot in his taale! Come quiet, me good haythen, and I'll dale aisy wid yer."

Hu Dra securely manacled to a scented gum, Tim dealt with the baskets, capsizing the contents and belabouring them with the bamboo until they looked as if they had been the playthings of a baboon. Hu Dra watched the foundation of his fortune vanish. He wailed.

"Come away, me bhoy! I arrest ye, Tsing Hi, fer escaping from lawful custody. Ye may be charged also with resisting the pollis in the execution of dooty. It's a sarious charge. If ye come quiet I'll maake it aisy fer ye. If ye maake it a haard job for me, be gorra I'll inuake ye sorryful!"

Hu Dra gathered that it was a case of mistaken identity. He endeavoured to explain that he was Hu Dra, and not Tsing Hi. Tim curtly informed him that he was none other than Tsing Hi, that he had been convicted of stealing gold, and while on the way to Cooktown had wilfully and with malice aforethought escaped from legal custody. He would be taken to Cooktown at once. Hu Dra understood but little of the harangue, but being a pious Buddhist, having once climbed the Holy Mountain to gain merit, and being in the hands of a strong man armed, he accepted the fate of the moment. Meekly he followed Tim to the spot where the horses had been left, and was hoisted into the saddle and manacled. It was all a dreadful mystery, but he was sage enough to accept hard facts.

"Me Hu Dra," he explained over and over again, in vain repetition.

"Ye're Tsing Hi, I tell yer. Ye're Tsing Hi in the name of Her Majesty. Haven't I arrested ye as sich?"

"Me Hu Dra," reiterated the captive as they jogged on. "Me come Coo'tow' one yar."

"Shut yer mout! Didn't I tell yer before that ye're Tsing Hi? Didn't yer wilfully and knowingly escaape from me whin I was having a bite to ate, and I had yer tied to the post at the shanty back beyant there! Naw, I'll hear no more of yer Hu Rahin'. Kape a civil tongue betune yer taath, or, be gorra, worse 'll happen yer."

Hu Dra was patient. He thought of his pilgrimage long ago to the top of Mount Omei. Was this the reward he had gained?

He solaced his soul by murmuring the pious invocation which all pilgrims to the Sacred Mount have perpetually on their lips—"Om mane padme om!"

Torn from his secluded garden and happy and profitable toil, bruised and manacled, bundled on to a fear-provoking horse, hurried off he knew not whither, through a drought-stricken land under a searing sun, the road reeking with dust—what a plight for a devout Buddhist, who had sought to avert calamity and prolong life by the ascent of the chill mount where, alone in all the world, is revealed the "Glory of Buddha."

Mystic that he was, he found sure comfort in pious meditations. Present pains of body and mind vanished as with half-shut eyes he drifted into the chill realm where he hearkened to chants of priests, the tinkling of the temple bells, the fervent response of hundreds of pilgrims as meek as himself—"Om mane padme om!"

Such was the potency of the mechanical repetition of the all-healing words that Tim presently found himself echoing them, and brought himself up with a jerk.

"It's all haythen rubbish and cussing. The pore fule's daft wid the hate and the dust and the welt I give him. Shure it's the way I have to be sorry for the crature."

Like the refrain of an infectious song, the musical phrase would not be banished from Tim's mind and lips, and so the tough, rough Irishman and the gentle exile from the Flowery Land went on their way, scarce conscious of the grimy miles, both dreamingly hailing the jewel in the lotus.

Three days later the travel-stained pair arrived at Cooktown, where Hu Dra— henceforth to be known officially and authoritatively, and in spite of all protest, as Tsing Hi—was duly consigned to the custody of the lock-up keeper, to await escort to the town where his sentence was to be served.

"He's that quare in his hid," Tim informed Jock Egan, who now had charge. "He's bin Tsing Hi-in and Hu Rah-in' and Paddy Om-in' (d'ye know the maan, Jock?) all along the thrack till it's fair fascinated I am. And barrin' him bein' the very thafe o' the wurrld, it's a poor honest body he be. Shure it's little enough truble he give me, and me all alone be meself. An' the swag of him! Glory be to God, I dunno but it's wort five hundred pounds if it's wort a sint! Yirra! but it's weery I am. It's little slape I've had. Shure the whole beesely thrack be lousy wid shnaakes; and show me the man as cud slape shweet wid maybe four of the varmint all ascroodging and squaaking nath his blanket!"

"It's quare in yer head yerself," ye're exclaimed Jock. "Be off to bed wid ye. If the sargint gets ye a-talkin' like that, he'll be afther thinkin' ye're in dhrink."

"Then, me sowl to glory; he'll jist be thinkin' fwhat I'm wishful for. It's that farefull dhry up there on the Palmer I could dhrain a bucket."

"Get to bed, yer fool! Ye're talkin' that wild, ye'll have no care for yerself. It's meself that'll git the good woman beyant there to git ye a cup o' biling hot tay."

With that Jock got him out, with papers all in order.

Hu Dra had disappeared from the tableland as suddenly but not as' tracklessly as a phantom. Lonely men in their tents and three or four mothers of families in their slab humpies looked out vainly for him for three days, anticipating necessary vegetables, and, being disappointed, slandered him courageously, while they found consolation in the reflection that if he ever came his round again they would distress and vex him by withholding payments for the vegetables of the past. Not a customer but owed him something. His country men gave notice of his disappearance to the police, and black-trackers off-hand told a graphic and obvious story. Hu Dra had begun his weekly round when he had been attacked by myalls. They had capsized his baskets and wantonly battered them to pieces. For him had been reserved the customary fate. He had been hustled off to the gorges contiguous to Hell's Gates, to be killed and eaten in peace and comfort. His hut, his cherished garden were forthwith occupied and tended by another of the race-claiming cousinship. The newcomer even demanded payment of debts owing to his unfortunate relation, but the whole population sniffed with such vigour that the claim was not persisted in. Once a Chinaman had left the district unceremoniously, more especially at the forcible persuasion of flesh-hungry blacks, his dues lapsed by unanimous consent. He became merely a fragrant remembrance. It is so still, and the virtue is as virile as the odour of musk.

To himself Hu Dra was always so. Be his official and authoritative title for the time being what it might, he was determined not to sacrifice his identity.

The gaoler found him a docile and obedient creature with an abiding affection for plants, which sprang up under his hands like magic. Within two months corners of the desert yard began to blossom, to bear cucumbers and radishes, and to be fragrant with shallots.

The pride of the gentle gardener lay in a few plants of zinnias close to a dripping tap. In bright red, gold, and white, he accepted them as substitutes for the sacred lotus, and prison flowers never flaunted more freely. As innocent as they, he deftly, tirelessly trained each plant, caressed each opening bud, cherished it as if it were a jewel, and found surcease of the pangs of exile, easement for the restraints upon liberty, and blissful consolation. Tendance upon the garden under the strait shadow of wall was to him, not a duty, not a pastime, but a ritual. The captive was happy, for here was the end of his pilgrimage.

Exemplary conduct, combined with the art with which he forced salads from the boorish soils, found him favour and earned privileges and concessions.

Hu Dra kept no count of the passing months. What was time to a contemplative Buddhist whose being was permeated with the hope of release from delusions and sorrow and of attaining final sanctification?

One morning he was summarily marched into the presence of the big loud-voiced man whose orders were obeyed with instant smartness, who told him, to his amazement and despair, that he must depart with his property. The seals of a sack were broken before him, and its contents displayed and duly accounted for—a sleeping-mat, a small red blanket, the elastic-side boots, two scrolls of sinfully painted silk, a hard round hat stuffed with gaudy handkerchiefs, three watches and varied jewellery in a ginger-jar, the quaintly carved toilet devices, the jam-tin full of nuggets, and a chamois-leather bag delusively heavy with fine gold.

The same authority which had ordered his affairs ever since he had been torn from the burnt hills now commanded him to begone.

For nigh upon two years he had dwelt passively in dream-land. This was but another wonderment entrancingly agreeable. Without endeavouring to elucidate the incomprehensible, he accepted the gifts of the gods, and asked for a yellow zinnia. It was a reality, a guarantee, an assurance.

Good, though gruff, the gaoler was wont to say that his departing guest gazed on the flower with almost religious fervour and mumbled over it a prayer; and the gaoler's insight was true, for in comparison with a flower, the masonic emblem, the pride of Tsing Hi's life was to Hu Dra but tinsel.

It passed all understanding.,

Hastening to escape from the land of bewilderment and easily gotten riches, Hu Dra-the quietest, the happiest, the wealthiest of a great company of his fellows boarded a steamer for Hong-Kong.

Many a long year after, Tim, who had blossomed into a sub-inspector, had retired on pension, and had lost most of his brogue in the process, confided in me the whole story.

"You see, my friend, it was either the sack or Chinkee for me. I got the Chinkee. There were plenty of 'em!"

TIME'S FINGER

"The more cleer and the more shynynge that Fortune is, the more brutil and the sooner breketh she."—CHAUCER.

High up on the auspicious shoulder of the Island mountain stands the Sentinel, a coarse, truncated pinnacle of granite, roughened and wrinkled by the toll of the moist breezes, alternating with the scorching flames of the sun. It overlooks the league-long sweep of the treacherous bay, with its soft and smothering sands, the string of islets of the Yacka Eebah group, while Bli and Coobie lie close under foot, set in a swirling sea.

One aspect of the Sentinel commands all the map-like detail of Pun-nul Bay, with its labyrinthian creeks among a flat density of mangroves, like lustrous, uncertain byways in a sombre field, erratic of shape, magnificent of proportion. Beyond are many islets—dark blue on a lighter plain. In the distance, on the other hand, islands and islets trail away until lost in the vague blending of sea and sky; and for a background is all Australia. In front alone does the Sentinel peer over uninterrupted space, and not always, for at times patches of white filigree mark the outliers of the Great Barrier Reef.

Looking up from Pun-nul Bay before sunrise, the base of the Sentinel 'was swathed in white—night's rumpled draperies not yet tossed aside. As the east glowed it stained the mist pink, and so warmed it that it parted into patches of luminous fluff which floated up and dissolved into crystalline air, and the great lumbering rock stood naked and bold in the sunshine.

Then it was that the apex of a splintered peak beyond the Sentinel glittered, and that Chutter-murra Wylo, the one survivor of the truculent natives, told once more of the wonderful stone for which many had ventured, which had caused the disappearance of several, which decoyed man and beast, and stored their bones close to the awful hole whence issued the smoke which made the rain, and the dread lightning, and the thunder.

None ever ventured there now; but sometimes in the early morning the stone twinkled for a moment like a malignant sprite, watchful all night, but abashed yet impudent to the authoritative sun.

Chutter-murra Wylo had so often indicated the exact locality of the stone, and had described its dire influence with such sincerity that, when it twinkled, a resolution which had been long in the back of my mind became wilful and imperative. He said that it was "on top, along oo-nang-mugil"—a gloomy place among rocks—and that the old men of the country had been wont to say that this particular "oo-nang-mugil" was the favourite resort of the "debil-debil," the to whose arrogance and awful deeds the bones of man and beast bore terrifying testimony.

Between the Sentinel and a spur to the south is a narrow ravine, from which in the rainy season mist rises like jets of steam, and this was the very spot whence the lightning and thunder ranged when the "debil-debil" lifted the mighty stone which blocked the entrance to the cave of the winds. All about was fantastic ground, peopled by evil spirits who resented the intrusion of human beings and inflicted upon trespassers peculiar punishments. Ill befell everyone who invaded that remote, almost inaccessible, uninviting region, at the very centre of which the alluring stone glittered. Of those who rashly determined to gaze at the prodigy at close quarters, some never returned. Those who did come back were vexed with burning and smarting pains; they suffered illnesses; their skin broke out into blotches; they became old and enfeebled prematurely and all, whether they survived for a few irritating weeks or a few sad years, wore to the end a startled, awe-struck air. "That fella no more sit down quiet; him frait all time," Wylo explained. And the stone was good to look at. Sometimes it was white like water; sometimes blue, like the sea; sometimes red, like "carrie-wy-in-gin" (sunrise). Sometimes it shook, and then it became so bright that the eyes were dazzled. The star-like stone had been on the rock for all time, protected by distance and mystery. Was it not, indeed, the eye of the "debil-debil" who had custody of the lightning and thunder imps, and could it not be elevated or depressed like the eye of a sand-crab? No intruder had ever escaped its vigil or the consequences of his temerity.

We were camped under the lee of a low sand-dune, the top of which commanded Pun-nul Bay. As the wind swayed its scalp-lock of twisted shrubs, the dune quivered, and rivulets of singing sand, almost as fluid and as unstable as water, trickled down, for it was one of the rubbish-heaps of the sea, over the brink of which waste was unceasingly shot.

The maze of mangroves whence weird hoots and bubbling cries and sharp clicks came at night, the stealthy sand marching over the land, the barren slopes of the mountain, and the misshapen rock, gave one's thoughts a twist in the direction of the vague and mysterious. Wylo's continual harping on the wonderful stone renewed the old longing for adventure. He had seen it from a safe distance, but from the present aspect only the indecorous glint at sunrise was visible.

The stone was a crystallised fact, but why had the blacks invested it with such ill omen? Here was a worthy quest—a beautiful if not precious crystal betokening the actual presence of a wary demon guardant over the mouldering skeletons of Wylo's forefathers! What quest could be more sensational or likely to be so famously rewarded?

Wylo was prepared to climb the mountain to the base of the Sentinel, but no higher. Secrets hidden from his intemperate, insistent gaze must surely be inconsequent. Once and for all, the legend of the crystal might be disposed of at the cost of two or three hours' climbing. I would bring it back to prove to Wylo that no irreverent "debil-debil" would ever again blink at the sun from that particular spot. As for the skeletons, they were, without doubt, as mythical as the evil spirit, and in any case a few old bones were not to scare me from venturing to the boldly obvious summit of the mountain.

Wylo went wellnigh naked, carrying a day's provisions and the rifle. I, too, was lightly clad, but wore thick-soled boots, freely studded, and with a tomahawk felt efficiently armed.

Beyond the entanglement of the beach scrub the way was open, though rough, with granite boulders half hidden among rampant blady grass. The country was decidedly hostile to the climber, though far from actually forbidding, and with Wylo in the lead—for I held myself in reserve for the final clamber up the ravine, to which the ascent to the base of the Sentinel was merely a prelude—the pace was respectable and sure. Closer acquaintance forced a certain sort of respect for the Sentinel, which was more massive, more venerable and time-worn than could be imagined from afar off, while all the scene below seemed softer and smoother and more fairyland-like than in reality.

Having indicated what he deemed to be the direct route, and firmly resolving to take no risks by peering into the domain of the "debil-debil," Wylo sat in the shadow of a huge boulder whence he could command a view of the entrance to the rock-bestrewn gorge. Not more than eight hundred feet separated the spot from the summit of the peak. A couple of hours at most and I would be down again, and, semi-seriously, I counselled Wylo to stop where he was until late in the afternoon, and if I had not then appeared to return to the camp, where he was to remain for a couple of days, when he would be at liberty to make his way to the head of the mangrove creek where the boat was anchored, with the design of bringing help to kill the "debil-debil" that detained me in his clutches. He was not too cheerful in his parting injunctions. "No good you fight'm that fella. Suppose he catch'm you, he kill you one time—finis. No good me come back. Me clear out quick!"

In all seriousness he undertook to "sit down" for two days, and finally imparted advice which might enable me to out-manoeuvre the "debil-debil," and either curb him or throw him out from his lair "with wondrous potency." Up the gorge I would find a prickly bush, from which I was to cut a leafy branch as a frontal shield. Then, when the fiend swooped upon me, its long arms and pliant hands, furnished with needle-like nails, would become embarrassed by the "nails," of the branch, and while it howled and danced I could "kill'm alonga leg" with the tomahawk. I was to be careful not to look up, for the eye of the "debil-debil" was so bright and hot that it burnt up mortal sight, leaving the intruder a blind and hopeless victim.

Discreetly valorous, Wylo was quite enthusiastic, anxious, indeed, that the quest should be accomplished by an audacious white man and at no risk to himself. Therefore did I accept his counsel gravely, and in parting promised to bring down one of the hands of the long-standing terror of the mountain as proof that I had exacted the last penalty for many demonic deeds.

Thus, good-humouredly, I began to clamber up the ravine through a perplexity of shrubs growing among loosely packed stones, thankful for strong boots and hands toughened by the sun. Overhanging trees and shrubs almost converted the ravine into a tunnel, but here and there a greenish light wrought changeful patterns on the gloomy rocks, and ferns of sombre green with unfolding fronds of ruddy brown occupied crannies and crowned rocks favoured by drips. No sound of animal life came to my cars, but an ever-increasing current of air was perceptible as the walls closed in and became almost precipitous.

The narrow footway was swept bare of loose stones and vegetable rubbish, save where the wet-season torrents had scooped out basins, or where a ledge of resisting rock made a wet-season water fall. Such places had to be discreetly scaled, for the rock was worn to polished smoothness and hand and foot holds were few and far between. Aerial roots, thin as whipcord, hung from the branches of trees crowding on the brink of the ravine, and with tasselled terminals sopped up moisture. A melancholy, humming monotone pervaded the ravine, seeming to increase in remonstrance and warning the higher I ascended. Wylo had told of the noise like a steamer's whistle a long way off. His local knowledge was being authenticated at every step. Such a sound was almost uncouth in such a locality; and there, overhanging a jutting angle of red rock, was the predicted bush with keen prickles thickset on limber branches. Half amused, I climbed to the spot, and, clinging precariously to the principal stem, cut off a branch which, falling into the ravine, slipped several yards down the smooth floor. It was not worth recovering, but a certain half-humorous sense of obedience to the black boy's cautions induced me to return for it; and as I trimmed off some of the prickles that it might be grasped comfortably, a stone clattered down, bouncing on the rock almost at my feet.

A substantial mystery! What invisible agency had given this hard fact its force? A gleeful chuckle followed by a discordant crow dissipated doubt-the stone had been dislodged by an industrious scrub fowl raking on the brink of the ravine. A sense of fellowship with the harsh-voiced bird manifested itself. A transient sensation of relief—I had not been conscious of the least mental depression—followed the thought that in and about the ravine there were other living things besides myself and snakes. The death adder, the head of which I had fatally bruised just now, had been the only sign of life, and it had been as dull-coloured and almost as inert as the rock on which it lay—an emblem of death at home in this almost lifeless seclusion. Dwelling with amusement on Wylo's suggested precautions, I bore the branch before me as I climbed a steep face, the tomahawk in my belt, intent for the time being, and as cautious and suspicious as a black boy. On the lip of what seemed to be a hollow a fig-tree grew, the naked, interlacing roots of which made the final stages of the ascent easy and safe. Briskly hauling myself up, I stepped over the edge of the depression, and the solid rock lapsed and slid underfoot.

In a flash the head of a python arose, and with gaping jaws struck as the branch fell from my hand.' In a moment I had whipped the tomahawk from my belt and slashed at the body of the snake squirming at my feet, as, baffled for a moment by the falling branch, it gathered itself for a second attack.

Few of the enemies of man are more easily disabled than a snake. Always zealous in obedience to the Biblical law, it is honest to confess to a decided preference for elbow-room when engaged in its actual fulfilment. This was a fight with man's first enemy in close and awkward quarters—a precipice behind, walls of rock in front and at either hand. Three times my length, strong enough to constrict to death a giant, wily enough to seek the cover of the matted roots of the tree, several points were in favour of the snake. My first wild haphazard stroke, which had merely scored its flesh, seemed to have roused its vindictiveness. Once in those coils, the chances of victory would be remote indeed.

Part of the python's still gliding length was within reach, while (the forepart resting on a branch) the head was but slightly higher than mine, though beyond the radius of the tomahawk.

The bulging head drew slowly back, as the snake released sufficient of its length to encompass me. The yellow, blinkless eyes, with knife-edge pupils, flashed with the hate of agelong feud as I edged against the wall. My arm was free. The lust of battle tightened every nerve. Neither flashing eyes nor strangulating length made for fear. The hitherto all-conquering snake, lord and master of the ravine, bade defiance, joining issue with the craft of its kind.

Slowly the pendant portion increased as the subtle beast seemed to concentrate all its energies on one triumphant, invincible effort.

Anticipating the fateful instant, I slashed with all my force at the portion of the body within reach, ducking simultaneously. Shooting over me, the head of the enemy struck the rock with brain-bemuddling impact. For once the serpent had been foiled. With jaws awry, the head swung limply, like a ceasing pendulum. One blow with the back of the tomahawk established the right of man to wander at will among the rough and secret places of the mountain.

Still did the swaying reptile cling with a single coil round the figtree's branch, while chill blood dripped and splashed among the intertwined and snake-like roots. A sudden tug brought the body down a squirming mass. With rough-shod heel, I fulfilled the letter of the law, bruising the battered head, and then were revealed the bosses by which, with the tail, the snake had sustained its dead weight.

Was this the "debil-debil" which had scared so many from the quest—a python which any man might kill in the open without running any risk, and which a black boy, with time on his hands, would joy to eat? Yet I own that I was somewhat flustered, and not a little tired and bruised and angry, because such an impediment had had to be cleared from the track. Was there not cause for indignation? Why should a gormandising serpent, full to repletion, lie slothfully across a highway open to all, to the checking of a holiday-making mortal in lawful pursuit of a demon-protected crystal? Let me once more vindictively stamp on its head.

But which way? Here was a dead and unscalable wall to right and left and in front, and all in deep shadow. I estimated that another one hundred feet would take me to the mountain-top, whence it would be possible to survey the scene in relation to the bejewelled rock. Descent was the only practicable preliminary towards further ascent. Utilising the interlacing roots of the fig-tree, the way down was easy enough, and, choosing the left wall of the ravine, I began a perilous climb out of gloom into sunshine, upon a conglomeration of immense granite boulders, over which the Sentinel cast a shadow. This shadow indicated that the ascent had occupied at least three hours, and in my self-complacency I had calculated to beard the "debil-debil" in his den, dislodge the crystal, and be back at the camp gloating over the escapade to open-eyed Wylo in less time.

Though a night was to be spent in the haunt of the evil spirit, yet would I proceed. I found not one but many "oo-nang-mugils," lowering caves and clefts in which scores of fearsome "debil-debils" might lurk, but which, as far as a vigilant mortal could detect, were given over to innocent bats and those sun-loving swiftlets which rear their young in nests adherent to rocks in dusky places.

Over and beneath boulders, squirming through bolt-holes and up flue-like openings, bruised and with bleeding hands, at last the top was reached, harsh with granite, and there to the right, on a gigantic splintered boulder which seemed to block the end of the ravine and to peer down into the blue bay below, was the crystal glinting in sunshine. It was not more than fifty yards away, and, easeful of mind, I sat down to munch a piece of damper. Close by a patch of vivid green moss indicated the existence of moisture and the further possibility of water. Sure enough, twenty yards down spongy moss and fern spread over a lip of rocks, and from dangling tufts and drooping fronds water dripped in melodious splashes into a shallow depression, and overflowed in a fan-shaped film. The facets and apex of the crystal reflected harsh brightness as unsullied as the moss-filtered, unstable drips which gathered second by second and were gone. How like those drips, how unlike the scarred, time-chastened rock, that steadfast slip of light which since the dawn of creation had flashed messages across the unresponsive sea.

From a ledge in which ferns and orchids grew in careless profusion—bird's-nest fern and polypodium and white-flowering orchid—the crystal might be reached by a little manoeuvring. But why hurry? Every minor crevice was embossed with spongy moss, from which sprang modest little flowers, a flower of mountaintops alone, lacking a familiar name, but which in its dainty form and rich mauve is none the less precious. While all the rest of the way had been barren or gloomy, here was brave sunshine and space, a jewel-like crystal, and moss and ferns and flowers, and calm and cool serenity which' bespoke remoteness from the "debil-debil" and all his works, and from the noisy cave of the winds. Magic there was in plenty-the air tingled with it—that exhilarating, mind-expanding silence of mountain-tops which is the most thrilling magic of all.

Leisurely glances at the mass of granite from which the crystal shone showed that from the ferny ledge it would be beyond reach, and that unless care was exercised in the dislodgment it might fall among a confusion of boulders far below and be lost for ever. My plan was of to build a buttress of loose stone on which to stand to tap it with the tomahawk. Like a miniature railway cutting, the ledge ran out on the face of the rock, so that standing upon it one looked down into the ravine; but it was broad enough to afford safe and even convenient footing.

As a final preliminary to the beginning of operations, I clambered up on to the ledge. Ferns grew among decaying vegetable matter in masses difficult to push through. Polypodiums with brown, oak-leaf like, infantile fronds clung tightly to the rocks with furry fingers, and the birds'-nests were big enough to conceal a man. A broad and comfortable path it was, leading directly under the crystal, and with haste and confidence I pushed along, smiling inwardly at "shynynge" fortune, to be in another moment dismayed by her "brutilness." The earth sank under me. I shot into an acute fissure with ferns and dust piled overhead!

Gasping and coughing, I cleared away the smothering rubbish, to find myself a fixture—jammed fast between walls of granite. Deceptive ferns had masked the crevice. I had walked along a treacherous track until at a weak spot it had given way as the gallows' trap beneath the feet of a murderer.

Light came from ahead, too. There the lancehead-shaped fissure opened on the ravine, whence it was flushed with cool air.

Was ever mortal in such a plight? A drop of eight from the spacious top of the mountain had lodged me a prisoner in the narrowest of cells. Dismayed but not despairing, I struggled frantically, working with shoulder and arms against the walls of granite. The right foot was firmly fixed, while a sensation of easiness was perceptible with regard to the left. Gently yet firmly, and fearful lest the slight grain of comfort might be fraudulent, I felt the weight of my body on the left foot, while scrutinising in detail the horrible trap into which the crystal bait had lured me.

There, a few feet below and further towards the ravine, was the skull of a human being, and still further down, where space was more confined, other bones were fixtures. There was a weird fascination about the skull, for at noon it would receive the benediction of the sun, and the diurnal glare into the secrets of the crevice had made a patch of white desert in an oasis of grey mould. The bones below, green and earthly with age, lay in disorder and confusion—poor fragments of the framework of man and harmless beasts, sharing a common fate.

Though fast a prisoner, nothing to live on but hope and fresh air, a sense of relief, somehow, sometime, established itself in my mind. Most of the significant features of the adventure had been faithfully foretold by Wylo— the prickly bush, the snake (archetype of the fiend), the mocking delusive stone, the stored bones of man and beast-all as he had described. He must have known more than he had voluntarily told, and assuredly would he come', when he would coo-ee, and I would shout for very joy. In the meantime would I possess my soul in patience and conserve all the strength of my lungs and power of endurance.

Just beyond the platform of ferns a splash of lovely tints illuminated the edge of the time-recording shadow—the solar spectrum produced by the prism which had beckoned from afar. Was there no escape from the wizardry of the crystal? No hope of evading comparison of its beauty and permanence with the muddy and fleeting passions of mankind? Yet how fruitless its functions—to glorify for aeons the intractable rock, and to leave it ever unstained! For once in all the centuries may not a human hand be interposed between those ineffectual flames and the surly rock? Cannot even that small measure of space be overcome?

A few inches from the tips of my outstretched fingers were the prismatic tints with which the crystal daily registered the decline of the day; but not for all my striving and all my wit could I get within reach. They were as remote as the creating sun!

The narrowness of the cleft forbade effort to reach down so that I might unlace my boots. There wan but one chance of deliverance—the coming of Wylo. And would he, agitated by superstitious awe, dare to venture into the haunt of the evil spirit when he began to realise that I, too, had fallen into the clutches he so much dreaded? Yet he must come! Of what special impiety had I been guilty that so rare and terrible a fate should have been reserved for me. He must come!

Yes. Listen! I hear his coo-ee far below! He is making his way up the ravine! And with, all my vocal power I coo-eed and yelled. But the muffling rocks stifled all noise at lips. Listen! Yes! The sound again—merely the mellow cadences of a swamp pheasant whooping among the blady grass.

Wylo dared not venture to the very door of the cave of the winds. I was alone with my fate! Could I master it?

The clean-cut shadow crept up the rock, and with it the colour splash receded. As I gazed it glittered and was gone. It would not be visible again until the next afternoon. Would I be here to watch it illuminate the rock once more? Could I contain myself until then, and perhaps after, and for day after day, until the last? And were my bones to be added to the secret horde mouldering within a few feet of the mountain-top? A few feet of nothingness—mere empty space—separated me from lost and lovely liberty, and with frantic hands I strove against the hard face of the rock, and cried aloud in agonising protest.

The old rock had disregarded similar protests and supplications, and had endured like infantile pushings! Call, and who shall listen? Push and shove and fight, and what availed it?

In my delirium I cursed and blasphemed, and "full of shriekynge was that sory place."

Darkness followed brief twilight, and up the ravine came the murmuring I had heard below—a sobbing sound which at first affrighted and then soothed, for it could be nothing but the echo of the sea on the curving beach below; and in its comfort that lulled all ineffectual clamour, and eventually to fretful but frightful sleep. Always I awoke panting with thirst, stiff and strained, and with unmanly cries of fear and pain on my lips, while the chaste stars danced across the narrow slit as I strove to stem the turbid stream of despondency.

About midnight a singular peacefulness possessed me, overcoming me in spite of myself. Feverish impatience and resistance seemed futile, and in my resignation I began to realise that to avert cramp and disablement from cold—for a chill, moist breeze from the ravine played continuously on me—some sort of exercise must be undertaken.

My left foot was certainly not so compressed as the right. Though it could not be raised, it was possible to move it ever so slightly forwards and backwards. Might it not be possible, by never-ceasing friction, to so abrade the edges of the sole of the boot that it might be reduced to such dimension as would permit it to be raised?

With all the force of my mind concentrated on the one idea, I began to work in a passion of patience. At first the play of the boot was hardly to be registered; but hour after hour of ceaseless and calculated effort not only counterbalanced mental tension and imparted some degree of warmth to my body, but so amended the shape of the boot that it began to move with some degree of freedom. The more easy the fit, the more cautious and calm I became.

No insipid monotony pervaded the remote, cold crevice. The operation was lubricated with hope. Once every heart-beat—for I kept strict tally, as further mental relaxation—my boot rubbed against the rock, and each rub wore away minute particles of leather. As time passed and the work became still easier, it became more engrossing, until calmness gave way, and every nerve thrilled with excitement, and I was convinced that I would win a joyful passage from this narrow strait by dint of the resolute continuation of the simplest of processes.

But the long night was not to end with such placid and entertaining occupation. Absorbed in it, sternly waving off all sense of weariness or despair, I was staggered and stunned by the fall, among an avalanche of fern debris, of a heavy living body on my head and shoulders—a grunting, struggling thing which kicked and scratched.

With a despairing shriek, 'all my vibrant nerves collapsed, as in the darkness and confusion I fought against infernal odds. For one appalling instant I was convinced of the reality of Wylo's most diresome fact, and did furiously believe that I was actually entrapped in the stronghold of a demon at that moment, intent upon tearing me limb from limb. The most fantastic and horrific of nightmares was actually materialised.

But at that instant a familiar odour sluiced away all mystery. This struggling thing, from the shock of which my very soul still trembled, was but a fellow-victim—a wallaby which, feeding along the ledge, had happened on the trap made by my fall.

In a flash of remorseless energy, I seized the panting body, felt for the throat, and, expelling pity from my heart, gripped until all was still. How precious and comforting it was! And once again all my powers of will and muscle were centred on a single design and action as with machine-like rhythm the boot wore itself against the rock. Disengaged from every other theme, my mind dwelt on the one steady, inevitable purpose. Rub! Rub! Rub! And I fancied I saw leathern dust fall like filings from iron down deeper into the crevice. Before dawn the boot was working freely, and with one arm on the compressed body of the wallaby to case my weight, rest was possible. The plan for the disengagement of the right foot, painfully rigid and cold, was perfect in theory. Would it hold in practice? When the left was free I would, by friction of the iron studs In the sole, wear away the laces of the engaged boot so that the foot might be withdrawn.

But physical weakness became imperious. The distraction of cramped and bruised flesh had to be withstood the while the constancy of the function was maintained. Continual comfort came from the dead body of the ill-fated wallaby—a sort of fellowship, and a feeling that with its co-operation the contest between living flesh and blood and the inert force of the mountain was not altogether one-sided. Light was certainly cheerful, but the crevice filled with mist which distilled on the rock, and a chill current of air benumbed my aching limbs.

Under the pressure of fierce determination the task persisted, until, quite unexpectedly as it seemed, the boot was free; and then, shoving and squeezing the wallaby as a cushion for my right arm, the sole of the left boot began to rasp away at the instep of the right. In such a constrained position the operation, which could be persevered in by fits and starts only, was exasperatingly slow. The sun sopped up the morning mist and boldly explored the crevice, revealing the marvellous precision of the space between the walls. No work of art could be more regular. The sheer simplicity of the trap made it the more effectual. The sunlight showed, too, that the fissure was the skylight of a cave which opened out on the ravine. Dry boulders were strewn about fifty feet below, while ahead I could catch a glimpse of a narrow ribbon of blue sea. This provoking sight of unattainable water aggravated thirst almost beyond endurance. Throughout the night had my longing increased, but now the pangs were extreme. The most gratifying of all drinks—cool, fern-filtered, flower-decorated water, water dripping in iridescent spangles from green moss soft as velvet—splashed incessantly into a hollow out there a few yards away in the free space of the mountain. Here, manacled with "adamant eterne," in an agony of impatience I quaffed the thirst-stimulating draught of unsatisfied longing as I strove fitfully to wear away the stubborn strips of leather which held me in bondage. In a doze or dream the action went on. Startled, I awoke to find myself pommelling with inane savagery the poor crumpled body of the wallaby, and to the realisation that the imprisoned foot was loose in the boot.

A luxurious stupor took possession of my mind. I was at liberty to work out of the crevice knees and shoulders; yet an impalpable force detained me. It was not that I was not master of my fate, but that out there in the glare of the sun was patient water, dripping for the refreshment and cleansing of my grimy lips. So enchanting a thought was not to be abruptly ended. Was it not deliciously dreamy to hold myself in suspense awhile, to linger over anticipated sweetness and prolong blest gratifications indefinitely?

Strange drowsiness and peace bewitched the sunlit chink. Why should I struggle more? Could I not, in fancy, hearken to the measured splash of the drops from the sodden moss? Could anything be more consoling than this cushion to my bruised and aching arms? Ease and sloth were sweet indeed. I was free, but not at large. The amazing adaptability of the human mind had reconciled me in a few suffering hours to this confined space. Verily do I believe that the overcoming of this subtle anodyne demanded the expenditure of more vital force than the sum of all the long-sustained automatic exertion by which I had won physical release.

One supreme mental tug and the baneful torpor was dispelled, and with stiffened legs and bruised hand@ I began to screw myself up to the free air cautiously and painfully; and there, in a beam of light from the crystal, was the slow-dripping flower-bedizened water-celestial nectar to parched lips.

Hours after I awoke as from a dream. Far below a column of smoke showed that Wylo still watched. My first act was to send up a responsive signal. In a fit of petty passion I flung the toil-worn boot into the ravine, and began the descent by way of the spur to the west.

Wylo seemed scared by the sight of the staggering and tattered scarecrow, barefooted, and stained with blood and dirt, who stumbled into the camp at dusk, too weary to talk, almost too spent to eat; and to this day he is convinced that I was actually detained by the "debil-debil," whom I had overcome by some means of which wonder-working white men alone have the secret.

After two days' rest I climbed the mountain again, blocked the fissure with loose stones, and built a buttress, standing upon which I tapped the crystal gently with the tomahawk. It quivered. A shaft of rainbow tints dazzled my sight. I tapped again. As I touched it it third time, the fragile finger with which the gaunt old rock had scorned the plodding centuries vanished in a splutter of spangles!

THE SOUL WITHIN THE STONE

"These ghosts of the living and of the dead assuredly illustrate in a striking manner the mysterious workings of the human mind, and the unsuspected influence of soul on soul."—PRODMORE.

Not more than a hundred yards from its mud-besmeared mouth the convenient mangroves disappear and the little creek assumes becoming airs. Huge tea-trees, with cushiony bark, straddle it, and ferns grow strongly in all its nooks and bends. When the big trees blossom in watery yellow, yellow-eared honey-eaters, blue-bibbed sun-birds, and screeching parrots in accordant colours, assemble joyously, for the aroma, as of burnt honey, spreads far and wide, bidding all, butterflies and jewel-backed beetles which buzz and hum, to the feast, until the aerial anthem is harmonic to the rustle of the sea.

The sturdy feet of the trees stand in black peat, through which the water from the wholesome hills oozes and dribbles, and the russet stain from discarded leaves is on their white bases. Russet, too, is the surface of the ever moist soil. Some element in the water derived from pacted roots of palm and fern tinctures whatsoever in it lies, so that the bottoms of the shallow, erratic pools are thick with russet slime. All above is bright and pure, and the water which flows over the slime-smudged roots limpid and refreshing. If you cut into the bark of the tea-tree you will find water in beads and trickles, water which sparkles with purity and has a slightly saline taste. The bare roots alone suffer defilement.

Many a tall tea-tree stands sentinel on the margin of the creek, and there are groves of slim palms with narrow truncated leaves—palms which creep and sprawl over vegetation of independent character, and palm& which coquette with the sun with huge fans. Orchid& display sprays of yellowish-green flowers, which contribute a decided savour to the medley of scents, and palm-like Cycads meander from the low bank out Into the forest.

But there is one tree which, if not superior to the rest in broadness of base, height, fairness of bark, and fullness of bloom, has especial endowment. It stands at the spot where generation after generation of the original owners of the soil has crossed the creek, wearing a waving path upon which ferns ever encroach and which every flood amends. In a recess in its massive roots reposes "Kidjo-bang," the restless stone—a boulder, man's-head size, stained with a rim of sober brown.

This is its accustomed scat. It roves the locality, returning, swallow-like, to the close-fitting hollow of the root. The embraces of the root are sometimes so strong that the dingy stone may not be moved. But the floods of the wet season maintain an unceasing cataract to its dislodgment, and then, according to the legends of the blacks, it begins to "walk about." It may rest a month just out of reach of the disturbing water among the ferns. It has been known to appear mysteriously on the sandy beach two hundred yards away, to which spot it is said to travel by way of the grass lands, avoiding the slur of the muddy creek.

Whether it seeks change of scene beyond the ripple of dead leaves and spoil of the flood, or whether it ventures out on to the open beach, where the breezes from the Pacific play upon it, the round white stone returns, independent of the agency of man, to the sanctuary which time, ever-flowing water, and the hospitable roots of the tree, have combined to afford. It is there this day. Should it be taken to one or other of the blue islands in the broad bay, sooner or later it will be discovered nestling cosily in the grotto in which the dyed slime smears it as with pale blood.

To the ordinary investigator of the whimsicalities of "Kidj-o-bang" the blacks betray no secret, though they would verify, with what to them is proof positive, that it does on occasion appear in unexpected places and unaccountably reoccupies its cell. Discreetly pursue the subject and peradventure you may be told precisely why the stone may not always rest in the one spot in the whole world which it fits as a kernel its shell. It has been, they assert, associated with an evil deed of which it is now the emblem. Among the many the mysteries of "Kidj-o-bang" dwell with the past, though it is still associated with the ceremonies of the bestowal of totemic names on the children of a certain father.

More than one legend concerning it is extant, and the young fellows of the present day frankly scoff at them all, while the old men believe each other's versions and repeat them with bated breath. They cannot discredit stories which were accepted as established facts when they were young, which no one then ever dreamed of doubting, and which provide a comfortably satisfactory account for otherwise perplexing incidents.

Musing on the spot, the legend of the roving stone usurped my thoughts. The trivial and uncertain notions of the black boy who was the first to tell it, and by theatrical gestures to illustrate its verities, became more and more indistinct. The soothsayers of the long past had been forbidden by Nature to doubt that which was the lore of the camp. Was it that Nature re-asserted her influence—that the essences of the scene, subtle and pervasive, had recurred, creating a receptive spirit, so deep a religion of assent that shadow and substance intermingled to my bewilderment? I was permitted to be a sensitive percipient in the midst of the ashes of shiftless folk who had passed away, catching but a casual and deceptive glimpse of the coming of the desolating white man.

Piln-goi, the black boy, had wandered up the creek. A thrilling silence prevailed. Stooping down, I laved my hands in the softly flowing water, idly intent on lifting the stone. The tawny slime defeated irresolute efforts, and my slipping hands bestowed a baptismal splash.

Instantly I became conscious of a strange presence, and, glancing over my shoulder, saw an unfamiliar black boy lurking behind a glistening-fronded Cycad.

The whole scene had undergone wishful transformation. The white-barked trees, purified of smears from the sooty fingers of fire, stood out in splendid contrast to a richer, thicker, a flowery undergrowth. Tall fern trees spread green cobwebs to entrap sunbeams. The Cycad under which the boy crouched was slim-shaped, and its foliage resembled that of one of the most beautiful of ferns, with languorous, dolorous fronds, while it was crowned with a huge fruit of golden-brown. All the scene had been wondrously transfigured. Time's treacheries had been defeated. A garden-like age had been restored. The sword-leaved orchid dangled yard-long sprays of brilliant yellow flowers, which saturated the air with delicate perfume. Fearless birds fluttered among and hovered over the pendant blooms, whistling and calling. Water-rats sported in the lily-bespangled stream, and a platypus basked, on the bank.

From the strained and expectant attitude of the boy, it was apparent that he was hunting. He stepped cautiously out of cover, and, using a wommera of dark wood with oval clutches of white shell, threw a spear into the long grass. A kangaroo, mad with fear and pain, staggered forward, knowing not whence fate had struck it, and, lurching helplessly, sank among the ferns on the margin of the water. Ignoring my presence the boy, having completed the hunter's office with a blow from a nulla-nulla, called in a thin, shrill voice:

"Yano-lee!" (We go this way).

In a few seconds a young girl of his own race stepped through the leafy screen. She cast casual glances at the dead kangaroo, and without saying a word to her companion came to the pool, stooped down beside me, and drank eagerly and noisily, using a scoop improvised from a leaf. Her back glistened with perspiration, and her coarse, fuzzy, uncleanly hair ceased in tufts on her neck. It was a slim and shapely little figure. The plumes of the orchid, golden and syrupy, swayed over her heedless head and seemed to caress it. Her eyes, round, large, and brimful of the bewildering eagerness of youth, relieved the unobtrusive expansiveness of her nose and almost atoned for her savage lips. Though almost touching me, the most shy, wild creature of the bush seemed unconscious of my presence. She was in fact and deed:

"We have the receipt of fern-seed; we walk invisible." I was the phantom—invisible, intangible. The pair beside, the unembarrassed realities.

Do phantoms reflect? That privilege was mine. Let memory treasure every detail of the scene, every vestige of its incidents.

"Kidj-o-bang" had vanished. There was its cell. A full and stainless stream, in a gurgling cataract, sparkled over the big root, while high among the blossoms birds clambered incessantly for nectar.

The primitive pair were at home, but not at case, In this Garden of Eden. They spoke in mumbling tones, of which I could catch but stray phrases, though I listened eagerly. Presently the girl took up two dry sticks, and, using one as a drill between the palms of her hands, essayed to make a fire.

The boy imperatively intervened. "Poo-nee imba!" (No fire).

The girl started up, and instantly both slid into the jungle as silently and as tracklessly as snakes.

The dead kangaroo, the expectant phantom (gifted for the time being with a faculty more subtle than any moral sense), remained alone among the birds and the orchids, while shy pencil-tailed water-rats began to sniff and peer among the sedges. So enthralling was the scene that time passed insensibly. The sun was overhead when the pair reappeared noiselessly. Smears of shell and grit betrayed an intervening meal of oysters. Swarms of green ants, in a scramble for food, almost obscured the blood-stains on the fur of the kangaroo, and, brushing them away, the boy made and enlarged with his fingers an opening in the body, and having torn out the heart, liver, and kidneys, made a fire, scarce a hand's-breadth wide and smokeless, on which the meat was singed prior to being munched with grim deliberation. They ate largely, some of the flesh from the hind quarters being also eaten, scrap by scrap.

Were they fugitives? Tall and strong, the boy was as alert and suspicious as a dingo. Every sense was strained. He seemed intent upon subduing the very noises in his head as he slowly crushed his food and gulped.

A forlorn cry, half appeal, half gurgle, filtered through the leafage as from the beach, and on the instant the jungle had soundlessly absorbed the affrighted pair. The handful of fire and the mutilated kangaroo remained as the only evidences of the handiwork of man.

What of the intruder? The cry was almost too weird to be human. Again it thrilled through the leafage, a trifle stronger, and seemed to convey a threat commingled with a prayer for succour.

The scene held me. I was powerless, but not indifferent; capable of sight, incapable of action or utterance. Something in the tone of the voice told of a member of my own race in sore distress. Yet I could not respond to his appeal or move to his aid.

Half an hour of intense silence passed, and then a lusty shout startled the air. Surely, I thought, the wayfarer who makes such outcry in this unpeopled wilderness is an uncouth fellow who has lost his way and thinks to dialogue with echoes for relief of loneliness. Presently the cracking of branchlets and a rumble of discontented phrases told of someone blundering along through the mangroves. Accustomed to the gentle sounds and the delicious silence of the jungle, the clumsy noises irritated while preparing me for the sight of the intruder—a big, aggressive, weather-scored man, his only clothing a pair of short pants of canvas, stained with wear and stiff and whitened with frost like sea-salt. The ocean had but an hour ago cast him like its scum on the beach.

He burst on the scene to plunge his broken lips into the water at my feet. Like the natives, he drank long and noisily, and when his thirst was allayed called to an imaginary mate—"Pietro, Pietro!" cursed freely when no answer came, and whimpered like a babe.

Huge of body, strong of limb, bully and brute stamped on his coarse features, yet did his dread of loneliness piteously overcome him. His bald pate, hung about with scant reddish ringlets, had been roasted by the tropic sun until it glowed, and eyes and nose strove for supremacy of inflammation. An unkempt moustache did not hide teeth of disreputable tint; chin and jowl were covered with a fortnight's growth of streaky hair.

Turning from the water, he saw the dismembered kangaroo, and, seizing one of the legs, tore the flesh from the bones and with ravenous greed began an uncleanly feast. The impure drank of the pure water and gulped the strong flesh until his gorged stomach swelled cask-shape, and then he slept as noisily as he had eaten and drank.

A leathern belt, cracked and whitened, furrowed his distended girth, and as he lay stretched with the sun scrutinising his face, flies and mosquitoes and carnivorous green ants feasted on his blood at will. Each leaden-tinted, lean fly revelled until it assumed similitude to a colouring grape, some "reeled to and fro and staggered like drunken men"; bloated mosquitoes and green ants, commingling, made a living mosaic on the skin of the unconscious man. What could the assaults and stings of myriads of insects avail against fatigue so formidable?

But a decree had gone forth that the sleeper should wake, and who is man that he should flout imperious commands? The merciless sun insisted. The strong man fidgeted under the persistent blaze. Perspiration poured from his skin; he snarled; his eyelids twitched and quivered; the veins of neck and forehead throbbed ominously. The sun does not tolerate disobedience. A thin trickle of blood issued from the grimy nose, and with a snort the man awoke, his flame-red eye% swilled with enforced tears. Dazedly he plunged his head into the water and drank greedily, and, sitting up, spat sullenly and with signs of disgust and contempt. What comfort could cold water afford so repleted a stomach?

Having disdainfully spurned the remnants of the kangaroo, he sat head between knees, grumbling against fate. To him the fruitful and pleasant land was disconsolate. A castaway, he had drifted on to its welcome shores, and all that it could offer was loneliness, cold water, the raw flesh of a strange animal, and denial of the solace of sleep. Out of the depths of his misery and dejection he called imperatively on his God, and taking from the lining of his belt a thumb-sized purse, of netted silver, displayed a glorious pearl, which he held aloft, and with an admixture of supplication and imprecation proffered it to the Most High as grudging ransom from a God-abandoned country.

Who is there that delights not in the susceptible purity of pearls? The gem which symbolises virginal placidity was like to be contaminated by the coarse handling of the fretful, bargaining castaway.

Did I lean forward acquisitively to accept it from the noisome fingers, reluctant that so serene a prize should be retained in so coarse a setting?

The man started, for the votive offering had vanished, and blasphemous lamentations and curses against the Supreme Being, whom he abused for defrauding him of fortune by trickery, shocked the quietude. Then a spasm of religious fervour jerked him to his knees as he patronised the Almighty for having accepted a pledge for safe-conduct from death-like solitude. After transports of impious piety, as uncouth and boisterous as his struggles through the labyrinth of mangroves to the purifying water, he sat bareheaded in the sun.

Steamy heat distilled strong aromatic odours from the myriad leaves; languid flowers gave copiously and of the best of their fragrance; ferns and lotus did obeisance to high noon. The birds had ceased to whistle, and the droning of bees gave to the upper air slumbering rhythm of its own.

Again the intruder slept. Again the sun commanded and he woke raging. Standing, he cursed both loud and long, eyes protuberant, face purpling under the strain of vindictive oaths.

What an unflattering contrast to the unclad natives who had dominated yet blended with the scene-the girl the prototype of a swaying palm, the boy that of a tough young bloodwood beside the creek, among the topmost branches of which a crimson-flowered mistletoe made a splash of colour in harmony with the single red feather from the wing of a black cockatoo which the soft-tongued youth had entangled in his hair.

This gross, profane, sun-smitten, sea-rejected herald of civilisation, disowned by his fellows, disinherited of the world, defiled the spot, and his voice created an inaugural discord.

With arms uplifted, he muttered ineffectual curses against his fellows, upbraided his saints, and defied his deity. But while his lips frothed with the passion of a stuttering tongue, the provoked but just genius of the spot passed sentence, and swiftly and silently the messengers of Death came. Four slender spear& penetrated his shaggy chest, as with a &cream which ended lit a gulp he splashed back into the water. His struggles and splutterings soon ceased. Silence resumed its fascination.

Blood welled from the mouth and nose and spear wounds, which the eager water carried off in wavy, independent streams, while the dead face whitened.

Many minutes elapsed before a dozen white-eyed natives cautiously oozed through the Jungle, stimulating each other's nervousness by reassuring gestures. Certain that the trespasser on their dominion was incapable of mischief, they began to chatter, showing fidgety interest in the body, which they touched and poked fearsomely with spears.

Dead eyes stared unblinkingly at the sun through a curtain of water, which had already cleaned them of heat and passion, and wisps of red hair drifted over the forehead.

The untimely yelp of a dingo some few yards in the jungle inspired a similar response from one of the men, and without shyness or reserve the boy and girl joined the throng, and all began to talk excitedly. Some of the men assumed threatening attitudes towards the girl, who stood submissively, while the boy talked in a rage of excitement. He had chosen his mate, and would not, even on pain of summary death, abandon her.

So trivial an incident as the love affairs of boy and girl could not compare with the phenomenon in the water. The crisis was momentary. Amazement was pictured in every face, and not a man but subjected the bleeding body to gross contempt and what passed among them for ridicule. They mimicked the high stomach as they stood, as the dead man had stood, with arms aloft in rebellion against his lot, and fell back, as he had fallen, screaming, to kick and wallow on the ground. Here was plot and matter for ludicrous corroboree, the first rehearsal of which took place on the scene.

Soon curiosity took possession of the unstable actors. The belt was removed, and on the purse being fumbled with, several small pearls fell out. They were disregarded; but the strong man of the party looped the belt about his own inadequate waist, the girl hid the purse (which had been passed from hand to hand) in her hair, while the men tore the bone buttons from the pants and fitted them into their ears as they strutted foppishly.

The dead eyes stared defiantly up into the sky, the face whitened, and the stains of blood seemed to settle on it.

A harsh sound came as an electric shock, and I heard as from afar off Piln-goi shout:

"You bin sleep long time, boss! Big low water. We fella look out pearl-shell!"

The scene had resumed everyday aspects. The sun concentrated its rays on my head through a rift in the jungle, and the stone, stained dull red, lay in its cell, while rootlets fringed with tawny slime wavered over it.

Had soul communed with soul on that illusive borderland we range in dreams, the emblem of a deed of blood eloquent to reveal its secret? And now that the tale is told, will it cease from bewildering the simple old men of the soil who with one hand grapple the magical past and with the other the realities of the present?

Piln-goi's impatience drew me from the spot and out on to the reef laid bare by the ebb. The beguiling pearl still eludes him, but memory holds a rarer treasure than all the fecund sea contains.

End

Milton Keynes UK
Ingram Content Group UK Ltd.
UKHW042144281024
450365UK00010B/610

9 789362 097170